The Printer as Author in Early Modern English Book History

This is the first book to demonstrate how mnemotechnic cultural commonplaces can be used to account for the look, style, and authorized content of some of the most influential books produced in early modern Britain. In his hybrid role as stationer, publisher, entrepreneur, and author, John Day, master printer of England's Reformation, produced the premier navigation handbook, state-approved catechism and metrical psalms, *Book of Martyrs*, England's first printed emblem book, and *Queen Elizabeth's Prayer Book*. By virtue of finely honed book trade skills, dogged commitment to evangelical nation-building, and astute business acumen (including going after those who infringed his privileges), Day mobilized the typographical imaginary to establish what amounts to—and still remains—a potent and viable Protestant Memory Art.

William E. Engel is the Nick B. Williams Professor of English at The University of the South: Sewanee. He has published seven books on literary history and applied emblematics, two previously with Routledge, *Chiastic Designs* (2016) and *Early Modern Poetics* (2016), and has contributed chapters to several Routledge volumes, including *The Birth and Death of the Author* (2020), *The Routledge Handbook of Shakespeare and Memory* (2017), and *Forgetting in Early Modern English Literature and Culture* (2004).

Routledge Studies in Early Modern Authorship

For more information about this series, please visit: https://www.routledge.com/Routledge-Studies-in-Early-Modern-Authorship/book-series/RSEMA

The Printer as Author in Early Modern English Book History
John Day and the Fabrication of a Protestant Memory Art

William E. Engel

NEW YORK AND LONDON

First published 2022
by Routledge
605 Third Avenue, New York, NY 10158

and by Routledge
2 Park Square, Milton Park, Abingdon, Oxon, OX14 4RN

Routledge is an imprint of the Taylor & Francis Group, an informa business

© 2022 William E. Engel

The right of William E. Engel to be identified as author of this work has been asserted in accordance with sections 77 and 78 of the Copyright, Designs and Patents Act 1988.

All rights reserved. No part of this book may be reprinted or reproduced or utilised in any form or by any electronic, mechanical, or other means, now known or hereafter invented, including photocopying and recording, or in any information storage or retrieval system, without permission in writing from the publishers.

Trademark notice: Product or corporate names may be trademarks or registered trademarks, and are used only for identification and explanation without intent to infringe.

Library of Congress Cataloging-in-Publication Data
Names: Engel, William E., 1957– author.
Title: The printer as author in early modern English book history: John Day and the fabrication of a Protestant memory art / William E. Engel.
Description: New York, NY: Routledge, 2022. |
Series: Routledge studies in early modern authorship |
Includes bibliographical references and index.
Identifiers: LCCN 2021049504 (print) | LCCN 2021049505 (ebook) |
ISBN 9780367145880 (hardback) | ISBN 9781032223988 (paperback) |
ISBN 9780429032431 (ebook)
Subjects: LCSH: Day, John, 1522–1584. | Printing–England–History–16th century. | Protestant literature–Publishing–England–History–16th century. |
Book industries and trade–England–History–16th century. |
Early printed books–England–16th century.
Classification: LCC Z232.D277 E54 2022 (print) |
LCC Z232.D277 (ebook) | DDC 686.2094209/031–dc23/eng/20220110
LC record available at https://lccn.loc.gov/2021049504
LC ebook record available at https://lccn.loc.gov/2021049505

ISBN: 978-0-367-14588-0 (hbk)
ISBN: 978-1-032-22398-8 (pbk)
ISBN: 978-0-429-03243-1 (ebk)

DOI: 10.4324/9780429032431

Typeset in Sabon
by Newgen Publishing UK

Contents

List of figures vii
Acknowledgments x
Note on quotation and spelling xi

Introduction: incarnating ideas   1
The early modern paperworld 2
Conceptual and analytical coordinates 8
Mnemotechnic cultural commonplaces 13
World orientation 20

1   The deluxe design of *The Cosmographical Glass* (1559)   30
"Arise for it is Day" 31
The printer as author and the aura of authority 38
*The business of printing and the promotion of
   new learning* 43

2   Renovating the *Catechism* (1553) and *Metrical Psalms*
(1562)   64
Instigating oral and visual mnemonic triggers 67
Instituting aural and somatic memory practices 84
The visionary printer as author 94

3   The grand enterprise of Foxe's *Book of
Martyrs* (1563)   103
*Remembering martyrs and the consolidation
   of history* 106
Making new memories and supplanting the old 115
The material conditions for propagating new memories 124

4   Underwriting England's first Protestant emblem
book (1568)   141
Conditions of trade and the emblematic context 142

vi *Contents*

> *Apocalyptic mythography* 147
> *Contextualizing the circulation of memory images* 152

5 The compelling visuality of *Queen Elizabeth's Prayer Book* (1569)   160
> *Hemming in the text with memory images* 165
> *Patterns of devotional reflection* 177
> *The circulation and transfer of memorable matter* 193

Conclusion: making history   209
> *Imagining Derricke's* Image of Ireland (1581) 211

Index   215

Figures

0.1 Camillo's Memory Theatre, working sketch by Frances Yates. London: The Warburg Institute, with permission. Photo credit © William E. Engel — 16
0.2 Camillo's Memory Theatre, prepublication draft by Frances Yates. London: The Warburg Institute, with permission. Photo credit © William E. Engel — 16
1.1 Portrait of John Day. *The Acts and Monuments* (London, 1563). Image used courtesy of The Lambeth Palace Library — 35
1.2 "Arise for it is Day." Day's Printer's mark on title page of The Bible (London: John Day, 1551). Beinecke Rare Book and Manuscript Library, Yale University — 36
1.3 Title page. The Bible (London: John Day, 1551). Beinecke Rare Book and Manuscript Library, Yale University — 37
1.4 Title page. *The Cosmographical Glass* (London: John Day, 1559). Image used courtesy of The Huntington Library — 44
1.5 Title page. *Euclid's Elements of Geometry* (London: John Day, 1570). Image used courtesy of The Huntington Library — 45
1.6 Day's *memento mori* printer's mark, last leaf of *The Cosmographical Glass* (London: John Day, 1559). Image used courtesy of The Huntington Library — 53
2.1 Multiple type fonts. *Short Catechism* (London: John Day, 1572), sig. A5^r. Image used courtesy of The Newberry Library — 71
2.2 Schoolroom scene. *Short Catechism*, frontispiece (London: John Day, 1572). Image used courtesy of The Lambeth Palace Library — 79
2.3 Schoolroom scene. *Short Catechism*, frontispiece (London: John Day, 1583). Image used courtesy of The Newberry Library — 80
2.4 Idle Dog. Albrecht Dürer, *Melencolia I* (1514). Image used courtesy of Princeton University Art Museum (object number: x1952–1) — 81

viii List of figures

2.5 Music notation for Psalm 6. *The Whole Book of Psalms collected into English metre* (London: John Day, 1584), sig. D3^v. Image used courtesy of The Newberry Library — 87
2.6 Hand mnemonic. William Samuel, *An Abridgment of … the Old Testament, written in Sternhold's meter* (London, 1569), sig. A5^v. Image used courtesy of The Folger Shakespeare Library — 91
3.1 Latimer and Ridley executed. *The Acts and Monuments* (London: John Day, 1563), f. 1938. Image used courtesy of The Lambeth Palace Library — 113
3.2 Burning martyrs. *The Acts and Monuments* (London: John Day, 1563), f. 2253. Image used courtesy of The Lambeth Palace Library — 122
4.1 Whore of Babylon. *A Theatre for Worldlings* (London: Henry Bynneman, 1569), sig. D4^r. Image used courtesy of The Folger Shakespeare Library — 148
5.1 Typological page layout. *A Book of Christian Prayers* (London, 1608), sig. C4^r. Private collection. Photo credit © William E. Engel — 163
5.2 Reaper *memento mori*. Little Garden of the Soul. *Hortul[us] Animae* (Mainz: J. Schöffer, 1514), fol. 147^r. Image used courtesy of the Newberry Library — 166
5.3 Vanitas *memento mori*. Little Garden of the Soul. *Hortul[us] Animae* (Mainz: J. Schöffer, 1514), fol. 142^r. Image used courtesy of the Newberry Library — 168
5.4 Elizabeth at prayer. *A Book of Christian Prayers* (London, 1608), sig. ¶1^v. Private collection. Photo credit © William E. Engel — 172
5.5 Elizabeth at prayer / prayer in first person. Hand colored presentation copy of *Christian Prayers and Meditations* (London: John Day, 1569). Image used courtesy of The Lambeth Palace Library — 173
5.6 Dance of Death hemming in Latin prayers. Hand colored presentation copy of *Christian Prayers and Meditations* (London: John Day, 1569), sig. Oo2^v–Oo3^r. Image used courtesy of The Lambeth Palace Library — 174
5.7 Dance of Death of Women. Book of Hours (Paris, *c.*1502). Loose page, printed on vellum. Private collection. Photo credit © William E. Engel — 175
5.8 Entombment typology. Biblia Pauperum. (*c.*1495). Loose page. Private collection. Photo credit © William E. Engel — 180
5.9 Resurrection typology. *A Book of Christian Prayers* (London, 1608), sig. L2^v. Private collection. Photo credit © William E. Engel — 182

List of figures   ix

5.10 Industry over Sloth/Memory over Oblivion. *A Book of Christian Prayers* (London, 1608), sig. S4ᵛ–S5ʳ. Private collection. Photo credit © William E. Engel   184

5.11 Death visits Youth and Infant. *A Book of Christian Prayers* (London, 1608), sig. Gg4ᵛ. Private collection. Photo credit © William E. Engel   188

5.12 Death visits Compositor and Pressman. *A Book of Christian Prayers* (London, 1608), sig. Gg1ᵛ. Private collection. Photo credit © William E. Engel   192

5.13 The Triumph of Death. William Burch, *A Book of Drawing* (c. 1590), fol. 85ʳ. Canterbury Cathedral Archives (Lit Ms/A/14). Image used courtesy of Canterbury Cathedral Archives   194

5.14 Day of Judgment. William Burch, *A Book of Drawing* (c. 1590), fol. 88ʳ. Canterbury, Cathedral Archives (Lit Ms/A/14). Image used courtesy of Canterbury Cathedral Archives   195

5.15 "Imago Mortis." William Burch, *A Book of Drawing* (c. 1590), fol. 141ᵛ. Canterbury Cathedral Archives (Lit Ms/A/14). Image used courtesy of Canterbury Cathedral Archives   196

5.16 Dance of Death Panels. William Burch, *A Book of Drawing* (c. 1590), fol. 85ᵛ. Canterbury Cathedral Archives (Lit Ms/A/14). Image used courtesy of Canterbury Cathedral Archives   197

Acknowledgments

The primary research for this book was conducted prior to the Closing of the Libraries during the global pandemic of 2020–21, and I am grateful to the curatorial staffs at Canterbury Cathedral Archives, The Folger Shakespeare Library, The Huntington Library, Lambeth Palace Library, London College of Communication, The Newberry Library, and The Warburg Institute. Thanks are due to the Office of the Dean at Sewanee, The University of the South, for authorizing travel grants and a year of research leave; and to the Alderson-Tillinghast Fund for supplementing summer travel to conferences and archives abroad 2017–19, in Warsaw, London, and Tübingen. I am indebted to colleagues in the profession both far and near who responded to my periodic queries: Stephanie Batkie, Elisabeth Chaghafi, Thomas Herron, Andrew Hiscock, Matthew Irvin, Maha Jafri, Rory Loughnane, Scott Lucas, James Ross Macdonald, Ben Mangrum, Kirk Melnikoff, Jennifer Michael, Scott Newstok, Mark Rankin, Anita Gilman Sherman, J. Christopher Warner, and Grant Williams. Joel Harrington and Mara Wade were instrumental in helping me frame my project on John Day for a successful bid to finish writing this book at the Herzog August Bibliothek in Wolfenbüttel. Heather Hirschfeld, Laurie Maguire, and Rory Loughnane, the editors of Routledge Studies in Early Modern Authorship, have been encouraging from first to last. By way of a dedication, I would mention those of my mentors (of blessed memory) who put me on the trail of John Day early in my career and urged me to persevere: Roland Mushat Frye, Charles B. Schmitt, J.B. Trapp, and Jonas Barish. Finally, whatever work–life balance there has been during the 16 months sequestered high atop a mountain in Tennessee, I owe to Rory, always eager to find new trails and patiently waiting for me to catch up: *canis bonus, tibi gratias.*

Note on quotation and spelling

To make this book more accessible to contemporary readers, spelling and punctuation in quotations from early modern texts have been modernized and silently regularized (i for j, v for u, w for uu, and so forth), printers' abbreviations expanded, and compositors' accidentals corrected; the same applies to titles in citations of works from the period, except in those cases where retaining the original orthography or typesetting preserved or helped bring out some special meaning otherwise lost. For example, the spelling of "theatre" is used throughout for book titles in which it originally appeared (such as, *A Theatre for Voluptuous Worldings*) and, in keeping with the conventional designation of special terms of the period, terms like "memory theatre" and "theatre of God's judgment." Short versions of early modern titles are used unless it was judged that giving the longer or in some case the full title helped clarify a book's contents, stated aims, or market audience, or perhaps revealed some subtlety pertaining to the work in question. When and where possible, all early modern works cited have been examined in person (see Acknowledgments); otherwise, quotations refer to facsimile sources whether in a reprint series or in *Early English Books Online* (via ProQuest). At all events, Short Title Catalogue (STC) numbers and for later works Wing numbers are included in the bibliography section at the end of each chapter. Square-bracketed material in quoted excerpts indicates editorial interpolations or textual lacunae; ellipses signal material omitted from quoted sections of target texts. Every effort has been made to remain faithful to source material in the editions from which they are quoted.

Introduction
Incarnating ideas

Ernst Cassirer has had such a lasting influence on my thinking about language, culture, and myth over the years that when I have an original thought about the "unconscious life of images," it is hard for me to say whether it is my own idea or something half-remembered from Cassirer. Although Cassirer won't be cited at every juncture, much of my understanding about how one might process and make sense of Reformation thought—especially what I am calling the fabrication of a Protestant Memory Art in early modern England—is indebted to his philosophy of symbolic forms. An extended passage, by way of a belated epigraph, will serve to indicate some of Cassirer's (1977 [1923]) fundamental themes upon which my own investigation is built.

> For it is not the content of a doctrine, but solely its form, that can serve as a criterion for its classification as a religion: what stamps a doctrine as religion is its affirmation not of any being, but of a specific "order" and meaning. Any element of existence … can be negated, provided the universal function of religious symbolism is maintained. Here the basic act of religious synthesis is such that only the process itself is ultimately apprehended and subjected to a definite interpretation, while every supposed substratum of this process dissolves and finally sinks into nothingness. In its whole development Christianity also fights this battle for its own peculiar definition of religious "reality." Here release from the world of mythical images seems all the more difficult because certain mythical institutions are so deeply embedded in the fundamental doctrines, the dogmatic substance of Christianity, that they cannot be removed without endangering the substance itself. […] The form of tropological thinking transforms all physical reality into a mere trope, a metaphor, but the interpretation of this metaphor requires a special art of religious hermeneutics, which medieval thought seeks to reduce to a set of rules. Yet such rules can be drawn up and applied only if there is *one* point at which the world of spiritual, transcendent meaning and that of empirical-temporal reality come into contact, despite their inner divergence and antagonism—and if at this point they directly permeate each other.

DOI: 10.4324/9780429032431-1

All allegorical-tropological interpretation relates to the basic problem of redemption, and thus to the historical reality of the redeemer as its fixed center. All temporal change, all natural events and human action, obtain their light from this center; they become an ordered, meaningful cosmos by appearing as necessary links in the religious plan of salvation by taking a significant place in it. And from this one spiritual center the circle of interpretation gradually broadens. [...] The meaning of the world opens up to us only when we rise to a standpoint from which we view all being and change as rational and symbolic at once. [original emphasis]

(pp. 247–8, 257, 259)

Cassirer arrived at this formulation of what undergirds religious thought as an offshoot of cultural history while affiliated with the Warburg Library then in Hamburg, where, as he wrote a century ago, he "found abundant and almost incomparable material in the field of mythology and general history of religion, and its arrangement and selection, in the special stamp which Warburg gave it" (Cassirer 1977 [1923], p. xviii). Aby Warburg's unique collection of books, "which in its scope bore an uncanny resemblance to Cassirer's intellectual goals," resulted in the transformation of his "innovative and comprehensive 'morphology' of culture into a three-volume opus" (Levine 2013, p. 109). My first serious engagement with questions about the formation of early modern notions of cultural history likewise was shaped by the organizational pull of Aby Warburg's approach to texts and images in the perennial transmission of ideas and myths when, 40 years ago, I was a dissertation fellow at London's Warburg Institute. In such an intellectually stimulating environment, there was no escaping the metacritical insight that the foundational notions of Renaissance "thought images," "idea formation," and "world orientation" had from the outset been fast-tracked and subsequently shaped by the printing press.

The early modern paperworld

Printing was singled out by Cassirer (and by many others, of course) as one of the most obvious changes affecting early modern intellectual and spiritual life, indissolubly linked as it was to shifts in religious practices and, concomitantly, to communal, collective, and even confessional memory during the period. Paul Oskar Kristeller (1988) has characterized the humanist movement as being driven by an attitude toward learning and an approach to virtuous living "that affected more or less deeply all aspects of the culture of the time" (p. 11). Much of the impetus of early Renaissance humanism stemmed from the antiquarian enterprise of rediscovering and copying ancient texts and architectural remains including mosaics, statuary, and tomb sculptures. The ensuing twin exercise of filtering and repackaging the pagan classics was a major part of the growing interest among humanists to make available (and later, to do so in print) the best versions (and later, translations) of the ancients for an increasingly large audience of new readers. Consistent with the humanist impulse to extend the boundaries of what can be known and accomplished, reinforced by the strength of reason and actualized by the force of will, was an ever-widening view of the world occasioned by mercantile voyages, opening trade routes, and maintaining outposts (which has direct bearing on the key text examined in Chapter 1). For example, Johannes Stradanus's 1580s *Nova Reperta* is remarkable for its 20 detailed engraved illustrations and the practical information disclosed about such "new discoveries," globalization, recent inventions, as well as updates on older ones—most notably the processes of engraving and printing (Markey 2020).[1] Indeed, it is by now commonplace to observe that ongoing discoveries in the heavens, around the globe, within the human body, and in smaller worlds still, were made available to a wide range of new readers by virtue of advances in print technology, and especially as pertains to the mechanical reproduction of images (Engel 2020, pp. 77–8). Situating John Day's place within early modern print culture is the first step toward understanding how the material products of his ingenuity ended up shaping the reformed religious views that bolstered an emergent national consciousness in Tudor Britain.

Books and pamphlets, spreading new ideas about religion and defending old ones, became makeshift repositories for both doctrinal beliefs and could be used to broadcast up-to-the-minute views that challenged traditionally received knowledge, whether from Aristotle or the Bible. Manuscripts preserved and conveyed in uniquely crafted artifacts the words, deeds, and wisdom of the ancients along with a backlog of accreted authorial commentaries, while the printed book both represented and was itself a new kind of visual and mnemonic aid resulting from, as Elizabeth Eisenstein observes, the confluence of a range of new technologies (2012, pp. 54–7). The Protestant reformer and logician, Peter Ramus, tellingly conceptualized the book as a "memory machine" (Ong 1991, p. 134). Printing, which could reproduce hundreds of more or less exact copies of a text, led to a revolution in Western memory though, as Jacques LeGoff (1992) argues, obviously not all once (p. 81). The cycle drew strength from itself; and, incrementally, there came a change in reading practices and habits of book acquisition conducing to an increase in the number of people involved with the industry, which in turn was linked to a development of a range of new activities and trades associated with the production and distribution of printed materials (Febvre and Martin 2010, p. 234; Pettegree 2011, pp. 65–6). With the advent of printing, readers (as well as auditors) were confronted by a newly enlarged collective memory, the subject matter of which could not easily be assimilated on its own. I stress here (and will continue to do so implicitly throughout this investigation) the importance of auditors of the printed word being read aloud, mindful that the audience of published works was much larger

4 Introduction: incarnating ideas

than the records of book sales, let alone the number of copies in a given print-run, might suggest. Readers and hearers, as Roger Chartier (1994, p. 3) explains, "are never confronted with abstract or ideal texts detached from all materiality; they manipulate or perceive objects and forms whose structures and modalities govern their reading (or their hearing), thus the possible comprehension of the text read (or heard)." The estimated circulation of specific books is complicated further by the fact that some books deemed by governing bodies too heterodox or controversial were hunted down and burned (Fudge 2007, pp. 75–128). A good case in point (discussed in Chapter 3) is Tyndale's piecemeal translations of the Bible, which had to be printed on the continent during his lifetime and surreptitiously trafficked into England (Daniell 2001, pp. 283–332). We also must consider the multiplier factor, namely, that, through public readings and commentaries as well as the circulation of printed works within one's circle of friends and confidants, the actual number of people affected by a book, pamphlet, or new translation of a work was "far in excess of the number of copies printed, especially as the sale price fell in line with the reduction of production costs" (Barbier 2016, p. 256).

Accordingly, new approaches—many of which were modeled on old methods newly adapted to accommodate changing circumstances—were required for the culling, handling, and organizing of that information now flooding the market and finding its way into what might be considered public consciousness (Blair 2010, p. 13). As a result, one's memory no longer was wholly interiorized but, in due course, came to be conceptualized and experienced as being reposited in and projected onto exterior things, such as books and pamphlets. Indexes and lists of topical headings with corresponding section or page numbers, as well as comparable kinds of postproduction apparatus for creating a kind of artificial memory for the readers to access from within the work itself, became valued and expected features of longer printed works. Taking its precedent from an earlier manuscript tradition, this led in short order to the production of concordances and extracted commentaries on "common places" to be found in larger works, or *loci communes*, as exemplified in Melanchthon's (1521) extremely influential reformist work given that very name. The full title of Philipp Melanchthon's book is *Loci communes rerum theologicarum seu hypotyposes theologicae* [Common Places in Theology or Fundamental Doctrinal Themes], and, as advertised, it distills the proper Protestant understanding of the Bible following Luther's teachings as drawn principally from Paul's epistle to the Romans (MacCulloch 2005, p. 140). Among the results of the expanded marketplace of ideas owing to commercial printing was that the author, like the translator and publisher, became yet another reader of the memorial register of the thoughts being set down on paper. Rudolf Agricola provides an exemplary case study. His *De formando studio* (1484), originally a long letter concerning a private educational program addressed to his disciple and friend, Jacob Barbireau (Agricola 2018, pp. 282–309), was printed as a small booklet 30 years later (Agricola 2002). The resulting work was to have an enormous impact on 16th-century pedagogy, especially with respect to using *florilegia* as a moral filter for the pagan culture that humanists were transmitting in their translations and commentaries, treatises, and discourses (Mack 1985, pp. 23–41; Moss 2002, p. 88). The keeping of a commonplace book in the 16th century was an essential part of the humanist pedagogic mode (Burke 2013, pp. 153–77). This practical exercise, essentially grounded in medieval scholasticism, came to be part and parcel of early modern "new learning"; and, as such, figures as a recurring leitmotif in my study, concluding, in Chapter 5, with the case study of a unique visually enriched commonplace book based on Day's printed work. The commonplace book, however, was both a repository and a record of one's committing to paper the "facts" one had accumulated from "an indefinitely larger and disparate range of sources," and, as Ann Blair (1992) has further shown, treating "each fact, whether traditional or of recent origin, bookish or directly observed, as equivalent to every other" (p. 545). It is in this light that we should consider Montaigne's (1965a) comment that the commonplace book approach to learning accounts for his decision to write and eventually publish his *Essays*: "For want of natural memory I frame some of paper" (p. 356).[2] Notwithstanding Montaigne's frequent protestations of self-confessed forgetfulness, though (Frisch 2016, pp. 648–9), as Wolfgang Neuber (2009) has shown, printing manifestly made possible a wholly new kind of private as well as public "collective memory" (p. 71). An instructive case in point is *L'Exemplaire de Bordeaux* (painstakingly and expertly edited by Philippe Desan), a copy of Montaigne's printed essays interlaced with several layers of handwritten additions reflecting the author's further animadversions, thus making visible the traces of his ongoing creation of and engagement with a textual artificial memory made of paper. Along with this new kind of private as well as public collective memory made possible through printing came a reorientation to—what Neil Rhodes and Jonathan Sawday aptly call—"the Renaissance paperworld" (2000, pp. 1–6).

Of this "Guttenberg Galaxy," Marshall McLuhan (1969) long ago explained how the printed book became a "teaching machine" that "rendered the older education obsolete," making the "manuscript a crude teaching tool only" (p. 176). At the same time, as Angus Vine (2019) has shown, the broader intellectual context of manuscript culture persisted and even thrived in new ways, especially as regards "the notion of the notebook as both a spur to the memory and a kind of external memory in its own right" (Vine 2019, pp. 7, 17). The printed book, as a new kind of "teaching machine," still relied on old learning even as it looked forward to new domains for collective cultural memory, resulting in a daunting influx of information in need of organization beyond what traditional topical headings could provide. Humanist commentators and educators were busy finding, translating, and publishing ever-more recently rediscovered works of classical learning, and yet they also recognized that there was something unsettling about accumulating and putting into circulation these often antiquated and sometimes discredited preserves of ancient knowledge. They were, in Katherine Eggert's estimation, "skeptical about a system while still functioning wholly within it" (2015, p. 30). Comparably, and more germane to my larger argument about what counted as usable knowledge in the mnemotechnical registers of one's thoughts whether based on discoveries in nature or in one's reading, as Ann Blair (1992) has argued, "the method of commonplaces explains how critical judgment can coexist with blatant inconsistencies" for, in "sorting incoming information, the commonplace book offers opportunities for new critical confrontation of material; on the other hand the indefinite multiplication of separate headings can easily harbor contradictions which seem to belie the very critical faculties demonstrated elsewhere" (p. 547).

The Printer as Author, therefore, takes up such questions of literary judgment, textual authority, and questions of authorship while entertaining the heuristic value of thinking about one printer in particular, John Day, as a new kind of author made possible by the so-called second age of printing (usually, if somewhat artificially, designated as commencing in 1550). The first 50 years of printing (and here, in the English context, one thinks of Caxton, de Worde, and Pynson) gave rise to a new breed of mechanically inclined artisans known for both canny business acumen and, more often than not, the promotion of whatever polemical and religious views they tended to favor when their books or pamphlets were published (Green 2003, p. 23; Coldiron 2015, p. 103). For example, at the time when Luther's pamphlets were beginning to circulate widely, the most lucrative and cost-effective activities of the German printing houses was the production of indulgences (associated with the remission of sins equated to shortening one's time in purgatory) which, in turn, were to be sold by designated papal representatives ostensibly as fund raisers for, among other projects, the construction of St Peter's basilica and a crusade against the Ottoman Turks (Pettegree 2015, pp. 53–60), While some printers may have had qualms of conscience about printing indulgences as sanctioned by Roman Catholic Church officials, it was after all good for business. And yet there is no indication that John Day ever dealt in the printing of indulgences during the reign of Catholic Queen Mary. There is however some typographical evidence that, early in her reign and following Day's mysterious release from prison presumably for his expert skills previously displayed as a printer of psalters (Blayney 2013, p. 804), he did assemble type for primers and devotional works supervised by the Catholic printer John Wayland who had been granted a patent to produce just such texts (Carefoot 2019, pp. 24–5; King 2011, p. 173). Arranging and reproducing the words and works of others cannot help but reflect the otherwise sometimes hard-to-trace aesthetic tendencies, level of technical knowledge and material conditions of one's craft and,

Introduction: incarnating ideas 7

to some extent, expressions of the polemical views of a printer like John Day. And these are precisely the kinds of material traces that combine to form the basis of my analysis of his contribution to the fabrication of what I shall argue constitutes a Protestant Memory Art.

There are plenty of reasons to draw on this key aspect of humanistic and rhetorical training adapted to early modern intellectual and literary activity, especially in the light of Kyle Pivetti's (2015) contention that the various schemes associated with the traditional memory arts "offer too powerful an understanding of recollection as a process controlled through signifiers and sequencing, and controlled with intent by those able to remake the signifiers with the aesthetics of literary form, to ignore" (p. 16). Although covered at length in the penultimate section of this Introduction, it will be helpful to have a working definition in mind as we proceed. A "memory art," generally considered, following the landmark exposition by Frances A. Yates (1978), names any simple system, or a repeated series of composite schemes, used to set up a pattern for recollection, often involving the imaginative disposition and sequential arrangement of images (*imagines agentes*), sometimes accompanied by abbreviated references to specifically tagged texts, that are deposited in fixed places (*loci*), conducive to their being revisited, retrieved, and used toward some end (pp. 18–24). This embedded cognitive retrieval mechanism derived from classical rhetoric required conscious and even diligent effort to recover the terms of such a system of reconfigured ideas; and yet a well-designed memory art might in fact activate very potent unconscious triggers along the lines of subliminal recall. It is the latter that John Day understood so well—especially with respect to typographical page layout, the mnemonic features of the catechism and metrical psalms, and the strategic placement of suggestive images (as will be disclosed more fully in the ensuing chapters)—and which he implemented with verve as a conscientiously Protestant printer, publisher, and author.

Day, however, proves to be something of an outlier with respect to his remarkable success in the book trade; even though, at the same time, his approach to literary production can be seen as having been fairly typical given what was possible and practical at the height of Tudor printing. For, unlike the majority of mid-16th-century English printers, as Kirk Melnikoff (2018) remarks, Day was able to rely on the profits from his patents "for small, cheap titles to bankroll his many larger projects" (p. 11). Further, Day does not conform to the modern image "or even seventeenth century image of a successful printer," according to Elizabeth Evenden (2002), insofar as no single printer "could print works on the scale that John Day did alone" such that, after his death, his place in the English printing industry "would be taken over by teams of printers funded by syndicates of booksellers" (p. ix). Day's work product, as will be discussed in Chapter 1, was peculiarly inflected by the especially challenging times during which he plied his trade in the service of advancing the still-developing aims of the reformed church in

England. Apropos of which, and considering the frequent misuse of and hence misleading blanket terms such as "Anglican" and "Puritan," I have sought throughout to be vigilant when characterizing key moments and movements in the religious transitions of the 16th century, taking my lead from Diarmaid MacCulloch (2005):

> Even that slippery term "Anglican" appears to have been first spoken with disapproval by King James VI of Scotland, when in 1598 he was trying to convince the Church of Scotland how unenthusiastic he was for the Church of England.
>
> (p. xx)

My book then, in the first three chapters especially, looks at the broader mercantile and proto-nationalist expressions of English collective identity, especially as they influenced ideas about authority—literary and otherwise. This builds somewhat on Patrick Collinson's (1988) claim that "religious myths have often made the most critical contribution to the nation as an idea" (p. 6). Also, even though the Tudor era long has been associated with the rise of a national consciousness ahead of much of continental Europe, the community imagined in its literature arguably was more "British" than English (Schwyzer 2004). This has special relevance to John Day's commitment to and promotion of a Protestant state through print (Shrank 2004), as well as to the authors in Elizabethan England concerned broadly with the emerging nation–state and who generated "experiences of a collective past" (Pivetti 2015 pp. 163–8). The first two chapters therefore will address, *en passant*, issues such as the acquisition of specific type fonts, how Day came to possess and use (and often reuse) his stock in trade, and the processes involved in commissioning and sometimes copying outright earlier images and border elements. That being said, my primary critical interest remains with larger symbolic, mnemotechnical, and cultural concerns. Each chapter, accordingly, attends to specific aspects of the broader implications of Day's fashioning and standardizing innovative ways of presenting printed words and images freighted with religiously imbued meanings and hence directed toward consolidating and projecting a unified sense of communally experienced national consciousness. Day's output, as will be discussed in what follows, was indelibly marked by the interplay of old and new forms of visuality, typography, and memory practices. As such, *The Printer as Author* is situated at the intersection of book history, authorship studies, and mnemonic criticism.[3]

Conceptual and analytical coordinates

The larger symbolic and cultural concerns of this study are approached through a set of concepts drawn from the "human sciences," in the traditional continental academic sense of that term, namely, as

Geistewissenschaften.[4] Literally meaning "sciences of mind," in pedagogical circles the term designates something like "the humanities," distinct from the natural sciences (*Naturwissenschaften*). Historically, *Wissenschaft* (a dominant ideology of 19th-century, especially German, universities) stressed systematic, which is to say "scientific," research methods, but the term always has had a much broader meaning than the modern English word "science." It embraces the totality of knowledge in general and involves those academic disciplines or areas of study dealing systematically with a derivable body of facts—or truths—that can be known through careful study and applied research (Nyhart 2012, pp. 250–5). In what follows then, I would single out three main concepts that animate and inform my treatment of Day's activities that will be used to explore and account for his prominent place in English book history as well as the history of thought. Initially, though, I want to clarify that in referring to "the history of thought" rather than "the history of ideas" at this point in the Introduction, I am mindful of Michel Foucault's (2001) methodological reason for distinguishing between the two.

> The history of ideas involves the analysis of a notion from its birth, through its development, and in the setting of other ideas, which constitute its context. The history of thought is the analysis of the way an unproblematic field of experience, or set of practices, which were accepted without question, which were familiar and "silent," out of discussion, becomes a problem, raises discussions and debate, incites new reactions, and induces a crisis in the previously silent behavior, habits, practices, and institutions. The history of thought, understood in this way, is the history of the way people begin to take care of something.
>
> (p. 74)

First, then, my analysis revives Aby Warburg's notion of the *psychogram*, a concept that incorporates aspects of what Cassirer would have considered cultural psychology and historical studies. The study of psychograms fundamentally drove Warburg's lifework, giving rise to his prescient reconceptualizing of "the afterlife of antiquity" so evident in his *Mnemosyne Atlas* presenting a series of "pathways" designed to stimulate "differently" (different from traditional, temporally linear approaches) the viewer's memory, imagination, and hence understanding of the products and artifacts of cultural expression.[5] Warburg's tapping into psychograms aimed to set in motion the affective forces of historical memory in such a way as to short-circuit the typical stasis of representation as such, and strive instead for, as Giorgio Agamben (1999) puts it, "an indissoluble intertwining of an emotional charge and an iconographic formula" (p. 90).

The second underlying concept guiding my analysis is the *mnemotope*, which usually comes into play with reference to religion and mythology.

10 *Introduction: incarnating ideas*

Mnemotopes involve a special kind of remembering, through site-specific materializations of the past in the present. Most often, they are discussed in connection with archaeological artifacts though they can apply to other "invented artifacts" as well; for, as Anthony Purdy has commented, mnemotopes "serve as a vehicle for personal and cultural memory" (2002, pp. 93–110). The contemporary critical use of mnemotopes builds on Mikhail Bakhtin's (1981) notion of the "chronotopic motif" with reference to how configurations of time and space are represented in language and discourse (pp. 84–5). Whether in a literary work or in the world upon which such artifacts are based, chronotopic analysis, as applied to mnemotopes, involves "the conscious or unconscious memory traces of a more or less distant period in the life of a culture or, metaphorically an individual" (Purdy 2002, p. 94). Basically then, mnemotopes activate and play off the memory that is tied to certain sites, artifacts, or other texts, creating what might be called public-access memory. Inevitably, they are therefore subject to the vagaries of shifting attitudinal values, such as, exemplarily, the evangelically committed catechism, domestic prayer book, and martyrology issuing from the workshop of John Day in the wake of persecutions of those dissenting from the beliefs and tenets of faith associated with the Roman Catholic Church.

The third and perhaps most important underlying concept in my treatment of Day's authorial projects (even if not explicitly referenced throughout in my ensuing analysis) involves *engrams* and *mnemic energy*. These linked terms refer respectively to the fundamental units of cognitive information accounting for how memories are stored, and the transmission of these discrete bits of stored memory. Engrams and mnemic energy are grounded in neuropsychology and evolutionary biology by way of Richard Semon's pioneering studies of the retentive basis in a mind or organism that accounts for memory, *The Mneme* (1921) and *Mnemic Psychology* (1923). For Semon, *mnemes* concerned more than mere recollection of facts or events by an individual. They were essential components in a larger theory that embraced the preservation of the effects of experience from one generation to the next. Hence the mneme, for Semon, is a fundamental organic plasticity that, in the organic world, links the past and the present in a living bond. It is in this sense that historical memory and the memory of history take on what might be thought of as an evolutionary valance that tacitly is invested in and played out through the cultural unconscious of a given community. This descriptive (if still metaphorical) model of mnemes and their recoverable traces as engrams, circulating in and constituting the flow of mnemic energy, gave Semon a way to discuss the activation of the affective powers associated with tapping into the immemorial reservoir of mythical thought and ritual practices by means of mnemonically charged symbols and emblems. Aspects of this model thus have been useful to me in unpacking the conceptual underlayer of Day's activities as a printer. This model, moreover, helps explain what is implied in referring to Day as an author in his own right, owing to his setting in place a series of affectively powerful engrammic-generating mechanisms for readers and viewers to take in and take to heart the words—and especially the images—of others, conducing to what I am discussing in terms of the fabrication of a Protestant Memory Art in Tudor England.

With these three mnemotechnically oriented concepts in mind, my book resumes and expands upon a premise succinctly articulated by Jean Seznec in his ground-breaking study, which first appeared in *Studies of the Warburg Institute* (1940). Seznec (1953) pointed out, with reference to the monumental artworks of the Renaissance (such as palace vaulting and chapel cupolas), that far from being merely decorative, "their true meaning and character may be understood only by establishing their connection with the immediate forerunners, the gods of the Middle Ages, who had survived as the incarnation of ideas" (p. 5). By the same token, even though a literary historian by training, I remain drawn to the visually motivated reconstructive enterprise practiced by those pioneers of modern iconography, cultural aesthetics, and especially intellectual history (*Geistesgeschichte*), who, like Ernst Cassirer, Jean Seznec, and Francis Yates, were attached to or otherwise beneficiaries of the Warburg Circle. Among the main background studies with a Warburgian lineage that have been integral to the development of my mnemotechnic approach to John Day are Erwin Panofsky's (1972) *Studies in Iconology*, Edgar Wind's (1958) *Pagan Mysteries of The Renaissance*, and Raymond Klibansky et al.'s (2019) *Saturn and Melancholy*. Nothing quaint or esoteric is intended by the main coordinates of my analytical approach to literary history and mnemonic criticism being derived from works originally published as long as a century ago concerning how myth and cultural memory can be said to operate. My aim has been to apply some of the more productive—if often suggestive—ways of coming to terms with the unconscious or hidden life of images in a given culture by going back to, remembering, and picking up the thread of this way of thinking about memory through the "human sciences." I seek to apply practically (if tacitly) those aspects of Cassirer's philosophy of symbolic forms concerned fundamentally with myth and religious imagery—specifically Christian imagery and, more particularly still, forms of emergent English evangelical thought and reformist dogma, which was, as William Dryness (2004) has commented, "sometimes systematic, sometimes impulsive" (p. 91), while remaining cognizant of the Warburg-inspired intellectual pursuit of the mental structures undergirding the affective activity of commonplace, everyday symbol-making. At the same time, I have kept current with recent work on the pan-European Renaissance book trade, as well as with contemporary scholarship in memory studies especially those models and approaches concerning "Extended Mind" (Menary 2012), "Distributed Cognition" (J. Sutton 1998; Tofts et al. 2004; Tribble and Keene 2011, pp. 2–6), and "Embodied Cognition" (L. Johnson et al. 2014). Taking such matters into account, my pursuit of special topics in literary history is intended as a kind of critical intervention; namely, a recognition of the heuristic utility of deploying the ideas represented by psychograms, mnemotopes, and engrams and mnemic energy with reference to early modern publishing practices and related cultural configurations of things theological, aesthetic, and material. Such is the backdrop of my contribution to the ever-increasing body of knowledge about 16th-century religious thought, the book trade, and early modern mnemonic culture.

This book therefore is not strictly about John Day's career as a printer, even though the five chapters and the Conclusion are arranged chronologically with regard to the output of his presses—and it is worth keeping in mind that he owned and operated as many as three at a time and had at least four available to him for the 1583 edition of Foxe's *Acts and Monuments* (Evenden and Freeman 2002, p. 25). Further, as will be discussed in the ensuing chapters, from time-to-time Day outsourced the production of parts of his projects, and even had others print works to which he held the rights and license, his "assigns." Several outstanding studies already have carried the day in this regard, works to which my own project deeply is indebted (Oastler 1975; N.S. Sutton 1993; Evenden 2008), thereby allowing me to focus more intensively on the mnemotechnical ends to which Day directed his energies—authorially— to bring out something of the hidden life of religious myth and memory in his printing projects. Neither does this book seek to rehearse in exacting detail the publication history of Foxe's *Book of Martyrs*, which Day saw through the press in four different versions during his lifetime; again, several major works already cover this important ground (Loades 2011; King 2011; Evenden and Freeman 2013). This present book, as the saying goes, stands on the shoulder of giants. My goal therefore has been to write about what remains still to be seen when one surveys the horizon of critical possibilities with respect to the unconscious life of memory images associated with the wider cultural impact of Day's lifework as a printer and publisher—and author. The printer as author (and all that this might entail conceptually and symbolically, materially and pragmatically), concerns the extent to which Day acceded to the authority of being a printer, stationer, and publisher who was in a position to authorize what the reading public took in (whether on purpose or, as it were, subliminally) when taking in hand, assimilating, and acting on the work of his ingenuity.

Several basic historiographical presuppositions also attend my argument about Day's lifework. First, the productive if at times apparently destructive interplay of the old and new forms of religious observance and polity persisted longer in England than the rest of Europe (Dowley 2015, p. 88). Second, religious "reform" obviously was older than the Reformation, and its former traces are never fully erased or forgotten (Marshall 2017, p. 193). Third, the carefully curated infusion of Protestant theology into earlier Catholic forms and modes of cultural expression emerges as a kind of canny existential expedient. In this regard, I concur with Peter Carlson's (2017) argument that "the anxieties expressed in the various types of literature all demonstrate the fundamental confusion of a world in which authority itself had lost much of its stability, affecting everything in life, including death," such that early modern English "Protestant theology had to adapt to pre-existing behaviour rather than the other way around" (pp. 635, 649).

Mnemotechnic cultural commonplaces

Insofar as this book, as the subtitle indicates, is concerned with the memory arts, some further remarks are in order with regard to memory as a subject of inquiry in the history of thought.[6] As already has been discussed with reference to "the method of commonplaces" (Blair 1992, p. 541), memory in the early modern period was especially Janus-like, looking back to earlier models and ahead toward new approaches in the interest of taking care of all manner of information encountered, uncovered, and created. An additional advantage of looking at "the history of thought" (Foucault 2001, p. 74) where the memory arts are concerned is that many of the existing histories of memory, and more particularly of the Art of Memory, excel at "describing what they consider to be new features of engagement with the past than in specifying what cultures of memory these replaced" (Pollmann and Kuijpers 2013, p. 3). Pierre Nora (1989), for example, sees the historian's task as decoding the hybrid aspects of what amounts to the mnemonic schemes that often unwittingly are employed by those who previously have given a nation or culture its sense of history and identity (p. 19). It is all too easy and erroneous "to conflate pre-modern mnemonic theory with actual memory practices in early modern European societies" (Pollmann and Kuijpers 2013, p. 3). With such methodological matters being foregrounded here (and which come into play in each of the ensuing chapters), this section of the Introduction is devoted to reconstructing something of the recessed assumptions underlying and guiding the typical wit, style, and mental operations of the memory arts associated with the main 16th-century visualization practices whether concerning primarily secular or sacred material.

Following Jean Seznec, I maintain that the essential function of the culturally significant visual image "is the summing up of trends or currents of thought" (1953, p. 7). Complementarily, certain verbal expressive forms, most notably adages and proverbs, at once draw on and activate internalized memory images. Owing to their pithy if rudimentary summing up of some grain of truth observable in the world and reflective of human experience, proverbs take on a kind of universalizing effect. On the one hand, they mean what they say; and, depending on the context in which they are deployed, proverbs have the capacity to speak beyond themselves (Mieder 2008, pp. 251–76). In all their venerable simplicity, moreover, proverbs in the 16th century were literary analogues of commonplace visual tropes—and vice versa. For example, Pieter Bruegel the Elder, banking on while also skillfully parodying the perennial truth of this parallelism between the mediums of word and image, famously literalized over a 100 proverbs and idiomatic expressions in his 1559 painting, *Nederlandse Spreekwoorden* [*Netherlandish Proverbs*]. Bruegel's busy and visually rich *jeu d'esprit* based on popular everyday expressions admirably captures the self-reflexively ludic interplay between the verbal and the visual especially where proverbs are concerned. It was deemed sufficiently popular (and hence lucrative) to have been copied and sold no fewer than 16 times by Breughel's son, and had many later imitators among a wide range of printmakers (Sullivan 2017, p. 33).

In remarking on this conceptual parallelism between the verbal and visual registers of thought—and the playful, often intentional, overlapping of the two—the stage is thus set for proceeding with my mnemonic approach to Day's multimodal authorial achievements. For it is but a short step from here, with proverbs, to seeing how the same sorts of mental operations and careful attention to the reservoir of commonplace everyday truths in the material world as well as the evangelically inclined religious truths current in Queen Elizabeth's England—the very stuff of mnemotopes—pertain to Day's printed images, emblems, and colophons or printer's marks. Further, the symbolic images under investigation in *The Printer as Author* typically are combined with attendant tag-words resulting in what can be construed as mnemotechnic placeholders that set in train the recovery of finer details of larger narratives, myths, and culturally specific stories. This was a common aesthetic choice of the period, reflecting and imitating mnemotechnically inspired architectural models (Evett 1990, p. 104). For example, in the judicious use of mnemonic loci by poets such as Edmund Spenser (whose literary designs are encountered in Chapters 2, 4, and 5), whole histories "can be compressed into compact narrative niches, resembling the instructive verses recited by human statues stationed along the route of a civic pageant or royal entry" (Engel 2016, p. 81). Such psychograms have a large role to play in John Day's scripturally based reformist program, as will be shown in what follows but especially as regards his production of Foxe's *Book of Martyrs* in Chapter 3, Van der Noot's Calvinistically inclined emblem book in Chapter 4, *Queen Elizabeth's Prayer Book* in Chapter 5, and Derricke's *The Image of Ireland* in the Conclusion.

Whether expressed through words (such as proverbs, like those discussed in this section) or pictures (such as Jonah being delivered from the great fish, typologically anticipating and prefiguring the resurrection of Christ and his ensuing fulfillment of prophesy as discussed in Chapter 5), or some combination of both, a complex associative memory image is being evoked in the mind's eye. With the apprehension of such

Introduction: incarnating ideas 15

a distinct frame of reference and its contents, the whole then easily might be lodged accordingly in an appropriate place within one's own Memory Theatre. As such, the memory image, as a placeholder in an extended chain of ideas, serves to fix or anchor the content, often with respect to some specific theme or topical message in a given context of "applied metaphorics" (Engel 1995, pp. 3–4, 206–9). The enunciating of proverbial or commonplace wisdom in succinct phrases, and sometimes more wittily expressed as subtle epigrams, was in the 16th century (and, indeed, still is) part of everyday experience. Or, as Stanley Fish (1970) challengingly declared with reference to "affective stylistics," the experience of an utterance "*is* its meaning" [original emphasis] (p. 131). It is in this regard that *The Printer as Author* is concerned with the uses to which commonplaces—whether visual or verbal, whether religious or folkish in origin—were called upon, co-opted, and mobilized, rather than with whether and the extent to which early modern writers had a coherent theory of myth (cf. Hartmann 2018).

The following proverb, culled from one of Erasmus's several collections (and hence not "original" to him beyond his role as compiler and commentator), speaks directly to how such mnemonic statements can be expected automatically to work: "Little fishes slip through nets, but great fishes are taken; so small things slip out of memory, when as great matters stay still" (Meres 1598, sig. Ii7^v). The mental image conjured up here is easy to visualize and therefore more likely to find a place in one's mind's eye: a net, analogized to memory, with tiny fish wriggling out, "small things," and disappearing into the murky depths, namely, toward oblivescence. For Renaissance humanists, and indeed anyone trained in the five canons of classical rhetoric,[7] those fish both large and small were points to be recalled and onto which they could have preset meanings attached. As a safeguard to preserve and retain even small matters, the details, serious advocates of the Renaissance art of memory, most notably Giulio Camillo, devised techniques for visualizing target information—large or small—grounded in place-system mnemonics using an architecturally tiered design with functional if imaginary storage cabinets (see Figure 0.1 and Figure 0.2).

The first figure is Frances Yates's draft sketch reflecting her progress as she set about working through the details to reconstruct Camillo's Memory Theatre. The second is her prepared "pen and ink" version of the finished chart for publication.[8] Her careful reconstruction of Camillo's design in effect recapitulates what any early modern mnemonist would have had to undertake in assuming, building, and using an already-given artificial memory system. Such "local memory" schemes involve the invention of backgrounds (*loci*, or places) and the fixing and arranging of a series of lively images, a visual shorthand that often combined associative wordplay. Classical rhetoricians and orators, for example, proposed imagining a stroll through a familiar street or building and all these places visited in turn, "the various deposits … demanded from their

16 *Introduction: incarnating ideas*

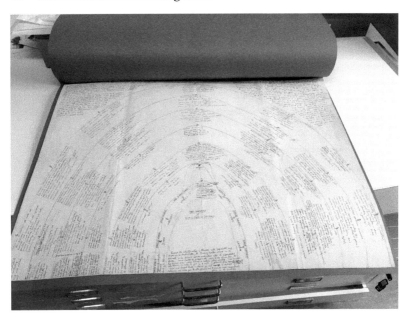

Figure 0.1 Camillo's Memory Theatre, working sketch by Frances Yates. London: The Warburg Institute, with permission. Photo credit © William E. Engel.

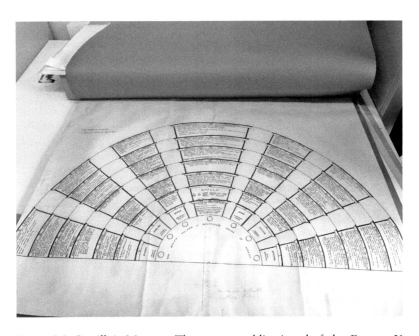

Figure 0.2 Camillo's Memory Theatre, prepublication draft by Frances Yates. London: The Warburg Institute, with permission. Photo credit © William E. Engel.

custodians, as the sight of each recalls the respective details" (Quintilian 1961, p. 223). Thus the old adage "God lies in the detail" apparently was revived in modern times by the visionary architect Ludwig Mies van der Rohe, known to have been quite familiar with mnemotechnic matters. "The German version of the adage, 'Der Liebe Gott steckt in Detail,' perhaps the original source for Mies's maxim, was used by Aby Warburg to indicate the foundation of the iconographical method for researching in art history" (Frascari 1984, p. 23).[9] This idea of "the process of signification" being in the details of the memory arts "can be traced through Leibniz" back to the combinatory memory machines of Ramon Lull,[10] such that, according to Frascari, the details "are then the *loci* where knowledge is of an order in which the mind finds its own working" and, further, they "are much more than subordinate elements; they can be regarded as the minimal units of signification in the architectural production of meanings" (p. 23).

The mnemonic image of big fish caught in a net of memory as little fish slip away can be found in, among other 16th-century English epitomes, Francis Meres's (1598) popular miscellany *Palladis tamia* (sig. Ii7ʳ).[11] The rich afterlife of this proverb and its easy portability from one anthology to another speaks to its suitability as an example of the transmission of cultural currency, consistent with Erasmus's own characterization of a proverb "by two features: common use and novelty" (Wesseling 2002, p. 84). Meres's several quite successful commonplace digests were published for a new generation of readers 50 years after the boom of translations of Erasmus's handbooks. He capitalized on and contributed further to the "surge in English collections based on Erasmus's works," partly attributed to "the gradual introduction of the new standards set by the humanist educational agenda" and coinciding specifically with "the introduction of Erasmus' proverb collections in the curriculum" (Juhász-Ormsby 2017, p. 47). And yet, as already observed, just as Erasmus did not create this instructive simile about the little fish but took it from earlier sources, so too this quotation attributed to Erasmus by Meres is one of several that he had culled and placed under the topical heading of "Memory." Meres looked to, among others, Erasmus, the humanist anthologer *par excellence*, and assembled a collection of commonplaces from already existing epitomes. Erasmus likewise, as a way of advancing the humanistic program he championed, had gathered and commented on over 4,000 proverbs and maxims, although he did not arrange them topically or alphabetically. Meres's more modest endeavor, however, does implement the mnemotechnical expedient and precedent going back to Aristotle and Cicero of organizing his treasury by discrete topics, such as "Virtue," "Poets," and (as in the example discussed above) "Memory." The quotations that he made available to Elizabethan readers thus granted them easily conned mnemonic access-points to lay claim to nuggets of wisdom mined from the usual humanist source texts. These terse cues provided a new class of aspiring readers with exactly what they were looking for: a predigested memory on paper that someone else had constructed for them in their native language. And the same may be said for John Day, the printer as author, similar in kind if different in degree, as will be discussed in Chapter 2 with respect to the catechism and metrical psalms.

The expected appropriation by new readers of the structures of thought no less than the specific content intentionally prepacked by anthologers like Meres and by Protestant printers as authors such as Day gave them a means by which they could participate individually—but, of course, also collectively—in the brave new paperworld. As such, the social reality of readers who were quite literally buying into the world of words and images on offer by the anthologer as well as by the entrepreneurial printer is yet another iteration of the commercial side of symbol-making and world-building in the early modern age of print. Kirk Melnikoff (2018) wisely cautions in this regard that "there's more to know about a given merchant beyond whether he or she is trying to make a living though buying and selling" because "the orientation toward profit tells us nothing useful about the particular business practices or products" (p. 10). Concomitantly, and with special reference to Day's lifework, we need to also understand the printing enterprise in terms of the incarnation (or indeed the reincarnation) of ideas drawn from forerunners, which is to say from prior textual ecosystems and print environments.

In line with this, Erasmus (1982), for example, recognized and promoted the printing of adages as an effective *aide-mémoire* for, he contended, "there appears to be no form of teaching which is older than the proverb. In these symbols, as it were, almost all the philosophy of the Ancients was contained" (p. 13). His compendious *Adages* begins with several hallowed definitions, including that of Diomedes, "A proverb is the taking of a popular saying, fitted to things and times, when the words say one thing and mean another" (p. 3), and eventually offers his own working definition: "A proverb is a saying in popular use, remarkable for some shrewd and novel turn" (p. 4). With this definition, we are provided a glimpse into the underlying structure of this intellectual enterprise, which in so many ways is bound up with memory and the attendant anxiety concerning oblivescence. It is this "shrewd and novel turn" to which I will be returning in my treatment of John Day whose images and page-layout preserved the familiar processes of mnemotechnical thought and recollection, which can be recovered through the material traces of his visually charged textual recreations. For the proverb, like the emblem (as will be discussed in each of the following chapters), was a ubiquitous feature of early modern European literary and mnemonic culture. Hence, my attention throughout to the mnemotechnic value accorded to recycled commonplaces including and especially scriptural points of reference excerpted and often set in new contexts and doctrinal configurations with—and hence with reference to—other texts. And the same applies to their visual counterparts, taking into account their dialogic function as catalyzing terms within a larger register of humanist epistemology that informed a variety of 16th-century cultural practices. This study therefore focuses on the inherently mnemonic aspects of such recycled words and images—at once common, which is to say easily recognized as such by a popular audience, and yet having "a shrewd and novel turn"—which made them ideally suited for being incorporated into a wide range of expressive forms of the period. I am interested principally in the textual reservoirs and visual repositories into which printers and authors, exemplarily John Day, tapped so as thereby to gain access to and repurpose these commonplaces for their own often polemical, devotional, and pedagogical ends. Although I am working for the most part with English sources, the wider application of my remarks reaches out toward other national, regional, and localized instantiations of these ready ways to acquire and plant mnemonically charged seeds of thought (Horowitz 1998, 5–12). Trading in proverbs was fundamental to the humanist method of collocation, the excerpting and placing side-by-side memorable sayings and deeds so as later to enliven one's writing and table talk with *copia*.

This practice of copia (a stylistic goal of having access to abundant and expansive richness and amplification of one's speech and writing) was, in fact, taken to task by Erasmus (2002) in his best-selling book on the subject, in the opening section headed "That the Aspiration to Copia is Dangerous" (pp. 11–12). Typical of his self-reflective pedagogy, he models in his writing the positive virtues he would have his students attain and inserts a well-placed proverb to fix the theme in memory. He thus delivers at the outset a proactive admonishment of what one should keep in mind while using his handbook, *On Copia of Words and Ideas*:

> For as there is nothing more admirable or more splendid than a speech with a rich copia of thoughts and words overflowing in a golden stream, so it is, assuredly, such a thing as may be striven for at no slight risk, because according to the proverb, "Not every man has the luck to go to Corinth."
>
> (p. 11)

He does not gloss the origin or meaning of this proverb, namely, that not everyone has the same opportunities or access to the same sources of information—specifically, in this case, classical rhetoric. An already learned reader, one who proverbially had been to Corinth, presumably would know that the adage derives from Horace's *Epistles* (1.17.36) and is echoed in Aulus Gellius's *Attic Nights* (1.8.4). But more to the point, as King and Rix also point out in their annotations to this work, "most of the ancient writers which Erasmus quoted as illustrations or examples, he repeated from the works of Quintilian or another, instead of directly from the works of the original author" (Erasmus 2002,

Introduction: incarnating ideas

p. 11). This is not to take anything away from Erasmus's achievement but merely to put it in context. The same principle of looking back to and repurposing previous words and stories, myths and legends, images and emblems, "with a shrewd and novel turn" applies as well to John Day. The affective mental structures that stand behind such an approach to bookmaking parallel those associated with seeking to accumulate, compile, select, and deploy the content of knowledge that previously had been accorded some degree of contemporary cultural cachet, but now giving it one's own "shrewd and novel" stamp, and thereby authorizing it—as if it were one's own.

World orientation

A few final theoretical considerations need to be raised before moving on to Chapter 1. They pertain to Day's printing-house activities, which, I shall argue, had direct bearing on his readers' ways of experiencing their encounters with the content of the books he produced as well as, by extension, their ensuing perceptions of the world—spiritual as well as secular—to which those experiences referred. One of the ideas that Cassirer brings forward in his critical analysis of mythical consciousness involves Hegel's understanding of *Wissenschaft* as a "linguistic and rhetorically based science that produces a systematic way of speaking about experience" (Bayer 2009, p. 208). With direct bearing on what already has been introduced about the memory arts in the sweep of early modern epistemological thought, Thora Ilin Bayer (2009) resumes the argument:

> In the final chapter of the *Phenomenology* on "Absolute Knowing," Hegel claims that the science of experience of consciousness is a memory theatre. His science [*Wissenschaft*] is accompanied by an art of memory (*Erinnerung*), and this art produces a Gallery of Images (*Galerie von Bildern*). This is in accord with the Renaissance art of memory as described by Frances Yates in *The Art of Memory* [see pp. 17–62]. The memory is a treasure house of master images from which we can draw forth the dialectical stages of experiences. These images are, so to speak, the middle terms of experience from which all *argumenta* or themes of consciousness can be entertained. They are the *topoi* or *loci*—the commonplaces—that hold consciousness together at its base.
>
> (p. 208)

This insight into Hegel's mnemotechnical description of the science appertaining to the experience of consciousness brings centerstage the classical rhetorical canon of *memoria*. Comparably, Oswald Spengler (1996) observed in his compelling and prescient critique of Western cultural thought (written incidentally at the same time as Cassirer's *Philosophy of Symbolic Forms*):

The picture of history—be it the history of mankind, of the world of organisms, of the earth or of the stellar systems—is a *memory*-picture. "Memory," in this connexion, is conceived as a higher state … a perfectly definite kind of imagining power, which enables experience to traverse each particular moment *sub specie aeternitatis* as one point in an integral made up of all the past and all the future, and it forms the necessary basis of all looking-backward, all self-knowledge and all self-confession [original emphasis].

(p. 103)

Somewhat less abstractly, recourse to a storehouse of commonplaces howsoever conceived gives the practitioner of the memory arts a point of departure—and of return—after the fashion of Aristotle's *topoi* and Cicero's *loci* as discussed and used in Renaissance memory treatises (Yates 1978, pp. 114–18). Hence, this book will single out a series of particularly telling commonplaces and recurring patterns in Day's work in the interest of attending to them as mnemotechnical nodes in a larger network of what can be reckoned as and in terms of a vast and expansive Protestant Memory Art. Rather than seeing such recycling of older images and texts merely as an expedient of book production (which to some extent undeniably it is), *The Printer as Arthur* makes a case for viewing and understanding this self-conscious printing house tactic as an essentially metacognitive mode for reflecting on Day's larger purpose as regards his approach to bimedial exposition and, in effect, argumentation. Conceptualizing Day's exemplary place in the early modern printworld along such lines provides a ready way, using the critical apparatus associated with research in the human sciences and material culture, to implement a method for thinking about the symbolic and unconscious life of images while, at the same time, taking into account and reading between the lines how topics in authorship and media studies historically have been formulated.

The overarching aim of *The Printer as Author* is to offer insight into the history and philosophy of symbolic forms, especially as pertains to early modern emblematic expressions concerned with mortal temporality and in response to the anxiety associated with oblivescence. The chapters that follow therefore will survey and analyze various expressions of what might be categorized, in the Hegelian sense, as "Absolute Knowing" in Elizabethan England, namely, those material and symbolic expressions steadily coming out from John Day's printshop and which tellingly stand out as reflections of his own authorial sensibilities. Collectively they will be shown to supply and in effect institute a reformed experiencing of consciousness—both secular and religious—by means of the paperworld brought to prominence and sustained by Day's emergent Protestant Memory Art. Chapter by chapter, then, we shall move as it were room by room through a "Gallery of Images," a metaphorical movement requiring a special art of religiously oriented hermeneutics by means of which we shall encounter the basic issue of "redemption," shown time and again to be related ultimately to the historical reality of the redeemer as its fixed center. To recall Cassirer's comment about allegorical-tropological interpretation (presented at the outset): "All temporal change, all natural events and human action, obtain their light from this center; they become an ordered, meaningful cosmos by appearing as necessary links in the religious plan of salvation by taking a significant place in it." This revisiting of the material and durable products of the paperworld associated specifically with John Day's indefatigable labor, risky capital outlay, and technical ingenuity is undertaken in light of the view outlined by Cassirer that the world of symbolic meaning gives us a hold on our evasive and evanescent conscious life and, thereby, "has a fundamental role in our world orientation and is the foundation of our cultural personal identity" (Schwemmer 2004, p. 11).

More specifically, this notion of "world orientation," especially as regards cultural life during the reign of Queen Elizabeth and also in and through the early modern paperworld, is brought out by looking at five moments in the career of John Day. First, a careful consideration of the aims and achievement of *The Cosmographical Glass* (1559) provides a way, in Chapter 1, to explore the issues of authorship and authority with reference to the business of printing and the promotion of new scientific learning that so often (and for good reasons) is associated with Renaissance England. Chapter 2 focuses on the combined nationalist and Protestant goals linked to Day's licenses for—and indeed his lucrative monopolies on—the printing of the most fundamental aspects of reformed Christian learning and shared religious experience from 1553 to 1572. This sets the stage for Chapter 3 concerning the quintessential Protestant martyrology of Elizabethan times, John Foxe's *Acts and Monuments* (1563) containing over 50 woodcut illustrations, the largest publishing project undertaken in England up at that time and arguably the most influential book of the period. Chapter 4 continues the investigation of how Day's polemically thematized use of images managed to fix, sustain, and reinforce an unflinchingly Protestant and mnemonically charged train of thought with his Dutch and French printings of Van der Noot's *A Theatre for Worldings* (1568), subsequently taken up by a fellow publisher and "Englished" by Edmund Spenser. Chapter 5 treats the preeminent book of domestic piety, known as *Queen Elizabeth's Prayer Book* (1569, 1578), as the crowning achievement in Day's lifelong program of self-consciously reconceptualizing earlier mnemonic forms, returning to and repurposing stock illustrations from the manuscript tradition and early printed block books so as to infuse them with new and affectively memorable Protestant content. The Conclusion looks at Day's last major handsomely illustrated production, John Derricke's *The Image of Ireland* (1581). This parting glance at Day's lifework offers an ideal way to sum up the range of mnemotopes on which he drew throughout his career as a printer and author, and which he set to work in the early modern cultural imagination.

Introduction: incarnating ideas 23

Notes

1 With special reference to what the engravings of "Philips Galle after Johannes Stradanus" (*c.*1588) disclose about 16th-century printing practices, see Bowen (2020), Imhof (2020), and Viljoen (2020).
2 Montaigne's verb *forger* (1962, p. 1071) is translated by John Florio as "frame" (1965a, p. 356), which Donald Frame renders as "make" (1965b, p. 837). On Montaigne's relation to the literary digesting of one's reading along the lines assumed here, see Engel (1995, pp. 100–1); and on his "constant quotation of excerpts mainly from Latin authors" and his having marked up books known to have been in his possession "in the manner of the commonplacing reader," thus making the *Essais* "that most uncommon of commonplace-books," see Moss (2002, p. 213).
3 On the utility of mnemonic criticism applied to early modern literature, see Engel (1991).
4 With the connotation of "cultural sciences," *Geistewissenschaften* more literally can be rendered as "human sciences" (Cassirer 2021, pp. xxxv and 322).
5 On the theoretical importance of "the subtle logic of the *Atlas*" as anticipating Gilles Deleuze's "concept of the 'rhizomatic,'" see C.D. Johnson (2012, p. 116).
6 This field of intellectual inquiry has blossomed considerably in recent years; with special reference to the English literary Renaissance, see Helfer (2018, pp. 315–17); on the movement from the claim that artificial memory was "vital to intellectual life in the period" to taking this "as a starting point in a literary-critical enquiry," Lyne (2016, pp. 4–7); and, with respect to "Renaissance systems of memory" that locate knowledge "in terms of schematized place," Marcus (2000, pp. 18–22).
7 Namely, *inventio* (invention), *dispositio* (arrangement), *elocutio* (style), *memoria* (memory), and *pronunciatio* (delivery), following the main ancient sources for composition, oratory, and memory training; see Yates (1978, pp. 20–2) and Engel et al. (2016, p. 5).
8 On Camillo's Memory Theatre, see Yates (1978, pp. 163–96). The finished, printed version of Yates's design of Camillo's Theatre usually appears as a fold-out diagram at the back of *The Art of Memory*. I am indebted to William Sherman for bringing to my attention the existence of these preliminary sketches in the Yates Archive at The Warburg Institute.
9 With reference to and quoting P. Johnson (1964, p. 137).
10 On the historical and ideational sweep from Lull to Leibniz in this genealogy of mnemotechnical signifying processes, see Heckscher (1974, pp. 101–34).
11 On Meres's place in the English memory arts tradition, see Engel et al. (2016, pp. 125–7).

Bibliography

Primary sources

Agricola, R. 2002. *Letters (MR 216)*. A. van der Laan and F. Akkerman, eds. Tempe, AZ: Arizona Center for Medieval and Renaissance Studies.
———. 2018. *Écrits sur la dialectique et l'humanisme*. M. van der Poel, ed. and trans. Paris: Classiques Garnier.

Cunningham, W. 1559. *The Cosmographical Glass*. London: John Day. STC 6119.
Derricke, J. 1581. *The Image of Ireland*. London: John Day. STC 6734.
Erasmus, D. 1982. *Adages Ii1 to Iv100*. In: R.A.B. Mynors, ed; M.M. Phillips, trans. *The Collected Works of Erasmus*, vol. 31. Toronto: University of Toronto Press.
———. 2002. *On Copia of Words and Ideas*. D.B. King and H.D. Rix, trans. Milwaukee: Marquette University Press.
Foxe, J. 1563. *Acts and Monuments*. London: John Day. STC 11222.
Melanchthon, P. 1521. *Loci communes rerum theologicarum seu hypotyposes theologicae*. Basel: Adam Petri.
Meres, F. 1598. *Palladis tamia: Wit's treasury, being the second part of Wit's common wealth*. London: P. Short. (STC 17834).
de Montaigne, M. 1962. *Oeuvres Completes de Montaigne*. A. Thibaudet and M. Rat, eds. Paris: Gallimard.
———. 1965a. *The Essayes of Moral, Politicke, and Militarie Discourses of Lo: Michael de Montaigne* [1603]. trans. J. Florio. London: J.M. Dent & Sons.
———. 1965b. *The Essays of Montaigne*. trans. D. Frame. Stanford: Stanford University Press.
———. 2011. *Reproduction en quadrichromie de l'Exemplaire de Bordeaux des Essais de Montaigne, texte établi avec une introduction*. P. Desan, ed. Paris: Classiques Garnier.
Quintilian [Quintilianus, M.F.]. 1961. *The Institutio oratoria*. H.E. Butler, trans. Cambridge, MA, and London: Harvard University Press and William Heinemann.
Stradanus, J. *c.*1588. *Nova Reperta*. Florence: Philips Galle.
Van der Noot. 1569. *A Theatre Wherein be Represented as well the Miseries and Calamities that Follow the Voluptuous Worldlings*. London: Henry Bynneman. STC 18602.

Secondary Sources

Agamben, G. 1999. Aby Warburg and the Nameless Science. In: *Potentialities: Collected Essays in Philosophy*. trans. D. Heller-Rozaen. Stanford: Stanford University Press. pp. 89–103.
Bakhtin, M. 1981. Forms of Time and of the Chronotope in the Novel: Notes toward a Historical Poetics. In: M. Holquist, ed. *The Dialogic Imagination: Four Essays*. trans. C. Emerson. Austin, TX: University of Texas Press.
Barbier, F. 2016. *Guttenberg's Europe: The Book and the Invention of Western Modernity*. trans. J. Birrell. Cambridge: Polity Press.
Bayer, T.I. 2009. Hegelian Rhetoric. *Philosophy and Rhetoric*. **42.3**, 203–19.
Blair, A. 1992. Humanist Methods in Natural Philosophy: The Commonplace Book. *Journal of the History of Ideas*. 53.4, 541–51.
———. 2010. *Too Much to Know: Managing Scholarly Information Before the Modern Age*. New Haven: Yale University Press.
Blayney, P.W.M. 2013. *The Stationers' Company and the Printers of London, 1501–1557*, vol. 2. Cambridge: Cambridge University Press.

Bowen, K.L. 2020. Philips Galle's *Nova Reperta*: A Case Study in Print Prices and Distribution. In: L. Markey, ed. *Renaissance Invention: Stradanus's "Nova Reperta."* Chicago, IL: Northwestern University Press.

Burke, V.E. 2013. Recent Studies in Commonplace Books. *English Literary Renaissance*. **43.1**, 153–77.

Carefoote, P.J. 2019. *Confusion of Printers: The Role of Print in the English Reformation*. Eugene, OR: Wipf & Stock.

Carlson, P. 2017. The Art and Craft of Dying. In: A. Hiscock and H. Wilcox, eds. *The Oxford Handbook of Early Modern English Literature and Religion*. Oxford: Oxford University Press. pp. 634–49.

Cassirer, E. 1977 [1923]. *The Philosophy of Symbolic Forms*. Vol. 2: *Mythical Thought*. R. Manheim, trans. New Haven: Yale University Press.

———. 2021. The Philosophy of Symbolic Forms. Vol. 2: Mythical Thought . trans. S.G. Lofts. New York: Routledge.

Chartier, R. 1994. *The Order of Books: Readers, Authors, and Libraries in Europe between the Fourteenth and Eighteenth Centuries*. trans. L.G. Cochrane. Stanford: Stanford University Press.

Coldiron, A.E.B. 2015. *Printers Without Borders: Translation and Textuality in the Renaissance*. Cambridge: Cambridge University Press.

Collinson, P. 1988. *The Birthpangs of Protestant England: Religious and Cultural Change in the Sixteenth and Seventeenth Centuries*. New York: Palgrave Macmillan.

Daniell, D. 2001. *William Tyndale: A Biography*. New Haven: Yale University Press.

Dowley, T. 2015. *Atlas of the European Reformations*. Minneapolis: Fortress Press.

Dryness, W.A. 2004. *Reformed Theology and Visual Culture: The Protestant Imagination from Calvin to Edwards*. Cambridge: Cambridge University Press.

Eggert, K. 2015. *Disknowledge: Literature, Alchemy, and the End of Humanism in Renaissance England*. Philadelphia: University of Pennsylvania Press.

Eisenstein, E.L. 2012. *The Printing Revolution in Early Modern Europe*. Cambridge: Cambridge University Press.

Engel, W.E. 1991. Mnemonic Criticism and Renaissance Literature: A Manifesto. *Connotations*. **1.1**, 12–33.

———. 1995. *Mapping Mortality: The Persistence of Memory and Melancholy in Early Modern England*. Amherst, MA: University of Massachusetts Press.

———. 2016. *Chiastic Designs in English Literature for Sidney to Shakespeare*. New York: Routledge.

———. 2020. Knowledge: Science and Education. In: A. Arcangeli and M. Tamm, eds. *A Cultural History of Memory in the Early Modern Age*, vol. 3. London: Bloomsbury. pp. 77–96.

Engel, W.E., Loughnane, R., and Williams, G. 2016. *The Memory Arts in Renaissance England: A Critical Anthology*. Cambridge: Cambridge University Press.

Evenden, E. 2002. "Patents and Patronage: the life and career of John Day, Tudor Printer." Ph.D. Thesis. University of York.

———. 2008. *Patents, Pictures and Patronage: John Day and the Tudor Book Trade*. Aldershot; Burlington, VT: Ashgate.

Evenden, E., and Freeman, T.S. 2002. John Foxe, John Day and the Printing of the "Book of Martyrs." In: R. Myers, M. Harris, and G. Mandelbrote, eds. *Lives in Print: Biography and the Book Trade from the Middle Ages to the 21st Century*. New Castle, DE and London: Oak Knoll Press and The British Library. pp. 23–54.

———. 2013. *Religion and the Book in Early Modern England: The Making of John Foxe's "Book of Martyrs."* Cambridge: Cambridge University Press.

Evett, D. 1990. *Literature and the Visual Arts in Tudor England*. Athens: University of Georgia Press.

Febvre, L. and H.-J. Martin. 2010; repr. 1958. *The Coming of the Book: The Impact of Printing, 1450–1800*. D. Gerard, trans. and G. Nowell-Smith and D. Wootton, eds. London: Verso.

Fish, S. 1970. Literature in the Reader: Affective Stylistics. *New Literary History*. **2.1,** 123–62.

Foucault, M. 2001. *Fearless Speech*. J. Pearson, ed. Los Angeles, CA: Semiotext(e).

Frascari, M. 1984. The Tell-The-Tale Detail. In: P. Behrens and A. Fisher, eds. *VIA 7: The Building of Architecture*. Cambridge, MA: MIT Press. pp. 23–37.

Frisch, A. 2016. Montaigne on Memory. In: P. Desan, ed. *The Oxford Handbook of Montaigne*. Oxford: Oxford University Press. pp. 648–62.

Fudge, J. 2007. *Commerce and Print in the Early Reformation*. Leiden: Brill.

Green, I. 2003. *Print and Protestantism in Early Modern England*. Oxford: Oxford University Press.

Hartmann, A.-M. 2018. *English Mythography in Its European Context, 1500–1650*. Oxford: Oxford University Press.

Heckscher, W.S. 1974. Petites Perceptions: An Account of "sortes Warburgianae." *Journal of Medieval and Renaissance Studies*. **4,** 101–34.

Helfer, R. 2018. The State of the Art of Memory and Shakespeare Studies. In: A. Hiscock and L.P. Wilder, eds. *The Routledge Handbook of Shakespeare and Memory*. London: Routledge. pp. 315–28.

Horowitz, M.C. 1998. *Seeds of Virtue and Knowledge*. Princeton, NJ: Princeton University Press.

Imhof, D. 2020. Stadanus's Print Shop and the Practice of Printing in Sixteenth-Century Antwerp. In: L. Markey, ed. *Renaissance Invention: Stradanus's "Nova Reperta."* Chicago, IL: Northwestern University Press. pp. 55–60.

Johnson, C.D. 2012. *Memory, Metaphor, and Aby Warburg's Atlas of Images*. Ithaca, NY: Cornell University Press.

Johnson, L., Sutton, J., and Tribble, E.B., eds. 2014. *Embodied Cognition and Shakespeare's Theatre: The Early Modern Body-Mind*. New York, NY, and London: Routledge.

Johnson, P. 1964. Architectural Details. *Architectural Record*. April, 137–47.

Juhász-Ormsby, Á. 2017. Erasmus' *Apophthegmata* in Henrician England. *Erasmus Studies* **37,** 45–67.

King, J.N. 2011. *Foxe's "Book of Martyrs" and Early Modern Print Culture*. Cambridge: Cambridge University Press.

Klibansky, R., Panofsky, E., and Saxl, F. 2019. *Saturn and Melancholy: Studies in the History of Natural Philosophy, Religion, and Art*. New Edition. P. Despoix and G. Leroux, eds. Montreal and Kingston: McGill-Queen's University Press.

Kristeller, P.O. 1988. Humanism. In: C.B. Schmitt and Q. Skinner, eds. *The Cambridge History of Renaissance Philosophy*. Cambridge: Cambridge University Press. pp. 111–38.

LeGoff, J. 1992. *History and Memory*. S. Rendall and E. Claman, trans. New York, NY: Columbia University Press.
Levine, E.J. 2013. *Dreamland of Humanists: Warburg, Cassirer, Panofsky, and the Hamburg School*. Chicago, IL: University of Chicago Press.
Loades, D., dir., 2011. The John Foxe Project. Humanities Research Institute, University of Sheffield. www.dhi.ac.uk/foxe/.
Lyne, R. 2016. *Memory and Intertextuality in Renaissance Literature*. Cambridge: Cambridge University Press.
MacCulloch, D. 2005. *The Reformation: A History*. New York, NY: Penguin.
Mack, P. 1985. Rudolph Agricola's Reading of Literature. *Journal of the Warburg and Courtauld Institutes*. 48, 23–41.
Marcus, L.S. 2000. The Silence of the Archive and the Noise of Cyberspace. In: N. Rhodes and J. Sawday, eds. *The Renaissance Computer: Knowledge Technology in the First Age of Print*, London: Routledge. pp. 18–28.
Markey, L. 2020. Introduction. In: L. Markey, ed. *Renaissance Invention: Stradanus's "Nova Reperta."* Chicago, IL: Northwestern University Press. pp. 25–39.
Marshall, P. 2017. Britain's Reformations. In: P. Marshall, ed. *The Oxford Illustrated History of the Reformation*. Oxford: Oxford University Press. pp. 186–226.
McLuhan, M. 1969. *The Gutenberg Galaxy: The Making of Typographic Man*. Toronto: Signet.
Melnikoff, K. 2018. *Elizabethan Publishing and the Makings of Literary Culture*. Toronto: University of Toronto Press.
Menary, R., ed. 2012. *The Extended Mind*. Cambridge, MA: Bradford Books.
Mieder, W. 2008. *"Proverbs Speak Louder than Words": Wisdom in Art, Culture, Folklore, History, Literature and Mass Media*. New York, NY: Peter Lang.
Moss, A. 2002. *Printed Commonplace-Books and the Structuring of Renaissance Thought*. Oxford: Oxford University Press.
Neuber, W. 2009. Mnemonic Imagery in the Early Modern Period: Visibility and Collective Memory. In: D. Beecher and G. Williams, eds. *Ars Reminiscendi: Mind and Memory in Renaissance Culture*. Toronto: Center for Reformation and Renaissance Studies. pp. 69–81.
Nora, P. 1989. Between Memory and History: Les Lieux de Mémoire. *Representations*. 26, 7–24.
Nyhart, L.K. 2012. *Wissenschaft* and *Kunde*: The General and the Special in Modern Science. *Osiris*. 27, 250–75.
Oastler, C.L. 1975. *John Day, the Elizabethan Printer*. Oxford: Oxford Bibliographical Society.
Ong, W. 1991. *Orality and Literacy: The Technologizing of the Word*. New York, NY: Routledge.
Panofsky, E. 1972. *Studies in Iconology: Humanistic Themes in the Art of the Renaissance*. London: Routledge.
Pettegree, A. 2011. *The Book in the Renaissance*. New Haven, CT: Yale University Press.
———. 2015. *Brand Luther*. New York, NY: Penguin.
Pivetti, K. 2015. *On Memory and Literary Form: Making the Early Modern English Nation*. Newark, NJ: University of Delaware.
Pollmann, J. and Kuijpers, E. 2013. Introduction: On the Early Modernity of Modern Memory. In: E. Kuijpers, J. Pollmann, J. Müller, and J. van der Stehen,

eds. *Memory Before Modernity: Practices of Memory in Early Modern Europe* Leiden: Brill. pp. 1–23.

Purdy, A. 2002. The Bog Body as Mnemotope: Nationalist Archaeologies in Heaney and Turner. *Style.* **36.1**, 93–110.

Rhodes, N. and Sawday, J. 2000. Paperworlds: Imagining the Renaissance Computer. In: N. Rhodes and J. Sawday, eds. *The Renaissance Computer: Knowledge Technology in the First Age of Print.* London. Routledge. pp. 1–17.

Schwemmer, O. 2004. The Variety of Symbolic Worlds and the Unity of Mind. In: C. Hamlin and J.M. Krois, eds. *Symbolic Forms and Cultural Studies: Ernst Cassirer's Theory of Culture.* New Haven, CT: Yale University Press. pp. 3–18.

Schwyzer, P. 2004. *Literature, Nationalism, and Memory in Early Modern England and Wales.* Cambridge: Cambridge University Press.

Semon, R.W. 1921. *The Mneme.* L. Simon, trans. London: George Allen & Unwin.

———. 1923. *Mnemic Psychology.* B. Duffy, trans. London: George Allen & Unwin.

Seznec, J. 1940. *La survivance des dieux antiques: essai sur le rôle de la tradition mythologique dans l'humanisme et dans l'art de la Renaissance* (Studies of the Warburg Institute 11). London: The Warburg Institute.

———. 1953. *The Survival of the Pagan Gods: The Mythological Tradition and Its Place in Renaissance Humanism and Art.* B. Sessions, trans. New York, NY: Pantheon.

Shrank, C. 2004. *Writing the Nation in Reformation England, 1530–1580.* Oxford: Oxford University Press.

Spengler, O. 1996 [1926]. *The Decline of the West.* C.F. Atkinson, trans. New York, NY: Knopf.

Sullivan, M.A. 2017. *Bruegel and the Creative Process, 1559–1563.* New York, NY: Routledge.

Sutton, J. 1998. *Philosophy and Memory Traces: Descartes to Connectionism.* Cambridge: Cambridge University Press.

Sutton, N.S. 1993. "Arise for it is Day": The John Day Imprints and the English Reformation, 1549–1559. *The Journal of Religious and Theological Information.* **1.1**, 29–58.

Tofts, D., Jonson, A., and Cavallaro, A., eds. 2004. *Prefiguring Cyberculture: An Intellectual History.* Cambridge, MA: Massachusetts Institute of Technology Press.

Tribble, E.B. 2011. *Cognition in the Globe: Attention and Memory in Shakespeare's Theatre.* New York, NY: Palgrave Macmillan.

Tribble, E.B. and Keene, N., eds. 2011.*Cognitive Ecologies and the History of Remembering: Religion, Education and Memory in Early Modern England.* New York, NY: Palgrave Macmillan.

Viljoen, M.C. 2020. Diligent Labor in Stradanus's Engraving Shop. In: L. Markey, ed. *Renaissance Invention: Stradanus's "Nova Reperta."* Chicago, IL: Northwestern University Press. pp. 61–73.

Vine, A. 2019. *Miscellaneous Order: Manuscript Culture and the Early Modern Organization of Knowledge.* Oxford: Oxford University Press.

Warburg, A. 2020. *Bilderatlas Mnemosyne: The Original*. R. Ohrt and A. Heil, eds. Berlin: Hatje Cantz.
Wesseling, A. 2002. Dutch Proverbs and Expressions in Erasmus' Adages, Colloquies, and Letters. *Renaissance Quarterly*. **55.1**, 81–147.
Wind, E. 1958. *The Pagan Mysteries in the Renaissance: An Exploration of Philosophical and Mystical Sources of Iconography in Renaissance Art*. London: Faber and Faber
Yates, F.A. 1978. *The Art of Memory*. Harmondsworth: Penguin.

1 The deluxe design of *The Cosmographical Glass* (1559)

> Thou that mak'st gain thy end, and wisely well,
>   Call'st a book good, or bad, as it doth sell,
> Use mine so, too: I give thee leave. But crave
>   For the luck's sake, it thus much favor have,
> To lie upon thy stall, till it be sought;
>   Not offer'd, as it made suit to be bought.
>   —Ben Jonson, "To my Bookseller"[1]

There were many material and pecuniary aspects of the production, circulation, and trade in books in early modern London, and John Day was engaged in nearly all of them. Above all else, though, he was a printer. Indeed, he has been felicitously dubbed "the master printer of the English Reformation" by John King (2011, p. 80). The term "master printer," however, had very specific connotations in the guild structure of the day. The research of Peter Blayney (2013) bears out that of "seventy-three master printers known to have worked in England in the first half of the sixteenth century, only fourteen had been trained by serving apprenticeships with the Stationers"—and Day was not among them (p. 931). It is only by including "two widows, five redemptioners, and John Day" (originally with the Stringers' Company), that "we can pad the Stationers' contribution to twenty-two out of seventy-three" (pp. 931–2). Such data compromise the traditional view of home-grown London Stationers as dominating the British printing trade.

As early as 1403, there was something like a guild of stationers in London, long before official record keeping of the works produced and regulations about who had the right to print which books as well as regarding who would stand to profit from subsequent reissues and reprintings. Real profits, Ian Green (2003) contends, did not come from the first edition, "when initial overheads such as payments for the manuscript, authority to publish, license, and registration had to be covered, but from the second, third, and further editions (and even then competitors might try to produce pirate copies)" (pp. 14–15). In the earliest days of the guild, membership embraced people from a variety of crafts and trades,

DOI: 10.4324/9780429032431-2

including those who wrote texts or otherwise provided content drawn from earlier sources or translations; those who decorated and colored manuscript and block book pages called *lymners* (illuminators); as well as bookbinders, who were themselves often booksellers and tended to carry out their trade at a designated location, hence the term *stationarius* (literally, someone based in a single place), which in this case was near to the wall of St Paul's Cathedral. It was not until May 1557 that the Stationers received a royal charter as London's 47th livery company, based in Peter College, which they recently had purchased from St Paul's.

Although publishing was not yet a profession as such, and "remained a very risky enterprise, undertaken to enhance rather than replace the publisher's main source of income" (Green 2003, p. 14), those of any standing tended to be "stationers—members of the Stationers' Company," which soon became "the key body for controlling the trade" with government support. Further, books increasingly were being published by "stationers whose daily trade was bookselling, and who used their own shop as an outlet to the public and other booksellers" (p. 14). Recent critical work on early modern London stationers by cultural bibliographers such as Marta Straznicky (2013) suggests we see stationers—the "collective term for printers, publishers, and booksellers in the modern period"—not only as practitioners of "any of the trades involved in book production, including binding, parchment making, and copying," but additionally as "readers of the texts they ushered into print," who, in performing acts of critical judgment about what works to publish, may also have "had motives that were not exclusively financial" (p. 3). Such background information about the place of stationers in London's early modern paperworld, both as tradespeople and as discerning readers of the works they ended up deciding to bring to market, helps set the scene for my examination of the material conditions of production and prevalent terms of trade undergirding the cultural significance of Day's "lifelong commitment to the dissemination of Protestant books and pamphlets" (King 2011, p. 180).

"Arise for it is Day"

As was discussed in the Introduction, there was hardly a monolithic notion of Protestantism in mid-16th century Britain beyond very general support of the Elizabethan Church with its state apparatus based in Westminster, and the eschewing of Roman Catholic practices and Eucharistic ideology (MacCulloch 2005, p. 288). As Marshall and Ryrie (2002) have characterized the situation, "English Protestantism ... was subversive, combative, intellectual and individualistic, drawing on the printshop and the pulpit; and at the same time hierarchical, universalist and eager to ally with the magistrate" (p. 13). In the earlier days of the Henrician Church, aspects of what has been termed "the non-Lutheran Reformation" by Diarmaid MacCulloch seem effortlessly to have "crossed cultural and linguistic boundaries" and Henry VIII appointed "evangelical-minded tutors" for his son and heir, the future Edward VI, such that, at his accession and with Thomas Cranmer's guidance, "England was suddenly poised to act as a refuge for prominent European Protestants" and welcomed many "overseas reformers who had been displaced by Catholic victories in central Europe" (MacCulloch 2005, pp. 254–6). Andrew Pettegree (1986) estimates that as many as 50,000 foreigners immigrated into England between the 1440s and 1550s (pp. 76–9). Among those seeking refuge in London, especially from Antwerp owing to Charles V's intensified persecution of Protestants in the Low Countries (MacCulloch 2005, p. 596), were members of a skilled artisanal class of printers, typefounders, binders, and all manner of craftspeople associated with publishing and distributing books. Extant records of the lay assessments indicate that Day had no fewer than four Dutchmen working for him (McKitterick 2003, p. 98), veterans of the printing industry, who from at least 1563–71 were registered as lodging in his then new and more commodious residence at Aldersgate (Evenden 2004, p. 76; and Evenden 2008, p. 17).

Prior to setting up his quality printshop in the parish of St Anne and St Agnes, coincident with his transferring from the Stringers' to the Stationers' Company, Day had been based in Cheapside from about 1549 (Alford 2002, pp. 119–20). By 1551, he made his mark reprinting a deluxe edition of the Bible (discussed further in what follows), with his former Cheapside partner, lifelong friend, and sometimes collaborator, William Seres. So even though Day from time to time was away from his place of business following up on patronage leads and in legislative venues looking after his interests (mainly to enforce his privilege to produce specific books and pamphlets and to shore up the monopolies he had been granted), his center of operation was the printing house. Daily tasks included commissioning or otherwise acquiring state-of-the-art woodblocks; supervising if not himself recasting the matrices for press production; proofreading, correcting, and casting off pages for the press; acting as an agent between Matthew Parker and the type-founders responsible for cutting Anglo-Saxon fonts in brass at the Archbishop's expense (Day printed four books wholly or partly in Anglo-Saxon);[2] as well as playing his civic role as Master of the Stationers' Company in the 1580s. All such activities, and many more besides, need to be factored into how we imagine Day's role in the bustling and far-from-tidy early modern English bookworld, keeping in mind Peter Blayney's (2013) apt assessment that of all the Edwardian printers who survived Mary's reign, the one whose career "presents the most puzzles and contradictions is John Day" (p. 798).

A few examples will serve to illustrate the sweep of the different kinds of authority involved with Day's becoming "master printer of the English Reformation." There are more than a few instances when he silently served as the ostensible author—or, more properly, as the producer and hence authorizer—of an astonishing array of publications already ascribed to others (Sutton 1993). Typically, after having made what he considered the necessary licensing agreements, he would supervise and assist members of his workshop in the translation and setting of English type font for the printing of works originally published in other languages, whether the approved catechism in English (the subject of Chapter 2) or a new version of the psalms in Dutch[3] (treated further in Chapter 4). One documented case (and for every one that is documented, there are perhaps a dozen more that have slipped into the mist of historical surmise) came about because of Day's presuming upon patents he had received during the reign of King Edward to print any works by two popular religious writers, Becon and Ponet—patents that were "obviously no longer useable" (Blayney 2013, p. 807). He was taken to task for encroaching on a preexisting patent, namely, for printing Ponet's Catechism. A resulting compromise, in the wake of involved and acrimonious legal wrangling, assigned the Catechism in Latin to Reyner Wolfe and in English to Day (Evenden 2008, pp. 25–6). As Day had expected, given how the winds of the reformist desire for religious books in English were blowing at the time, he came out on top. And, as will be discussed in more detail in Chapter 2, he continued to generate a steady stream of revenue from this work throughout his life (Evenden 2008, pp. 170–3). Enough so that he was able to fund his larger, more labor-intensive and time-consuming projects, such as his "landmark editions of textual *monuments* by Protestant luminaries" (King 2001, p. 67) [original emphasis], and *The Book of Martyrs* (the subject of Chapter 3),which tied up no fewer than three of his presses dedicated solely to finishing this work, which was something of a gamble owing to the long delay before any profits on it could be realized (Oastler 1975, pp. 65–9).

Day's authority and authorial status not only derived from but also extended beyond his role as a printer. There are instances, for example, of his being recorder and translator, and what today we might think of as a reporter. Epistolary evidence confirms that, after the third printing of Foxe's *Book of Martyrs* (to use its popular designation), Day collected and transcribed information told to him from surviving Protestant martyrs and witnesses of the harrowing Marian executions that was included in the fourth edition of *Acts and Monuments*—a work he envisioned as being a lasting monument to his skills, no less than to his own life as a printer devoted to the Protestant cause (Evenden 2008, p. 173). Insofar as the first edition of 1563 had leaned heavily on the genre of firsthand testimony, Day was thereafter the regular recipient of material from informants from all stations and social rank eager to set the record straight about what had happened, albeit from their personal recollections suffused with trauma. Such up-to-the-minute reporting both made for good copy and proved to be valuable additions in later editions of Foxe's *Book of Martyrs*. Day's exact process for getting this newly recovered information into print is difficult to determine. Additionally, he was adept at seamlessly presenting material while at the same time effacing his personal participation. A good case in point is Day's inclusion of the calendar of "saints' days" in *Acts and Monuments* (Evenden and Freeman 2013, p. 126), which directly imitates and explicitly subverts traditional—which is to say Catholic—lists of "approved" luminaries in the Church (a theme resumed in Chapter 3). That Day tacitly authored such material buttressing the book's main aims by way of, in this case, a summary account at-a-glance of the main figures to be considered and kept in mind by readers reflects his role as an author and not just as the printer of this monumental undertaking that captured and, to a large extent, shaped the early modern English Protestant imagination, quickly becoming "one of the cornerstones of English Protestant identity" (MacCulloch 2005, p. 285).

Along these lines, the most famous surviving and certainly the earliest known portrait of Day is his right-facing profile included in Foxe's *Book of Martyrs* (see Figure 1.1). The accompanying chiastic motto, not unusual in this period given to serious if witty contemplative exercises, turns his image into a moral *memento mori* emblem: "Life is Death and Death is life."[4] His authorial textual contributions for the most part remain unattributed within the larger work, as with his collected interviews from witnesses of the harrowing persecutions in recent memory. However, when Day wanted to alert readers to his hand in a book's production, he readily crowed about it. His distinctive motto, identifying colophon, and complex *memento mori* end-page printer's device are among the ways in which Day marked the products of his ingenuity and labor. They serve as both self-advertisement and as a metaphorical "wake-up call" to his evangelically minded readers. Day knew well how to convey his absent presence graphically, typographically, and allegorically. Typical of the witty verbal-visual conceits and canted puns of the day, and consonant with the rebus tradition to which William Camden devoted a whole chapter in his celebrated *Remains*,[5] Day developed and used several proprietary printer's marks—or colophons—to identify the books from his press as distinctive products of his own industry. Perhaps the most celebrated of which shows a sunrise with a sleeper being awakened, with the motto "Arise for it is Day" (see Figure 1.2; and, for its placement on the title page of Day's (1551) printing of The Bible, Figure 1.3).[6]

One of the characteristic aspects of such emblematic devices is that they lend themselves to being read in several ways at once, even as they keep their own counsel as it were. Generally, though, Day's motto is taken to be an allusion to the Reformation, with the clarion call to awaken from one's spiritual slumber and greet the new dawn of the changing times. King (1982) among others has noticed that the background can be interpreted as an evocation of the vision of New Jerusalem, continuing the symbolism of resurrection and revelation, which is further reinforced by the commonplace conceit of linking Christ to the rising

Deluxe design of The Cosmographical Glass 35

Figure 1.1 Portrait of John Day. *The Acts and Monuments* (London, 1563). Image used courtesy of The Lambeth Palace Library.

sun (p. 187). Day's motto and device, taken together, exemplify the intertwining of his printing career and religious faith (King 2001), which is clarified further through an allusive reference to the apocalyptic exhortation in I Thessalonians 5:5. This passage, following the wording of William Tyndale's translation of the New Testament in the Bible that Day printed (1551, fol. xxiii[v]), reads as follows: "You are the children of light

Figure 1.2 "Arise for it is Day." Day's Printer's mark on title page of The Bible (London: John Day, 1551). Beinecke Rare Book and Manuscript Library, Yale University.

and the children of the day. We are not of the night, neither of darkness." The symbolism thus betokens "the end of the world as the dawning of a New Day," such that the "reference affords a network of puns on the publisher's name" (p. 72).

Somewhere along the way, a few fabulous stories came to be associated with Day's motto, concerning his manner of handling his apprentices; stories that even if not documentable nonetheless reveal something about what contemporaries wanted to believe about the legendary hospitality of this "master printer" whose shop offered sanctuary and lodging to traveling humanists as well as foreign workers with reformed inclinations. Tradition has it that part of Day's morning rounds included rousing those who were residing at his premises and urging them to get on with the business of the day—or indeed, the business of Day.[7] Hence the admonitory double-pronged summons: "Arise for it is day," meaning also "get up, Day's here!" And Day was nothing if not industrious, with upward of 300 titles attributed to the printshop associated with his name. It could also be an allusion that only those closest to Day would apprehend at a glance for, apropos of his motto "Arise for it is day," Day started his printing firm "at the sign of the Resurrection," then located above "the Conduit in Holborn" (Isaac 1932, p. 81), having moved to Aldersgate by 1549. It should be kept in mind however that from the beginning, with his laboring "at the sign of the Resurrection," Day would go on to oversee several businesses in various parts of London (including properties he leased for his own use and some that he rented out), with an eye toward getting his products to market in a variety of ways. Day was a canny entrepreneur and a skilled printer devoted to the cause of religious reformation in England. As such, he was the originator and hence the author—whether acting as printer, publisher, overseer of

Deluxe design of The Cosmographical Glass   37

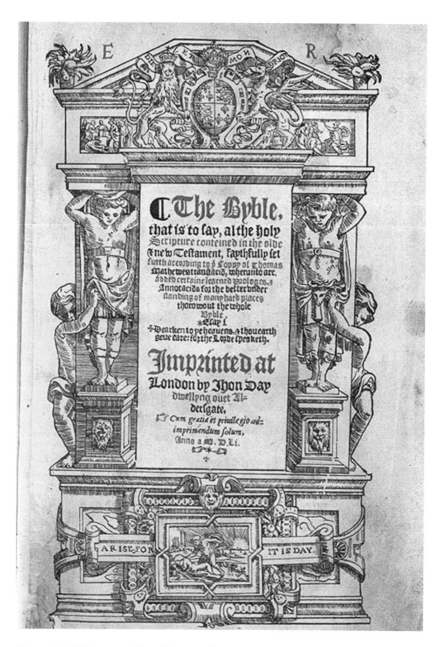

Figure 1.3 Title page. The Bible (London: John Day, 1551). Beinecke Rare Book and Manuscript Library, Yale University.

translations, outsourcer of works he had obtained the rights to reproduce—of hundreds of important works of the 16th-century book trade. Narrowing the scope to examine more carefully this phenomenon that was John Day, each chapter will take at least one of his works in particular to single out for scrutiny those traits that make him more than simply "master printer of the Reformation" (to echo once more John King's words), but also a key player in and also an author of the English Reformation in his own right. We are now in a position to press on and considered how movers and shakers of the Tudor paperworld, like John Day, warrant being considered authors.

The printer as author and the aura of authority

To understand what is meant by "the printer as author" as it is being used in this study, we need to go back to the classical origins of the term. Etymology and philology can help fill in some of the essential information encouraging us to entertain this perception of some 16th-century printers, exemplarily John Day, as rightfully arrogating the role and name of author. The Latin noun *auctor*, from the verb *augere* (meaning "to increase, originate, or promote") by way of the Old French *autor*, came into Middle English to denote someone who invents or causes something to be; acquiring the medial "th" perhaps owing to preference for Saxon diphthongs commonly used to naturalize English words from romance roots (Onions 1966, p. 63). Additionally, the term handily parallels the introduction of the word "authentic" into English, in use as early as the 1540s to mean "legally or duly qualified, authorized, licensed" (Oxford English Dictionary [OED] 1989). Hence, by 1611, the resulting translation of the Bible in English, set in motion by King James I and VI having convened the Hampton Court conference, will be called the "Authorized Version" (Nicolson 2003, pp. 110–23; Norton 2005, pp. 96–8). As James Raven (2007) rightly shows, "the 1611 Authorised King James Bible" was to become "the most familiar and legally protected of literary commodities in the English language" (p. 76). The expansive semantic field of the word "author" includes, originally, "creator, originator, source, person or thing which gives rise to something," which in the Middle Ages often was used "with specific reference to God as the creator of the universe"; and, by the 14th century, connoted "ancestor, parent" (OED 1989). Stephen Guy-Bray (2010) has summarized the teleologically driven metaphorics of male parthenogenesis in the Renaissance in terms relevant to this excursus on Day's authorial role:

> Like sexuality, textuality is supposed to lead to or continue something, and that something is chiefly the maintenance of the society in which the text was produced. The work of art, that is, does not reproduce itself: it reproduces social relations.
>
> (p. 21)

The word "author," then, derived from the Latin term for someone who produces something, carries with it the implication of a father or progenitor, of someone having the legal responsibility for, authority over, and perhaps even shame at what ends up being produced. Horace (1929) imagines his book is like a slave whom he has paternalistically nurtured to do good in the world but, once out of his care and protection, who can say what will happen (pp. 388–9):

> You seem, my book, to be looking wistfully toward Vertumnus and Janus,[8] in order, forsooth, that you may go on sale, neatly polished with the pumice of the Sosii.[9] You hate the keys and seals,[10] so dear to the modest; you grieve at being shown to few, and praise a life in public, though I did not rear you thus. Off with you, down to where you itch to go. When you are once let out, there will be no coming back.

The same trope is used by Chaucer for a somewhat different purpose in his extended envoy at the end of *Troilus and Criseyde* (V.1786–1806), and, by Spenser at the opening of his *Shepherd's Calender*, with an obvious nod to Chaucer. In the first case, the author, in a poetic gesture of wryly acknowledging his models, his venerable sources or *auctores*, sends the product of his ingenuity and labor out into the world with "Go little book" (l.1786), and seeks to impress upon it never to lose sight of its antecedents from whom it rightly should claim lineage, namely, Vigil, Ovid, Homer, Lucan, and Statius (l.1792). Spenser (1970) develops this conceit with reference to his book being some sort of enigmatic extension of himself in the following terms: "Go little book: thy self present, / As child whose parent is unkent" (p. 417), putting the emphasis on the self-consciously chosen archaic term at the end of the line that means of unknown parentage or otherwise unrecognized. Apropos of which Douglas Brooks (2005) contends correctly that the use of such procreative metaphors was "spectacularly suitable for articulating a range of emergent relations within a book trade radically transformed by the invention of movable type" (p. 2). Even so, such metaphors themselves have a lineage, whether or not acknowledged by Renaissance poets. The late medieval sense of the word *auctoritas* implied, according to Alastair Minnis (2010), veracity and sagacity, especially as regards a venerated source on whose authority some precedent can be established. The writings of an "*auctor* contained, or possessed, *auctoritas* in the abstract sense of the term" (p. 10). The role of the *auctor* was distinguished from that of scribe, compiler, and commentator, and, by the 16th century with the advent of the paperworld, a printer or publisher might take on all of these functions—and others as well—in order to produce a work considered new even if it was based on a text already in circulation. For our purposes then, as applied to printers like John Day, the term carries within it both the sense of the self-conscious littérateur and also one staking, authoritatively, a claim to the sole and (often) legitimate rights to the work being produced—and reproduced. The shape and form of the books Day printed all quite literally bear his unique stamp consistent with, but also in addition to, his ingenious printer's device. It is therefore important to trace how this came about and what his role was in the creative process, especially as regards the composition and selection of material to be printed, as well as his capitalizing the machines and overseeing the supplies that enabled him to fashion an oeuvre that left its indelible mark on the English literary Renaissance.

The kind of collaborative activity being discussed here, as pertains to what happened under Day's supervision, is similar in kind if different in degree from the practices of collaborative authorship that, as Harold Love (2002) remarks "is so common, and so often disguised, as to constitute a central concern of attribution studies," that notably is the case with much scholarly work on the plays of Shakespeare concerned "not with finding a single author but with teasing out the contributions of two or more working either as collaborators or as original author and reviser" (p. 37).[11] Our present focus is on the role of the printer who sometimes doubled as a publisher, but who also played the role of reader, reviser, and corrector of errors. The printer as author brought books into the world that indeed were written or translated by others and yet still managed to give them something of his own stamp of originality owing to layout, lettering, design features, and above all else his imprimatur—his seal of approval, attesting to his authoritative assessment of the viability of a text as a marketable commodity.

Any inquiry into what might be meant by "the printer as author" owes a debt to both dialectical anthropology and philosophical archeology with regard to the essential nature of what constitutes an author—in the modern sense of the term—along the lines suggestively presented during the height of "The Structuralist Controversy."[12] Michel Foucault's "What is an author?" tacitly in dialogue with Roland Barthes's "The Death of the Author," redirected the conversation to more material, less aureate origins of the "very notion of an author or singular voice that owns its utterance."[13] This strain of critical inquiry more recently has been resumed and extended by Seán Burke (2010), which has considerable relevance to my own concern with what is to be gained by looking at—phenomenologically and categorically speaking—the printer as author:

> Within the discourse of the death of the author, however, it is not enough to exclude the author but to recognize that the author has always been absent, that there never could be an author in the first place. Barthes, Foucault, and Derrida thus take anti-authorialism to the extreme of promoting authorial exclusion from a methodological prescription to an ontological statement about the essence of discourse itself. The appearance of writing is a priori identifiable with the disappearance of the author.
>
> (p. 15)

Accordingly, my situating Day's authorial role in the procedural generation of texts prior to a time when "authorship" had become an ideology[14] is consonant with the understanding, exemplarily articulated by Mark Rose (2002), that "cultural production is always a matter of appropriation and transformation" that elides "the role of the publisher" in cultural production (p. 135). Thus, in emending, expanding, and arranging the elements of a preexisting text—sometimes in his role as publisher and sometimes as printer—Day implicitly assumes the tasks traditionally and historically associated with an author, but in such a way that his own authorial voice, while not explicitly evident, is materially omnipresent in the works brought into existence by virtue of his ingenuity.[15]

This contention is borne out by the fact that court rulings and the tightening up of licensing and publication regulations in the age before copyright was directed at printers and publishers rather than the people who actually wrote the works, who were under a different kind of scrutiny altogether (Loewenstein 2002, p. 28). Leo Kirschbaum (1946) succinctly put all of this into perspective decades ago: "In Shakespeare's day, neither the Stationers' Company nor the government was interested in the rights of the author" (p. 43). The operative presumption then is that in Tudor England there definitely was a concern with regulating the printing trade, not with the rewards or tribulations of authorship. Moreover, Day was just as likely to suss out for himself what works would be sufficiently lucrative to offset production costs, whether by English authors or those from the continent—and it often was the case that books by people who had experienced famous deaths were judged to be especially marketable. The latter is certainly the case in one of Day's early and very successful ventures. In 1562, he published the complete sermons of Hugh Latimer, chaplain to Edward VI and who later, during the reign of Mary I, was burned at the stake in 1555, one of the three "Oxford Martyrs" memorialized in Day's printing of *Acts and Monuments*. To be sure, there already was a connection to and a licensing pact of sorts involving Latimer's reformist ideas about the English Church insofar as Day (in collaboration with William Seres) previously published Latimer's first sermon preached before the young king at the height of the Edwardian reforms in 1549.[16] The collaboration of Day and Seres resulted in over 100 books and pamphlets (in many of which Day's "I.D." monogram serves the purpose of a printer's mark) concerned principally with religious works, most notably those by Robert Crowley. Indeed, Day and Seres were known best in the trade for having produced books "largely related to theological controversies of the time" (King 1999, p. 176).

Day also profited from seeking to license and reprint works that had no single assigned or clearly identifiable author, as with his printing of "a number of editions of the Bible and parts thereof beginning in 1548" (Sutton 1993, p. 49; see also King 2001, p. 72). Many of the works from Day's press early on, including the 1551 Bible (Figure 1.3), bear the words "Cum Gratis et Privilegio ad Imprimendum solum," even though, as Oastler (1975) points out, there is no record of any earlier grants of such a Royal Privilege or Letters Patent (p. 70).

This seems to be something of a pattern with Day, as there are other instances of his using this wording claiming exclusivity to print a book while remaining heedless of or at least as a way of testing the limits of other printers' claims. After all, such licenses, even when granted, could cover rather broad categories. If no one called out Day on it, then he proceeded unchecked. In this regard, Richard Tottel, perhaps best known for his miscellaneous collection of English songs and sonnets (Warner 2013), "held the patent for the printing of all law books," and Byrd and Tallis "for all printing of music" (Loewenstein 2002, p. 29). Neither Thomas Tallis nor William Byrd were stationers, but still were given this exclusive right to print music for 21 years such that, in 1598, as Kirschbaum (1946) documented, the patent for music printing was granted to Thomas Morley (p. 45).[17] As will be discussed further in Chapter 2, irrespective of these printers being awarded the privilege "for all printing of music," Day had no compunction about printing musical notes—or meter, as it was termed—for singing the "metrical psalms," presumably because he believed his monopoly on the psalms warranted his investing in obtaining several sets of music fonts.[18] Indeed, the Sternhold and Hopkins Psalms published by Day in 1565 (STC 2434) was, according to Hannibal Hamlin (2004), "the most widely known volume of verse in English and made its way into the hands of English men and women of all social classes" (pp. 38–9). Insofar as Day is publishing texts geared principally toward promoting and advancing an English Protestant world orientation, his major works can be considered discrete exemplifications of mnemotopes (as discussed in the Introduction), for they involve site-specific materializations of the past brought forward into the present, serving thereby as a vehicle for personal and cultural memory.

Eager to establish himself as more than a job printer, Day took deliberate steps to gain a reputation for producing deluxe works. He sought to distinguish and advertise himself as a printer of books that would be esteemed culturally significant artifacts by both cognoscenti and court patrons. Still he never gave up making quickly produced and inexpensive pamphlets and other such short works as this meant steady income during the periods when he was producing deluxe folios. In a calculated step toward making prestige tomes, Day was commissioned to print an edition of Leonard Digges's *Tectonicon* (1556), a primer on how to use (as the title announces) "the carpenter's ruler," "quadrant," and "an instrument called the profitable staff," for surveyors, carpenters, and masons. Both in its association with the New Science of the age and in its precisely rendered diagrams, this book set the pace and tone for Day' follow-up project, William Cunningham's (1559) *The Cosmographical Glass*. In addition to including information on the title page of *The Cosmographical Glass* about where the book was printed, Day also indicated where it could be purchased, as well as issued a notice directing potential buyers where they could obtain "all the instruments appertaining to this book" (Evenden 2008, p. 182). Well on his way now, having secured a reputation for producing magisterial and practical folios, Day was approached to undertake a work involving even more intricate diagrams and special fonts, Henry Billingsley's (1570) translation of Euclid's *Elements of Geometry*. And so Day set his sights on being not just a master printer devoted to a reformed religious agenda, but also as one who produced or "authored" (in the senses discussed above) works that fed into the advancement of new learning in the secular world as well.

The business of printing and the promotion of new learning

The title page of *Cosmographical Glass* (see Figure 1.4) provides a suitable place to take the measure of Day's authorial role in bringing to market a special kind of deluxe book. Since the general look and page layout of the text is an important aspect of my overarching argument about Day's attention to setting up viable memory places for his readers by way of images and typographical features, it is important to remark first that Day reused the same exact title page engraving for Henry Billingsley's (1570) *Elements of Geometry*, substituting the central drop in block with the title of that work (see Figure 1.5).[19]

The reader of *Cosmographical Glass* is promised:

> In this glass if you will behold / The starry sky, and the earth so wide, / The seas also, with winds so cold, / Yea and thy self all these to guide: / What this type mean first learn aright, / So shall the gain thy travail [re]quite.

There is no comparable verse centered on the title page of *Euclid's Elements*, but rather an ornate advertisement for John Dee's preface to the book.

Day's using the same title page (with different central panels appropriate to each book) made good sense economically as well as in terms of labor saved.[20] It also tacitly invites a connection between the two books, Euclid's *Elements* and its forerunner in Day's printshop, *The Cosmographical Glass*. Once out of his shop and on the tables of booksellers and binders, the strikingly memorable title page designs would have declared to browsers that Day made quality books. The one called to mind—and advertised—the other. An expedient of the paperworld, yes; and yet Day seems to have made it work double duty in the service of promoting a certain ethos of the works he wanted to be known for having produced. While his métier had been and was to remain religious works (which, after all, had been very good to him and would continue to be an exceedingly lucrative part of his business model), he looked to the heavens in another way as well with his the

44 *Deluxe design of* The Cosmographical Glass

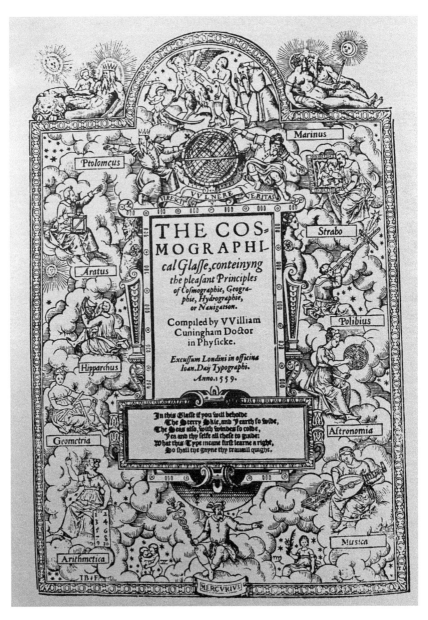

Figure 1.4 Title page. *The Cosmographical Glass* (London: John Day, 1559). Image used courtesy of The Huntington Library.

Deluxe design of The Cosmographical Glass 45

Figure 1.5 Title page. *Euclid's Elements of Geometry* (London: John Day, 1570). Image used courtesy of The Huntington Library.

publication of practical handbooks devoted to contemporary science. Like the involved design on the title page of *Cosmographical Glass*, Day's career is composed out of many interlinking facets at once political, mercantile, and humanistic.

The Cosmographical Glass came about in large measure owing to Day's ongoing favorable relationship with the courtly champion of Protestant reform in England, Robert Dudley (who was not yet the Earl of Leicester, which occurred in 1564 ostensibly to make him a more viable marriage match with Mary Queen of Scots). Dudley was responsible for brokering the meeting if not the proposed collaboration between Day and Cunningham, who was a noted physician (later appointed public lecturer at the Barber-Surgeons' Hall, one of the oldest livery companies in London), astrologer, and also an engraver. In recognition of Dudley's prominence in the genesis of this book and patronage, Day printed Dudley's full coat of arms on the page immediately following the title page. And, attesting to his skill as an engraver, Cunningham contributed a full-sized woodcut prospect view of Norwich, his hometown, which grounds his method of triangulation used to determine longitude by way of astronomical observations. Numerous other woodcut maps by other hands, diagrams, and figures abound in the volume, which is further enhanced by Day's large historiated woodcut initials.[21] Ultimately, this deluxe printed treatise would receive Queen Elizabeth's nominal patronage; in fact, "An extract of the Queen's highness gracious Privilege and License" is conspicuously featured on the penultimate page of the book, "Given at our Palace of Westminster the 28 day of October, the first year of our Reign" (sig. T3r). It serves as a stern warning to discourage literary pirates while declaring Day's royally sanctioned privilege.[22] As the subtle work of Mel Evans (2020) on "proclamation print" (familiarly called "English pica)" for disseminating the "royal voice" has shown, such texts function "on the immediate situation and—relatedly—on achieving the most appropriate representation of the monarch, such as foregrounding their honour, or their divine authority, according to the immediate, local purpose" such that "royal texts and the royal voices they construct were an intrinsic part of the dialogue of power between sovereign and subject" (pp. 239–40). Among the very specific terms of this particular patent, addressed by Queen Elizabeth to "all manner of printers, booksellers, and other our officers, ministers, and subjects," is that everything having to do with making this book is given

> only to the said John Day. Strictly forbidding and commanding by these presents, all and singular our subjects, as well printers and booksellers, as all other persons within our realms and dominions, whatsoever they be, in manner or wise, to imprint, or cause to be imprinted, any of the aforesaid books, that the said John Day shall by authorities of this our license, imprint, or cause to be imprinted, or

any part of them: but only the said John Day, and his assigns, upon pain of our high indignation.

(sig. T3ʳ)

The "all other persons" include, of course, the foreigners working in England, a great many of whom (as already discussed) were involved in the book trade and some of whom were linked to Day's printshop and would have had intimate, firsthand knowledge of this particular volume. That being said, Day's apprentices were not likely to try to go off on their own because as things stood even within the range of this proclamation concerning Day's exclusive publishing privileges, business for them was good; and, even if they were to do so, contravening a royal license so egregiously announced in the work itself was a strong deterrent from attempting a one-off theft of what amounted to the intellectual property of their master.

The title page in and of itself is not startlingly innovative with respect to the overall iconographic design,[23] even though it is certainly remarkable for its place in early modern English printing. It bears material witness to Day's unwavering commitment to bring Britain's publishing industry on par with the best of what was happening on the continent. And so it seems only natural that this elaborate gateway to the text directly resembles—and thereby nods to—the title page of Orance Finé's *De sphaera mundi* (Heninger 2004, p. 195, n2).[24] This is especially the case as regards its involved iconography, which evokes a network of compound associations,[25] including most prominently the four disciplines making up the quadrivium (music, athematic, geometry, and astronomy).[26] Moreover, like Finé before him who brought Euclid to French readers, Day followed suit and did the same for his English audience (as mentioned in the previous section). And yet, the title page to *The Cosmographical Glass* is less a piratical imitation as it is simply following the lead on something that was already a proven success abroad. The title page overall was conceived by Day in somewhat existential terms, physically standing out from and yet still a definite part of the book. While not actually made by him, he was known elsewhere to have designed such pages and duly took credit for them by marking them with his initials, "I.D." as is seen with his emblematic printer's mark placed at the end of the book (treated in the final section of this chapter).

And yet the title page functions as more than just a gateway into Cunningham's text. Day well knew, having already produced more than a few volumes with visual elements, that the title page was the first textual surface his readers would encounter. First impressions, especially for a potential buyer, need to be at once engaging and compelling. Of this key factor in the early modern book trade, Lucy Razzall (2017, par. 3) has remarked that such "title pages set themselves outside the book proper, as navigational starting points for finding a way into, and through the book." This is especially apropos of Day's self-conscious presentation of

Cunningham's dialogically framed treatise (master instructing student, as discussed in what follows), which was of special interest to navigators and others affiliated with trading consortiums, fleet management, mercantile networks, and commodity monopolies. The discussion then, as regards Day's calculations concerning the outsourcing and execution of this title page, can be instructively informed by the many—perhaps limitless—things that can be used to constitute what Gerard Genette (1997) has termed a work's "paratext." What all these prefatory elements bring forward, the title page especially, is an embodied directive, Genette argues, "to ensure the text's presence on the world, its 'reception,' and consumption in the form (nowadays, at least) of a book," such that, it is more "than a boundary or a sealed border, the paratext is rather the *threshold* … empirically made up of a heterogeneous group of practices and discourses of all kinds" [original emphasis] (pp. 1–2). The latter consideration is an especially apt way to think about the title page of *The Cosmographical Glass*, with its compartmentalized yet conceptually linked allegorical images, descriptive tags, and submerged stories drawn from a rich mythographic tradition, as being but the preliminary step toward a satisfactory hermeneutic exposition.[27]

The title page, therefore, should be accounted a document in its own right full of meaning-making potential. It certainly offers an enticing way to entreat the reader to learn more about the mysteries of cosmic matters represented symbolically on the surface and which the inset subtitle promises to demystify and clarify in the book itself. To this end the subtitle of the book advertises that readers will find information about "the pleasant principles of cosmography, geography, hydrology, and navigation" (see again Figure 1.4, central tablet). It is as if these four sciences, as old as Aristotle but now revivified, have supplanted the quadrivium of an earlier age by virtue of the new and better instruments they bring with them for discovering truths of the natural world. In their renovated forms, these four sciences are the prerequisites for going out into the world and undertaking successful nautical journeys and mercantile voyages. The science of book making, likewise, has a role to play in what kinds of information are disclosed here. For, again with reference to the title page as an index of Day's compound way of carrying out his successful navigation of the shoals and reefs of the book trade, experience had taught him (and as was standard practice of the day) the importance of working on the title page separate from the production of the text itself. Owing to the "physical and temporal separation" of its creation and yet given its centrality in imbuing the work with a kind of depth it otherwise might not take on, further attention thus is called to the distinctions between what is on the inside and what is featured on the outside (Smith and Wilson 2011, p. 3).[28]

In this regard, as well with respect the disposition of the printed parts of the text and numerous clear and well-cut diagrams, Day had a very specific plan in mind for organizing the reader's experience of this particular book. By all accounts quite popular in its own day, *Cosmographical Glass* subsequently has been judged one of the landmark English scientific texts of the period (Larkey 1937, pp. 105–14). Cunningham did for cosmography as it applies to navigation what Robert Recorde had done for celestial geometry,[29] in that both rescued their subjects from the exclusive province of scholars and schoolmen and brought them into the public sphere and, moreover, made them accessible especially to merchants, adventurers, and the gentry. So valued was this book beyond the schoolroom that *Cosmographical Glass* was one of only five English books Martin Frobisher took with him on his 1576 voyage in search of the Northwest Passage (Waters 1958, p. 99). *Cosmographical Glass* is set up to be deliberately seen as a new work of consequence, putting distance between itself and former times when treatises of serious intent were, as a matter of course, set in thick and heavy "black letter" or Gothic type, associated with the first age of print.[30] Other than the Latin passages, which are in small roman type, Day set the entire work (including "An extract of the Queen's highness gracious privilege and License") in a crisp, smudge-free italic font of the highest quality.[31] The typeface, in all likelihood, was produced for Day by François Guyot (Ferguson 1989, pp. 14–24).[32] Guyot was a highly respected French punchcutter and typefounder who had delivered letter types to the celebrated bookbinder and printer Christophe Plantin in Antwerp, and who for several years was in England making type expressly for John Day. Guyot and those he trained, most notably his son, Gabriel, who was working for Day at least by 1576,[33] supplied Day's presses with matrices that came to be associated with the overall look of his elegant imprints. *The Cosmographical Glass*, "the first masterpiece of English printing of the Elizabethan age," is impressive both for its pictures and "the first English appearance of Francis Guyot's handsome Double Pica italic type" (Evenden 2008, p. 59). I mention these visual and typographical features because this project secured Day's reputation as a master printer,[34] paving the way a decade later for his profusely and expertly illustrated *Book of Christian Prayers* (the subject of Chapter 5), and because of the precedent it set for state-sanctioned publication rights. *The Cosmographical Glass* thus marks the commencement of Day's distinctive if not outright revolutionary page layout that, in time and in other works, would come to be associated with standard expressions of the English Protestant faith in terms of domestic piety and the evangelical hagiography, which subsequently would be used to bolster its own self-declared origins (as discussed in Chapter 3). Also noteworthy in this regard is the way book historians of an earlier age singled out Day from among other Tudor printers. For example, Roberts (1893) judged Day "remarkable in being the first English printer who used Saxon characters, whilst he brought those of the Greek and Italic to perfection" (p. 79); and Esdaile declared in his *Manuel of Bibliography* (first published in 1931): "Except for John Day, few English type founders deserve praise" (Stokes 1981, p. 149).

Day judged that the high production cost for first-rate type font and expertly executed woodcuts was a small price to pay for the solidification of his reputation as a master printer. And, after all, as already discussed, Day had been awarded a patent for life to print Cunningham (the first such monopoly he was to receive under Queen Elizabeth). Along with the license, which as we have seen was prominently printed at the end of *The Cosmographical Glass*, came something that was potentially even more far-reaching and lucrative if Day was canny enough to act on it—and he did:

> also during the time of seven years, all such books, and works, as he hath imprinted, or hereafter shall imprint, being devised, compiled, or set out by any learned man, at the procurements, costs, and charge, only of said John Day
>
> (sig. T3^v)

Notwithstanding the somewhat vague and yet still *carte blanche* phrasing, Day here is being permitted to monopolize the production of any book "that he rushed into print so long as it was not subject to another patent" (King 2011, p. 204). With the publication of *The Cosmographical Glass*, then, also came an important privilege that set Day up in a more secure way than was generally the case for most printers of the period, affording him opportunities to accrue a steady income for the rest of his life. Not to put too fine a point on it, but it was to Day, and not to Cunningham, that the rights to produce and profit from this book had been granted. As far as records show, any and all remuneration went back into Day's business—and pocket. It can be assumed that Cunningham, like most people who supplied content to printers, was compensated for the text usually in the form of a onetime payment of some agreed upon amount. As this was not the first time Day had collaborated with Cunningham, presumably they went into *The Cosmographical Glass* already on amicable terms having established the previous year a mutually beneficial working relationship with *A new almanac and prognostication* (Cunningham 1558).

What then can be made of this productive symbiosis of Cunningham the compiler and Day the printer and bookseller? Roger Stoddard (1987) offers a way to pursue this inquiry, albeit in rather stark terms: "authors do not write books. Books are not written at all. They are manufactured by scribes and other artisans, by mechanics and other engineers, and by printing presses and other machines" (p. 4). Building on a comparable if more subtle materialist outlook regarding how books come into being, Roger Chartier (1992) has proposed the following, which has direct bearing on my argument about John Day, the printer as author:

> Against the representation developed by literature itself and repeated by the most quantitative histories of the book, according to which the text exists in itself, separated from all materiality, we must insist

that there is no text outside the material structure in which it is given to be read or heard. Thus there is no comprehension of writing, whatever it may be, which does not depend in part upon the forms in which it comes to its reader. Hence the necessary distinction between two groups of apparatuses: those which reveal strategies of writing and the intentions of the author, and those which are a result of the publishers' decisions or the constraints of the printing house. Authors do not write books. Rather they write texts which become objects copied, handwritten, etched, printed, and today computerized.

(p. 53)

The essentially dialogic and polyvocal nature of the book as discussed here is reinforced, moreover, by the narrative structure of *The Cosmographical Glass*, couched as a teacher instructing his apt pupil. The scene is prepared from the outset with what amounts to the *dramatis personae*, in the form of "The Interlocutors: Philonicus and Spoudaeus" (sig. B1^r). As such, it is reminiscent of the familiar pedagogical setup favored by Erasmus in his colloquies and also, to some extent, the structure of Platonic dialogues. The two-voiced organizing principle of the work (the schoolmaster or initiator and the pupil or neophyte) was typical of the textbooks of the day, as well as more sophisticated scientific treatises such as Robert Recorde's (1556) *The Castle of Knowledge*. Readers will notice at once the allegorical significance of the names of the interlocutors, which are, just to make sure everyone is one the same page before proceeding, glossed in the context of the opening scene. Readers familiar with the classical tradition would recognize in Philonicus, the one who brings forth gifts to be mastered, a reference to Philonicus the Thessalian, who presented the untamable horse, Bucephalus, to the young Alexander—a famous story treated among other places in Plutarch's *Lives*, that staple of Renaissance humanism and a runaway best seller during the first age of print (Pade 2007, pp. 89–112).

> SPAUDAEUS. God the giver of all sapience and science, save you, right reverent
> PHILONICUS. I accompt myself happy, that I have found you: for now my hope is, to be delivered, although not of all yet, of some of the bonds, and chains, of Ignorance.
> PHILONICUS. You are unfeignedly welcome to me at this present: *and like as your name* is Spoudaeus, so you do in no point degenerate from the same: but are diligent in seeking knowledge, eschewing idleness, and vain pastimes.
> SPOUDAEUS. That I learned, taking at you example: for you ever keeping perpetual war with ignorance, and vice of every kind: (for reward *whereof virtue also gave you that name*) do use to read, and revolve the treasure of Sapience, I mean, the secret works of Nature shut up, or rather contained, in the worthy and

ancient writers. And in reading certain of them, I have found not only matters of great difficulty, but also (as to me it seemeth) of much untruth. [emphasis added].

(sig. B1^v–B2^r)

This passage makes explicit something that often remains implicit in the typical reading of many a Renaissance text, irrespective of genre; namely, as Roger Chartier (1992) has argued, that it is to be

construed as a vocalization and its "reader" as the auditor of read speech [*parole lectrice*]. Thus addressed to the ear as much as the eye, the work played with forms and processes designed to submit the written word to the requirements of oral "performance."

(p. 58)

The link maintained between the text and the voice in written works certainly brings home to readers their place in the larger, more encompassing discourse (Chartier 1989). And yet, furthermore, in that very process, one also finds oneself reflected in a kind of literary *mise en abyme*. This link between the text and the voice, as in *The Cosmographical Glass*, at the same time tacitly gestures toward the unseen conditions of production operative in the work itself, which is to say embodied in the printer, as a kind of composite figure whose ingenuity and authority has enabled the voices, metaphorically speaking, to reach their target audience (Chartier 1994, pp. 25–60).

There is yet another way in which Day manages to speak as a figure of the author, again couched as a kind of dialogue both between himself and the reader by way of his emblematic *memento mori* printer's mark (Figure 1.6).[35] Significantly, it is the very last thing the reader encounters in *The Cosmographical Glass*, and indeed in many of his books from this point on in his career—enough so that it came to be identified with Day as much as did his "Arise for it is day" inset colophon (see again Figure 1.2). This allegorical woodcut on the final leaf of the book (Figure 1.6) neatly enframes the reader's encounter with another kind of dialogic structure—in this case, between the living and the dead; or, more accurately, the image presented freezes the moment in a conversation when one interlocutor apparently instructing another while the two regard one who is dead. Although more will be said about the compound ways in which emblems offer themselves to be read in Chapter 4 with respect to Day's only printed emblem book, it is worth noting here only that Day was very much attuned to the affective power inherent in images to portend and evoke thoughts of mortal temporality—and not just in prayer books and devotional texts. A less chilling and uncanny encounter with death is figured allegorically at the top of the lavishly illustrated title page (see again Figure 1.4), where a scythe bearing satyr having also the wings attributed to Saturn, as Chronos, walks with figures representing three

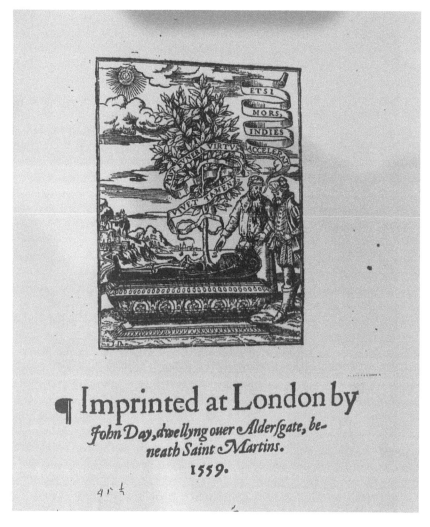

Figure 1.6 Day's *memento mori* printer's mark, last leaf of *The Cosmographical Glass* (London: John Day, 1559). Image used courtesy of The Huntington Library.

ages in the life of a person. This somewhat more benign version of the Dance of Death (discussed at length in Chapter 5) here is meant simply to represent the passage of time so fundamental to the numbering of our days ideally, as the psalmists says, in the pursuit of virtue and wisdom (Ps. 90:12). All the same, it is a theme explicitly foregrounded in the text itself with the initial meeting of Philonicus and Spoudaeus. Insofar as this title page served Day on more than one occasion, it is prudent to allege only the most general of hermeneutic connections between this gentle *memento mori* vignette and Day's more involved and personal emblematic printer's mark.

Still, from the first page literally to the last, Day promotes and confronts the reader with this allegorical and spiritualized register of thought conducive to right action in the world even in his works of secular enrichment such as *The Cosmographical Glass* and *Euclid's Elements*. What is it then that readers are encountering when they come upon such visual markers and textual banners in Day's books, as here with his printer's mark at the end of *The Cosmographical Glass* (Figure 1.6)? In effect, readers are given a window onto a scene that is at the same time a kind of mirror of their own mortal condition. Day's visual and emblematical parting gift to his readers upon completion of *The Cosmographical Glass* is a moment to pause and reflect both on the content of the book itself and on their own mortality—as well as, of course, on Day's technical ingenuity as a printer. Indeed, his initials at the bottom-left, "I.D.," leave no doubt that this printer's mark is his own design; he caused it to be brought into being. Indeed, he "authored" it.

Moving from the ground up, readers take in an elegantly stylized Greek sarcophagus bearing a skeleton lying on an ornate mat or carpet—whether set atop the tomb or itself a marmoreal part of it—reminiscent of the design of transi tombs of the period (Cohen 1973, pp. 5–9), depicting atop what the corpse interred within the tomb is in the process of becoming (Engel 1995, pp. 74–9). At the head of the apparently mostly skeletal corpse, our eyes are drawn to the two figures standing above and looking down at it. The sartorial markings of each figure differentiate the one from the other by their respective stations. By the 1520s, according to Tobias Capwell (2012), people of "elevated social status," noblemen as well as affluent and "upwardly mobile members of the middle classes, had begun to wear swords at all times in their everyday lives, whether a threat was anticipated or not" (p. 29). The gentleman on the far right has his *left hand* on his sword. Right-handed people wore their swords on the left for ease when reaching across their bodies to draw their sword for action,[36] but here the gesture is one of inaction, indeed of contemplation, with his *noncombatant hand* resting on the hilt. This same reflective posture was typical in full-length portraits of patricians and aristocrats, such as that of the "well-traveled Tudor courtier and MP John Astley" (pp. 42–3).[37]

The wearing of a sword in everyday life was both a sign of dignity and possibly rank, but the gentleman's august companion, attired in the apparel proper to a reverend doctor or schoolmaster, functions in this emblematic *mise en scène* as a guide; indeed, the admonitory speech banner issues from his apparently open mouth. The scroll rising upward in eight distinctive folds bears the words—represented as if painted after the manner of an inscription, in Roman capital letters—"Etsi mors in dies accelerat" [Though death hastens on daily]. And the rest of the sentence (both in terms of a syntactic unit and also carrying the sense of a weighty matter worth marking, or *sententia*), "Post funera virtus vivet tamen" [yet virtue will live on after burial], is conveyed on a second scroll, which, like the first, is read from top to bottom. The scroll that completes the composite sentence is wound within the branches of what iconographically is reminiscent of a holly growing out of a corpse. At first glance, the viewer might think it is a trick of perspective and the tree in fact is rooted behind the sepulchre. For how can such things be—a tree of virtue springing from the body of one long dead? And yet viewers must readjust and recalibrate their perspective, especially as regards the reading of such mnemotechnically charged images and words. For such designs squarely are rooted in the richly associative world of the emblem (the subject of Chapter 4), which presents a way to read and interpret the world that is at once rational *and* symbolic by virtue of a self-consistent kind of tropological logic of its own.

The holly, which flourishes and produces berries in European climes during the Yuletide winter months, therefore, evokes the theme of resurrection even as it connotes the timeless blossoming of virtue, consistent with the motto prominently displayed within the composite emblem. On the far left, the eye is drawn to a road leading toward a castellated town, which carries the viewer's attention away (ancillarily of course) from the foregrounded main set-scene, owing to the familiar operations of applied Renaissance perspective design typical of engravings and landscape paintings of the period. As Jean-Luc Marion (2004) has argued in this regard:

> This operation of perspective, which simply opens up the space of things as a world, is accomplished in a way that depends upon the ideality of space: an ideal space, more real [*effectif*] than real [*réel*], since it is the condition of possibility.
>
> (p. 4)

Further, the nautical vessels, visible in the river mouth or bay indicate—albeit in a tiny but highly suggestive way—that everyday commerce is taking place all around and at the same time as this reflective focal scenario. The distant city, formulaically rendered beyond the rocky shores in the left portion of the emblem, intimates that there is even more still going on *beyond what we can see represented* in this singular and intentionally directed glance afforded to the viewer. By extension, this principle of "more than meets the eye" likewise is signified by the moral matter Day has rendered through his colophon expressive of, among other things: "Though death hastens on daily, yet virtue will live on after burial."

An additional layer of meaning thus can be construed about Day's aspirations as a printer of useful, deluxe books that will stand the test of time, and also about the book industry more generally considered. For, in the upper-left corner, in the idealized space recognized by the viewer as being high in the sky, there is another even more idealized image: an anthropomorphic sun looking down on the whole tableau and out to the reader and viewer of this composite and tightly framed allegory. One cannot help thinking here about the rising sun in Day's other famous colophon (though without the markers suggestive of a human face), that likewise calls to mind the resurrection motif, especially in the light of the polysemous motto "Arise for it is day" (see again Figure 1.2). The intentionality of the connection is strengthened by the fact that Day himself designed this engraving and perhaps also had a hand in its production as is evidenced by, as already mentioned, his initials "I.D." at the bottom-left. As such, Day decisively is marking this as the work of his own ingenuity, and as something that, like the book itself, he has caused to be realized and brought forth into the world—and thence into the reader's own, individual Memory Theatre for future use and further reflection. This emblematic *memento-mori* printer's mark positioned at the end of *The Cosmographical* Glass is used by Day in most of his other works, although, as we shall see in Chapter 5, at times he astutely defers from including it. In the main, however, it is a telltale sign of Day's hand in a work, showing up on the last leaf of, most notably, John Foxe's (1563) *Acts and Monuments* and also on Roger Ascham's (1570) *The Schoolmaster* with the additional tag line that (as we have seen before) stakes Day's claim to her royal majesty's privilege for a set number of years, in this case ten ("Cum gratia & priuilegio Regiæ Maiestatis, per decennium"). It also appears in his extremely influential and lucrative *A Catechism, or first instruction and learning of Christian religion* (1570)— which is the next stop, with Chapter 2, in our itinerary following the material and visible traces of Day's fabrication of a Protestant Memory Art in Tudor England.

Notes

1 Jonson (2007, p. 29). This poem satirizes the fate—or luck—of a book once printed and offered for sale. The third poem in Jonson's book of epigrams (following closely the style of Martial), is self-consciously and chiastically bookended by the third-to-last in the collection, which muses further on the "afflictions of publicity." On the latter, see Riddell (1987, p. 53) and Barbour (1998, p. 500).
2 On Day's Anglo-Saxon type font, see Bromwich (1962, p. 270) and Oastler (1975, p. 34); on Archbishop Parker's workshop of binders and illuminators, see Grafton (2017, p. 28), and on Parker as "an impresario of scholarship" who built up and funded a team of scholars to rapidly acquire books and manuscripts for his collection, Grafton (2020, p. 131).
3 *Hondert Psalmen Dauids* was printed by Day in June 1561 (STC 2739); he also produced for the Dutch reformed congregation in London at least two other works that same year, *The Little Catechism* (STC 15261) and *A Brief Examination of Faith* (STC 18812); in all three cases of these works printed in Dutch, his name appears as "Jan Day."

4 On such engraved portraits of authors serving double duty as *memento mori* emblems for pious reflection, see Engel et al. (2022, entry I.11 on George Wither); and, on typical uses of such chiastic tropes in the English Renaissance, Engel (2016, pp. 2–5).
5 Camden (1605, sig. V1ʳ–V2ᵛ); even though attention is devoted to rebuses and similar verbal and visual historical curiosities, far from being a frivolous work (begun 1583 and completed 1597), Camden wrote what amounts to the first chorographical study of Britain "to restore antiquity to Britain, and Britain to its antiquity"; see Engel et al. (2016, pp. 195–7).
6 On this unique device, see McKerrow (1913; sig. h1ʳ [fig. 116]), and Roberts (1893, p. 79).
7 This apocryphal scenario is imaginatively recounted by, among others, Roberts (1893, p. 79).
8 Which is to say: in the booksellers' quarters in Rome.
9 The pumice was used to smooth the ends of the roll; the Sosii were well known as booksellers; mentioned also in *The Art of Poetry* (in Horace 1929, p. 479).
10 Referring here to the cupboards or cases in which books were kept under lock and seal.
11 On "authorial hands" and the murky space of early modern print production and proliferation, complicated further by unclear processes of collaboration, see Loughnane (2021, pp. 54–78).
12 For the collection of essays that most explicitly and succinctly articulates the terms and stakes of this turning point in the continental critical tradition, see Macksey and Donato (1970).
13 On the systematic critique of "the Romantic notion of the author as sole source of original meaning," in light of which the publication of Barthes's "The Death of the Author" in 1968 and Foucault's "What Is an Author?" in 1969 should be read, see Donovan et al. (2008, p. 9).
14 On the various ways this "ideology" historically has been anticipated, negotiated, and reconceptualized from the beginnings of print culture to the current moment, see Power (2021).
15 My use of the term "ingenuity" here and throughout is informed by the early modern notion of *ingenium*, especially as parsed and explored by Lewis (2014, pp. 114–17).
16 Moreover, prior to publishing Latimer's first sermon rehearsed before Edward in 1549, Day and Seres also had printed the Sermon of the Plough in 1548 (STC 15291), the first of Latimer's sermons after King Edward's accession—and Latimer's first public preaching since 1540; I am indebted to Matthew Irvin for helping me situate more completely the Sermon of the Plough in its proper historical context. On the amicable dissolution of Day's partnership with Seres and their cordial dealings thereafter, see Evenden (2008, pp. 19–22).
17 On the grant to Tallis and Byrd, see Arber (1950, p. II:15); on Morley's patent, see Pattison (1939, pp. 412–14).
18 On the creation and circulation of music fonts, see E[dwards] (1906, pp. 170–4); on the metrical psalm as "the perfect vehicle for turning the Protestant message into a mass movement capable of embracing the illiterate alongside the literate," see MacCulloch (2005, p. 308).
19 This was a fairly commonplace practice of the day; for example, the elaborate title page border design illustrating key episodes in *The Table of Cebes* made

58 *Deluxe design of* The Cosmographical Glass

by Hans Holbein famously shows up on a number of other consequential tomes including Tertullian's *Works* (1521), Erasmus's Latin New Testament (1522), and Strabo's *Geography* (1523); see Engel (2018, pp. 17–19).
20 Comparably, on Day's reusing elaborately rendered and carefully incised "head letters" from *The Cosmographical Glass*, most notably in his 1560s' devotional songs and psalms, *Certain Notes*, see Nixon (1984).
21 In fact, the lively designs used in connection with these initial capital letter woodblocks depicting subjects specific to the content of *The Cosmographical Glass* are singled out for special commendation by the eminent early 20th-century bibliographer Oscar Jennings (1908, p. 108).
22 On the pirating of Day's books, and the ways such piracy figured into the book trade, see Loewenstein (2002, pp. 32–6); and with special reference to Day, see Evenden (2008, pp. 171–2).
23 On architecturally disposed tropes as part of the visual literacy generally associated with such iconographical forays in early modern English book production, see Corbett and Lightbown (1979).
24 On Finé's work as editor of the *Sphaera*, see Axworthy (2020, pp. 185–96); on his activities as an engraver, such that "the reader is drawn to the figural aspects of his characters," see Bouzrara and Conley (2007, pp. 428–9).
25 Heninger (2004) provides an unsurpassed close reading of the images individually on this elaborate title page and goes on to explicate their relational groupings, which will not be rehearsed here as my argument is concerned not with unpacking the iconographic meaning but rather with Day's larger purpose in bringing together the eye-catching and the high-brow as part of his marketing ploy. Also, as already observed, insofar as Day reused this title page for other works, any attempt to make substantive connections between the visual program and the book's contents would be at best generic and hence tenuous.
26 On the medieval quadrivium and its later humanist context, see Stahl and Johnson (1971, pp. 245–50).
27 For a thorough gloss on the images, based not only on classical sources and mythology but also on alchemy and closely related subsidiary cryptograms, see Heninger (2004, pp. 2–4).
28 With special relevance to "surface matters" in book production, see Durrant (2021).
29 On Recorde's innovative treatment of applied mathematics in *The Castle of Knowledge* (1556), which incidentally endorses Copernican heliocentrism, see Engel (2020, p. 77).
30 On the four main classes of Gothic font (also known as Gothic bookhand and as Textura), descriptively and more generally called "black letter" at the time when "early printers came to produce their earliest designs," a type which, as one might expect, leaned heavily "upon the manuscript tradition," see Stokes (1981, p. 144).
31 Wynkyn de Worde is credited with introducing European style italic font into England with his edition of Lucian's *Complures Dialogi* (1528), modeled on the type cut by Francesco Griffo of Bologna for its designer and the first to use it in print, Aldus of Venice, around 1500, for his edition of Virgil (Stokes 1981, pp. 157–9).

32 On Day's close relationship with Guyot's family, see Vervliet (1968, pp. 26–7).
33 On the French Protestant punchcutter Gabriel Guyot who was working in London from 1576 to 1579 and again in 1583–1588, see Vervliet (1968, p. 28), Oastler (1975, p. 34), and Worman (1906, p. 26).
34 For facsimile examples and a list of the different kinds of type Day used from 1546 to 1558, see Isaac (1932, pp. 81–7).
35 The image is reproduced among other places in McKerrow (1913, No. 128) and discussed by Roberts (1893, p. 80).
36 On the issue "of 'wearing weapons'—that is weapons carried as part of one's everyday dress," as well as on the sword-bearing Englishman being trained to be ready instantaneously to draw his weapon (in accordance with the teachings of the celebrated Elizabethan Italian fencing master, Vincentio Saviolo), see Anglo (2000, p. 35).
37 The portrait mentioned here was painted by an anonymous English or Netherlandish artist in 1555; National Portrait Gallery, London (ref. 6768).

Bibliography

Primary Sources

A Catechism, or first instruction and learning of Christian religion. 1570. London: John Day. STC 18708.
Ascham, R. 1570. *The Schoolmaster*. London: John Day. STC 832.
Billingsley, H. 1570. *The Elements of Geometry*. London: John Day. STC 10560.
Camden, W. 1605. *Remains … concerning Britain*. London: G[eorge] E[ld]. STC 4521.
Chaucer, G. 1986. *The Riverside Chaucer*. L.D. Benson, ed. New York: Houghton Mifflin.
Cunningham, W. 1558. *A New Almanac and Prognostication*. London: John Day. STC 432.
———. 1559. *The Cosmographical Glass*. London: John Day. STC 6119.
De kleyne cathechismus [*The Little Catechism*]. 1561. London: John Day. STC 15261.
Digges, L. 1556. *Tectonicon*. London: John Day. STC 6849.5
Een korte ondersoeckinghe des gheloofs [*A Brief Examination of Faith*]. 1561. London: John Day. STC 18812.
Foxe, J. 1563. *Acts and Monuments*. London: John Day. STC 11222.
Hondert Psalmen Dauids [*Hundred Psalms of David*]. 1561. London: John Day. STC 2739.
Horace [Quintus Horatius Flaccus]. 1929. *Satires, Epistles, Art of Poetry*. H.R. Fairclough, trans. Cambridge, MA: Harvard University Press.
Jonson. B. 2007. *Epigrams and the Forest*. R. Dutton, ed. New York, NY: Routledge.
Recorde, R. 1556. *The Castle of Knowledge*. London: R. Wolfe. STC 20796.
Spenser, E. 1970. *Spenser's Poetical Works*. J.C. Smith and E. de Selincourt, eds. Oxford: Oxford University Press.
The Bible. 1551. London: John Day. STC 2088.

Secondary Sources

Alford, S. 2002. *Kingship and Politics in the Reign of Edward VI*. Cambridge: Cambridge University Press.

Anglo, S. 2000. *The Martial Arts of Renaissance Europe*. New Haven, CT: Yale University Press.

Arber, E. 1950. *A Transcript of the Registers of the Company of Stationers of London, 1554–1640*. New York, NY: P. Smith.

Axworthy, A. 2020. Oronce Finé and Sacrobosco: From the Edition of the *Tractatus de sphaera* (1516) to the *Cosmographia* (1532). In: M. Valleriani, ed. *"De sphaera" of Johannes de Sacrobosco in the Early Modern Period*. Cham: Springer. pp. 185–264.

Barbour, R. 1998. Jonson and the Motives of Print. *Criticism* **40**.4, 499–528.

Barthes, R. 1977. Death of the Author. In: S. Heath, trans. *Image Music Text: Essays*. New York, NY: Hill and Wang. pp. 142–8.

Blayney, P.W.M. 2013. *The Stationers' Company and the Printers of London, 1501–1557*, vol 2. Cambridge: Cambridge University Press.

Bouzrara, N., and Conley, T. 2007. Cartography and Literature in Early Modern France. In: D. Woodward, ed. *The History of Cartography*, vol. 3 (*Cartography in the European Renaissance*). Chicago: University of Chicago Press. pp. 427–37.

Bromwich, J. 1962. The First Book Printed in Anglo-Saxon Types. *Transactions of the Cambridge Bibliographical Society* **3**.4, 265–291.

Brooks, D.A. 2005. Introduction. In: D.A. Brooks, ed. *Printing and Parenting in Early Modern England*. Aldershot; Burlington, VT: Ashgate.

Burke, S. 2010. *The Death and Return of the Author: Criticism and Subjectivity in Barthes, Foucault, and Derrida*. Third Edition. Edinburgh: Edinburgh University Press.

Capwell, T. 2012. *The Noble Art of the Sword: Fashion and Fencing in Renaissance Europe, 1520–1630*. London: Paul Holberton.

Chartier, R. 1989. Leisure and Sociability: Reading Aloud in Early Modern Europe. In: S. Zimmermann and R.F.E. Weissman, eds. *Urban Life in the Renaissance*. Newark, NJ: University of Delaware Press. pp. 103–120.

———. 1992. Laborers and Voyagers: From the Text to the Reader." *Diacritics*. **22**.2, 49–61.

———. 1994. *The Order of Books: Readers, Authors, and Libraries in Europe between the Fourteenth and Eighteenth Centuries*. L.G. Cochrane, trans. Stanford: Stanford University Press.

Cohen, K. 1973. *Metamorphosis of a Death Symbol: The Transi Tomb in the Late Middle Ages and the Renaissance*. Berkeley, CA: University of California Press.

Corbett, M., and Lightbown, R.W. 1979. *The Comely Frontispiece: The Emblematic Title-Page in England 1550–1660*. London: Routledge and Kegan Paul.

Donovan, S., Fjellestad, D., and Ludén, R. 2008. Introduction: Author, Authorship, Authority, and Other Matters. In: S. Donovan, D. Fjellestad, and R. Ludén, eds. *Authority Matters: Rethinking the Theory and Practice of Authorship*. Amsterdam: Rodopi. pp. 1–22.

Durrant, M. 2021. *The Dreaded Name of Henry Hills: The Lives, Transformations, and Afterlives of a Seventeenth Century Printer*. Manchester: Manchester University Press.

E[dwards], F.G. 1906. A Famous Musical Printer: John Day. *The Musical Times.* **47.757**, 170–4.
Engel, W.E. 1995. *Mapping Mortality: The Persistence of Memory and Melancholy in Early Modern England.* Amherst, MA: University of Massachusetts Press.
———. 2016. *Chiastic Designs in English Literature for Sidney to Shakespeare.* New York, NY: Routledge.
———. 2018. *The Table of Cebes* and Edmund Spenser's Places of Memory. *South Atlantic Review.* **83.4**, 9–29.
———. 2020. Knowledge: Science and Education. In: A. Arcangeli and M. Tamm, eds. *A Cultural History of Memory in the Early Modern Age*, vol. 3. London: Bloomsbury. pp. 77–96.
Engel, W.E., Loughnane, R., and Williams, G. 2016. *The Memory Arts in Renaissance England: A Critical Anthology.* Cambridge: Cambridge University Press.
———. *The Death Arts in Renaissance England: A Critical Anthology.* Cambridge: Cambridge University Press.
Evans, M. 2020. *Royal Voices: Language and Power in Tudor England.* Cambridge: Cambridge University Press.
Evenden, E. 2004. The Fleeing Dutchmen? The Influence of Dutch Immigrants upon the Print Shop of John Day. In: D. Loades, ed. *John Foxe at Home and Abroad.* Aldershot; Burlington, VT: Ashgate. pp. 63–77.
———. 2008. *Patents, Pictures and Patronage: John Day and the Tudor Book Trade.* Aldershot; Burlington, VT: Ashgate.
Evenden, E. and Freeman, T.S. 2013. *Religion and the Book in Early Modern England: The Making of John Foxe's "Book of Martyrs."* Cambridge: Cambridge University Press.
Ferguson, W.C. 1989. *Pica Roman Type in Elizabethan England.* London: Scolar Press.
Foucault, M. 1969. What is an Author? In D. Lodge, ed. and J.V. Harari, trans. *Modern Criticism and Theory: A Reader.* London: Longman. pp. 173–86.
Genette, G. 1997. *Paratexts: Thresholds of Interpretation.* J.E. Lewin, trans. Cambridge: Cambridge University Press.
Grafton, A. 2017. Matthew Parker: The Book as Archive. *History of Humanities.* **2.1**, 15–50.
———. 2020. *Inky Fingers: The Making of Books in Early Modern Europe.* Cambridge, MA: Belknap Press of Harvard University Press.
Green, I. 2003. *Print and Protestantism in Early Modern England.* Oxford: Oxford University Press.
Guy-Bray, S. 2010. *Against Reproduction: Where Renaissance Texts Come From.* Toronto: University of Toronto Press.
Hamlin, H. 2004. *Psalm Culture and Early Modern English Literature.* Cambridge: Cambridge University Press.
Heninger, S.K., Jr. 2004 [1977]. *The Cosmographical Glass: Renaissance Diagrams of the Universe.* San Marino, CA: The Huntington Library.
Isaac, F.S. 1932. *English and Scottish Printing Types, 1535–58.* Oxford: Oxford University Press.
Jennings, O. 1908. *Early Woodcut Initials.* London: Methuen.
King, J.N. 1982. *English Reformation Literature: The Tudor Origins of the Protestant Tradition.* Princeton, NJ: Princeton University Press.

———. 1999. The Book Trade under Edward VI and Mary I. In: L. Hellinga and J.B. Trapp, eds. *The Cambridge History of the Book in Britain, 1400–1557*. Cambridge: Cambridge University Press. pp. 164–178.

———. 2001. "The Light of Printing": William Tyndale, John Foxe, John Day, and Early Modern Print Culture. *Renaissance Quarterly*. **54.1**, 52–85.

———. 2011. *Foxe's "Book of Martyrs" and Early Modern Print Culture*. Cambridge: Cambridge University Press.

Kirschbaum, L. 1946. Author's Copyright in England Before 1640. *The Papers of the Bibliographical Society of America*. **40.1**, 43–80.

Larkey, S.V. 1937. Scientific Glossaries in Sixteenth Century English Books. *Bulletin of the Institute of the History of Medicine*. **5.2**, 105–14.

Lewis, R. 2014. Francis Bacon and Ingenuity. *Renaissance Quarterly*. **67.1**, 113–63.

Loewenstein, J. 2002. *The Author's Due: Printing and the Prehistory of Copyright*. Chicago, IL: University of Chicago Press.

Loughnane, R. 2021. Shakespeare, Marlowe, and Traces of Authorship. In: A.J. Power, ed. *The Birth and Death of the Author: A Multi-Authored History of Authorship in Print*. New York, NY: Routledge. pp. 54–78.

Love, H. 2002. *Attributing Authorship*. Cambridge: Cambridge University Press.

MacCulloch, D. 2005. *The Reformation: A History*. New York, NY: Penguin.

Macksey, R. and Donato, E., eds. 1970. *The Languages of Criticism and the Sciences of Man: The Structuralist Controversy*. Baltimore, MD: Johns Hopkins University Press.

Marion, J.-L. 2004. *The Crossing of the Visible*. J.K.A. Smith, trans. Stanford: Stanford University Press.

Marshall, P. and Ryrie, A. 2002. Introduction: Protestantisms and Their Beginnings. In: P. Marshall and A. Ryrie, eds. *The Beginnings of English Protestantism*. Cambridge: Cambridge University Press. pp. 1–13.

McKerrow, R.B. 1913. *Printers' and Publishers' Devices in England and Scotland, 1485–1640*. London: Bibliographical Society.

McKitterick, D. 2003. *Print, Manuscript and the Search for Order, 1450–1830*. Cambridge: Cambridge University Press.

Minnis, A. 2010. *Medieval Theory of Authorship: Scholastic Literary Attitudes in the Later Middle Ages*. Second Edition. Philadelphia, PA: University of Pennsylvania Press.

Nicolson, A. 2003. *God's Secretaries: The Making of the King James Bible*. New York, NY: Harper.

Nixon, H.M. 1984. Day's Service Book, 1560–1565. *The Electronic British Library Journal*. www.bl.uk/eblj/1984articles/pdf/article1.pdf.

Norton, D. 2005. *A Textual History of the King James Bible*. Cambridge: Cambridge University Press.

Oastler C.L. 1975. *John Day, the Elizabethan Printer*. Oxford: Oxford Bibliographical Society.

OED. 1989. *The Oxford English Dictionary*. Second Edition. Oxford: Oxford University Press.

Onions, C.T. ed. 1966. *The Oxford Dictionary of English Etymology*. Oxford: Oxford University Press.

Pade, M. 2007. *The Reception of Plutarch's Lives in Fifteenth-Century Italy*. Chicago, IL: University of Chicago Press.

Pattison, B. 1939. Notes on Early Music Printing. *The Library*, Fourth Series. **19.4**, 389–421.

Pettegree, A. 1986. *Foreign Protestants Communities in Sixteenth Century London.* Oxford: Oxford University Press.

Power, A.J., ed. 2021. *The Birth and Death of the Author: A Multi-Authored History of Authorship in Print.* New York, NY: Routledge.

Raven, J. 2007. *The Business of Books: Booksellers and the English Book Trade, 1450–1850.* New Haven, CT: Yale University Press.

Razzall, L. (2017). "Like to a title leafe": Surface, Face, and Material Text in Early Modern England. *Journal of the Northern Renaissance.* 8 (2017), para. 3, www.northernrenaissance.org/like-to-a-title-leafe-surface-face-and-material-text-in-early-modern-england/.

Riddell, J.A. 1987. The Arrangement of Ben Jonson's *Epigrammes. Studies in English Literature.* **27.**1, 53–70.

Roberts, W. 1893. *Printers' Marks: A Chapter in the History of Typography.* London: George Bell & Son.

Rose, M. 1993. *Authors and Owners: The Invention of Copyright.* Cambridge, MA: Harvard University Press.

Rose, M. 2002. *Authors and Owners: The Invention of Copyright.* Third Printing. Cambridge, MA: Harvard University Press.

Smith, H. and Wilson, L. 2011. Introduction. In: H. Smith and L. Wilson, eds. *Renaissance Paratexts.* Cambridge: Cambridge University Press. pp. 1–14.

Stahl, W.H. and Johnson, R. 1971. *Martianus Capella and the Seven Liberal Arts.* New York: Columbia University Press.

Stoddard, R.E. 1987. Morphology and the Book from an American Perspective. *Printing History.* **9.**1, 2–14.

Stokes, R. 1981. *Esdaile's Manuel of Bibliography.* Fifth Revised Edition. Lanham, MD: Rowman & Littlefield (The Scarecrow Press).

Straznicky, M. 2013. Introduction: What is a Stationer. In: M. Straznicky, ed. *Shakespeare's Stationers: Studies in Cultural Bibliography.* Philadelphia, PA: University of Pennsylvania Press. pp. 1–16.

Sutton, N.S. 1993. "Arise for it is Day": The John Day Imprints and the English Reformation, 1549–1559. *The Journal of Religious and Theological Information.* **1.**1, 29–58.

Vervliet, H.D.L. 1968. *Sixteenth-Century Printing Types of the Low Countries.* Amsterdam: Menno Herzberger.

Warner, C.J. 2013. *The Making and Marketing of Tottel's Miscellany, 1557: Songs and Sonnets in the Summer of the Martyrs' Fires.* Farnham; Burlington, VT: Ashgate.

Waters, D.W. 1958. *The Art of Navigation in England in Elizabethan and Early Stuart Times.* London: Hollis and Carter.

Worman, E.J. 1906. *Alien Members of the Book Trade during the Tudor Period.* London: The Bibliographical Society.

2 Renovating the *Catechism* (1553) and *Metrical Psalms* (1562)

> This treatise, gentle reader ... is written for the behoove of the young children, which must be brought up with plain and short lessons. For we see daily by experience, that whosoever will teach children, must use much discretion and wisdom not to give them too much at one time (lest he dull and oppress their wits), and yet that which he giveth them he must often and many times rehearse and repeat unto them again, as near as he can after one manner of wise, and with the same words. For if they teach them now this, now that, now with these words, now with other, then the children learn little or nothing, they keep almost nothing in memory, and beside that they wax weary of learning and conceive a loathsomeness thereto and be more slothful and unapt to learn.
>
> —Preface to *Catechismus* (1548, sig. A1^{r-v})

The epigraph to this chapter sets the scene for tracking John Day's role in securing and establishing a solid religious foundation for English reformed habits of thought and related memorial practices. The paperworld of Elizabethan London both reflected and itself was a product of a highly stratified and authoritarian society. Debora Shuger (1997) makes the case that it was also, at the same time, "very small-scale and intimate by modern standards, and such personalization of power within small, relatively stable units cannot but have affected power relations by embedding them within a complex psycho-social web of needs and desires" (p. 190).

The catechism to which this epigraph refers supplied what was to become the original formulation of the state-sanctioned wording for what would become an inestimably influential work. The reformist imprimatur is ascribed to Thomas Cranmer, the first Protestant Archbishop of Canterbury, from 1533 until his martyrdom under Queen Mary in 1555. He was one of the "prime architects of the English Reformation" (Lindberg 2010 p. 307), responsible for the Book of Common Prayer, which, as Diarmaid MacCulloch (2016) explains, became "a vehicle for English worship which would remain almost unchanged for four hundred years" (p. 630). In tandem with his move to conduct services in English rather than Latin and doing away with masses for the dead (discussed

DOI: 10.4324/9780429032431-3

further in Chapter 5 in connection with *Queen Elizabeth's Prayer Book*), it was under Cranmer's purview that altars and doctrinally questionable iconography from churches were removed, and the monasteries restructured and, in most cases, dissolved.

Recalling the excursus in Chapter 1 on early modern notions of authorship and authority, we should not be surprised that this incalculably significant book, Cranmer's catechism (STC 5992.5), had no author as such. Textual comparisons clearly show it follows Justus Jonas's previous presentation of the essential reformed religious teachings, and yet Early English Books Online, for example, lists it as being "Anonymous." No one in particular can be said to be responsible for or identified as the originary author. The full printed title, however, gives a clear sense of its putative English point of origin, its intended audience, and prospective utility:

> Cathechismus, that is to say a short instruction into Christian religion for the singular commodity and profit of children and young people, set forth by the most reverend father in God, Thomas Archbishop of Canterbury, primate of all England and metropolitan.
>
> (1548)

The operative term here is "set forth." Given the extended title's naming of Cranmer as being behind the book, and taking into account that it is "Thomas, Archbishop of Canterbury" who signs the Dedicatory Epistle to King Edward (sig. (*)4^v), it is a sensible expedient to attribute the English *Catechism* to Cranmer rather than to its Dutch printer, Walter Lynn, who simply seems to have been in the right place at the right time. Lynn only briefly was a printer in London, having wrapped up his business by 1550 (Evenden 2008, p. 55). A rather different story, however, emerges with John Day's several printed editions of the ubiquitous English catechism that originated from his press. It is important therefore to keep in mind that "Day never worked for Cranmer" but instead, as MacCulloch (2016) affirms, "printed works of radicals," such as John Hooper, Bishop of Gloucester, who had more than a few confrontations with Cranmer.[1]

Conceptually then, as was discussed in the Introduction, in much the same way as proverbs and adages were considered the common property of those who seized upon and used them for their own ends, so too the catechism was up for grabs. But, of course, owing to the potentially controversial even incendiary material involved, only to a certain extent. Apropos of which, and also as was pointed out in the Introduction, Ernst Cassirer (1977) maintains that

> it is not the content of a doctrine, but solely its form, that can serve as a criterion for its classification as a religion: what stamps a doctrine as religion is its affirmation not of any being, but of a specific "order" and meaning.
>
> (p. 247)

The question-and-answer format associated with catechistic learning goes back to antiquity, often if dubiously referred to as the Socratic method,[2] and remains a perennially potent pedagogical mechanism. It gives the learner a way to reconstruct and further assimilate the lesson because some semblance of a logical or associative narrative trace marks the trajectory of the material covered. In this way, Diogenes of Sinope (404–323 BCE) famously helped his students "get by heart many passages" from poets and historians, teaching them "every short cut to a good memory" including a direct question-and-answer method (Diogenes Laertius 1929); and he is credited with an adage that clarifies the larger stakes in such an enterprise—as true then as it was during the 16th century: "The foundation of every state is the education of its youth" (p. 33). Another closely related classical pedagogical touchstone can be found in Plutarch (*fl.* 60–120 CE), whose words backup the claims alleged in Archbishop Cranmer's preface to the 1548 *Catechismus*:

> Above all, the memory of children should be trained and exercised: for this is, as it were, a storehouse of learning; and it is for this reason that the mythologists have made Memory the mother of the Muses, thereby intimating by an allegory that there is nothing in this world like memory for creating and fostering.
>
> (pp. 1–5)

The catechistic pattern for instituting and inculcating mutually reinforcing beliefs and dogma, especially as inflected by events in a people's collective memory and history, also is at the root of the Judaic tradition. For example, it figures prominently as a modality of inquiry in Talmudic learning and is retained in the Haggadah (the standard text for celebrating the feast of Passover), especially with reference to the "Four Questions" to which answers are accommodated to take into account the level of understanding attributed to the respondent.[3] So whether through its usage in medieval Catholic Spain where, as MacCulloch (2005) has observed, "it was a symptom of the militant Christian culture accustomed to dealing with often reluctant converts from Islam or Judaism" (p. 218); or by agents of the 16th-century Catholic Revival, most notably Ignatius Loyola, the catechism—more so even than preaching—was an essential element for building up and binding together a community of the faithful.[4] More fundamentally still, as Charlotte Appel (2007) has observed, the "teaching of the catechism was the starting point, the core, and in many ways the end goal of religious instruction" (p. 197).

As already indicated, the catechism that Cranmer brought before the English nation in 1548 was dedicated to the Reformation-oriented boy-king Edward VI. It was based on the efforts of Justus Jonas, the doyen of reformed German theology (Posset 2003, p. 14). Although Cranmer's state-approved version of the catechism for the most part follows Jonas's model, it also bears (if only cursorily) some resemblance to John Calvin's published in 1541 (Green 1996, p. 20). Jonas, who had translated *The Apology for the Augsburg Confession* and also the main texts of both Luther and Melanchthon, did not of course write the catechism as such. He did however give it a systematic and distinctively Protestant overhaul, even as Luther had done with his *Der Kleine Katechismus* of 1529 (still in print and very much still in use among Lutherans seeking confirmation). "The catechism," as Andrew Pettegree (2015) explains, "would continue to be one of the most popular and characteristic forms of instructional writing of the Protestant tradition and a steady source of work for its printers" (p. 262). Accordingly, the pattern of the catechism that Cranmer followed—as subsequently did those printers who took their lead from him on the way toward establishing what would become an English-reformed pedagogical tradition—includes the Ten Commandments, the Apostles' Creed, the Lord's Prayer, and the doctrine of the sacraments consisting only of baptism and the Eucharist.[5] The English "short catechism," as it was termed, was published in Cranmer's 1549 Book of Common Prayer (while the more expansive *Primer and catechism* had additional prayers taken mainly from the Book of Common Prayer),[6] such that the *ABC with catechism* "was an officially approved reading primer which contained alphabets in capitals and lower case in three typefaces, and in later editions arabic numerals as well" (Green 2003, p. 183). While this paradigm for presenting the foundational tenets of faith usually constituted the minimum of what was required to be learned (and demonstrated as having been learned) by those aspiring to take their first communion, it should be kept in mind that "over 750 different forms" of the catechism "were printed in England between the 1530s and the 1690s" (p. 190). And this is where John Day comes into the picture. His renovation of the catechism truly was a renewing by cleansing, by repairing, and in effect by rebuilding, not only the old text to fit new doctrinal needs of the emerging reformed English Church, but also of the minds—and memories—of faithful subjects of King Edward and later of Queen Elizabeth.

Instigating oral and visual mnemonic triggers

During his earliest years as a printer, Day produced and distributed a wide range of consequential Protestant works including sermons, most notably those by Hugh Latimer as already discussed in Chapter 1. He also had printed translations of the psalms, so vital to Protestant worship in both churches and homes, which is the subject of the next section of this chapter. Additionally, he brought out a range of generally affordable portions of the Bible in English, exemplarily his 1549 three-part Bible in octavo, innovatively "constituting half of a six-part Bible, whose other three volumes were printed over the next two years" thus making it, according to Eyal Poleg (2020) the smallest Bible printed in England up to that time (p. 160). Essentially, Day succeeded in creating "a cheap and affordable lay library, a collection of books to be bought gradually and consulted individually," which despite minimal margin space "did not stop zealous readers from annotating extensively" (p. 161). Day would do the same thing again when it came to the different forms in which he printed the psalms, a cagey marketing ploy to keep several versions in circulation at the same time. Beth Quitslund (2019) refers to this as "Day's multiply-reissued *First parte* of the psalms in meter," containing "about half the psalms and which sports a title page proclaiming (to the literate) that it is 'the first part' (rather than 'the whole book')" (p. 159).

At all events, Day's design for the layout of full-sized bibles truly "broke new ground in the presentation of chapter numbers" because, for the first time in England, the chapter numbers of biblical books were integrated into the running titles (Poleg 2020, p. 158). Additionally, by virtue of using lighter type, Day was able to give much more information at a glance and to do so in a more clear, legible, and user-friendly way: "his running titles include a summary, book and chapter identification, as well as a folio number (e.g. for 1Rg14: 'Saul | i.Samuel | The. xiiii. Chapter | fol. xxvi)" such that readers using Day's Bible "were able to identify the chapter divisions without recourse to the textual block itself" (pp. 160–1). Moreover, Day's high-quality illustrations in the 1549 folio Bible further advance his emphasis on lay education by whatever means were at his disposal as a printer dedicated to the evangelical cause. This included inserting descriptive "mnemonic couplets," which, as King (1982, p. 129) observes, "convert each Revelation image into a textual emblem"—a theme resumed in greater detail in Chapter 4. This same spirit of innovation, so evident in his mnemonic markers in an effort to streamline and enhance his devout readers' experiences with scripture, likewise infuses and animates his ongoing quest to produce clearly printed works that conformed as much as was possible to the newly reformed religious views—such as his printing (and frequently reprinting) Thomas Becon's *The Flower of Godly Prayers* (1550).[7] Also Day circulated his fair share of cheap pamphlets and shorter works, including many small-format and hence easily portable religious books, most notably the *Little Catechism* colloquially referred to as the *ABC* (King 2011, p. 81). This shorthand reference to learning one's ABCs is derived from the Latin *abecedarium*, an instructional practice exercise for learning the letters of the alphabet, a term that itself is an agglutinated word formed from the first two letters of the Greek alphabet, *alpha* and *beta*, recalling the Hebrew *alef-bet* and Perso-Arabic *alif-beh*.

Already inclined and eager to take up the printing of a work such as the *ABC with Little Catechism*, Day moved swiftly on it once he was assured of reliable support and sponsorship.[8] A work such as the catechism needed state approval in order to be mass produced and also required backing and patronage of court-savvy reform-minded nobles such as Robert Dudley (as discussed in Chapter 1 with reference to his arms being reproduced on the opening pages of *The Cosmographical*

Glass). Day was fortunate to have had the support—both openly and, as often as not, behind the scenes—of the Duke of Northumberland, John Dudley, who, it must be mentioned in passing, was frequently at odds with Cranmer.[9] Northumberland for all intents and purposes led the government of Edward VI from 1550 until his death in 1553. During that time, he had, albeit discretely, enabled Day to secure the valuable monopoly on printing a new catechism, which he managed to hold for the rest of his career, a grant that resulted ultimately "through the good offices of William Cecil" (King 1999, p. 167).[10] As the epigraph to this chapter indicates, English Protestant versions of the catechism already were in circulation, so what exactly distinguishes Day's contribution? What features are included and what memory traces are activated in this text designed to inculcate the ideology of an emerging state religion over which the reigning monarch was the nominal head, bearing in mind that Day now had the authority to print, market, and profit from the catechism? By virtue of his producing literarily tens of thousands of approved copies of this work during his lifetime, the *ABC with Little Catechism* exemplarily encapsulates how Day envisioned his role in the English paperworld. For all of Day's preemptive and stopgap legal posturing and squabbling to produce this book, his industrious streamlining of the look and format of this work for an English audience indicates his belief that it had the potential to not only serve as a primer for teaching the young and newly literate how to read but also become the bedrock upon which the mental habits and religious views of future generations might securely rest.

Due to a patent dispute and uneasy settlement (as discussed in Chapter 1), Day ended up with the exclusive right to print the catechism in English and Wolfe in Latin.[11] Both of these versions more or less followed the Calvinist-inclined text of the Marian exile, Alexander Nowell. Day relied on the English translation by Thomas Norton who had gained approbation for his English rendering of Calvin's *Institutes of the Christian Religion* (Green 2003, p. 17), and later would be one of the contributors to the *Metrical Psalms* published by Day (the main work discussed in the next section). Indeed, Day printed Nowell's version of the catechism in no fewer than six distinct forms, including three Latin versions, each of increasing difficulty. Nowell's catechism, widely circulated initially by Day, became the go-to text for this work in the period; for example, as Jean Brink (2019) has pointed out, between 1570 and 1647 Nowell's catechism went through "forty-four editions in Latin, English, and Greek" (p. 37). Watson (1908, p. 85) identifies six main versions: the larger catechism, a Latin version, the small edition, the middle edition as translated into English by William Whitaker (nephew to Alexander Nowell) as well as the same in Latin, and *A Catechism, or Institution of Christian Religion, to be learned of youth next after the Little Catechism: Appointed in the Book of Common Prayer* (1572).

This last-mentioned version is noteworthy for several reasons. First, because it was "a huge best-seller" (Green 1996, p. 175); indeed, it was among the most lucrative works Day produced from the time of the renewal of his Edwardian patents until his death in 1584 when the rights were transferred to his son, Richard. Second, it also reveals the extent to which Day's printing of the catechism had been sufficiently standardized in terms of its Protestant declarations of faith and brought into conformity with church doctrine under Elizabeth that it was the form printed in, and thus made a part of, the Book of Common Prayer—hence its later designation as "the Prayer Book catechism" (Green 2003, p. 39). Furthermore, and with special reference to the next section of this chapter, the Elizabethan Book of Common Prayer (a slightly modified version of the 1552 prayer book), regularly contained the ballad versions of the Sternhold and Hopkins psalms—which is to say, the metrical psalms on which Day held the monopoly (King 1982, p. 429).

Day was fully cognizant of and subsequently capitalized on the typographical possibilities as well as the typological ramifications of Nowell's *Catechism*. As the printer and seller of this work for which he held the patent, Day accumulated huge profits—and especially so from the *The ABC with the Little Catechism* in the 1580s. He also garnered no small amount of professional prestige for the public display of his technical, pedagogical, and aesthetic sensibilities in the production of this book, which was among the principal works on which students were examined in the Elizabethan classroom (Bushnell 1996, p. 59). And it was the foundational work from which many students first learned to read—initially the young but also, as already suggested, aspirational and socially fluid adult readers. Owing to its steady demand, not unsurprisingly, other printers sought to copy the format and sell the work in large quantities owing to the prospect of quick and ready sales. To protect his privilege, and at the same time set a precedent to discourage other potential unlawful publications, Day vociferously alleged that a small-time printer, Roger Ward, "had arranged for his apprentice to print about 10,000 pirate copies of that work," which in real terms amounted to the equivalent of, according to Green (2003), up to "eight editions of a normal work such as a sermon or treatise" (p. 175). The battle over protecting this privilege continued well after John's Day's death for his son and heir, Richard, charged specific publishers and printers with selling another 10,000 copies of the *Catechism*, and also brought allegations against three others, including "two senior members of the trade with printing yet another 15,000 pirated copies" (Green 2003, p. 175).

Typographically, there are three registers of punch-cut letter fonts on any given page of most catechisms, which makes them one of a "limited range of works in which the old black-letter type was often retained" (Green 2003, p. 255). By the end of the 16th century, the vast majority of books were printed in clear roman type (Cummings 2011, pp. lxii–lxiii). Most notably in this regard, the first English version of the Geneva Bible produced in the second year of Elizabeth's reign was printed in easy-to-read roman type along with copious margin annotations, glosses of words giving the sense of the original Hebrew or Greek, as well as polemical points stressing a Protestant interpretation of key passages. The Geneva Bible, which was the first English version to be divided into verses for easier study and commentary, as Gerald Hammond (2006) has commented, "may fairly well be described as the most influential book ever printed in England" (p. 188).

Day's first foray into the printing of the *Short Catechism* in 1553 uses a variety of type fonts reflecting the matrices available to him at the time. Specifically, thick black letter (or Gothic) type was used for both the Master's questions and the Scholar's responses. Their roles or parts, printed in italic font, are so named before each speech block as in play scripts. Topical indices appear in a smaller black letter font in the margins, and headers and the alphabetically arranged "Table" dividers appear in all capital letters using a crisp roman type. The most significant changes in the look of the *Short Catechism* as it went through various post-Edwardian editions concerns the selection of different type fonts to distinguish the words spoken by the Master and the Scholar (which follows the same dialogic pattern discussed in Chapter 1 with reference to the interlocutors in *The Cosmographical Glass*). In the 1572 edition, which became the preeminent model—we might even say the copy-text since most of the pirated editions follow this version perhaps owing to its improved legibility—the Master's role designation still appears in italics but his words now are in roman type. The Scholar's nominal designation likewise now is in roman type though his responses to the Master remain in the original thick, black letter (see Figure 2.1).

Over the years, Day's catechism shows a steady accretion of marginal references to biblical books rendered now in small black letter while

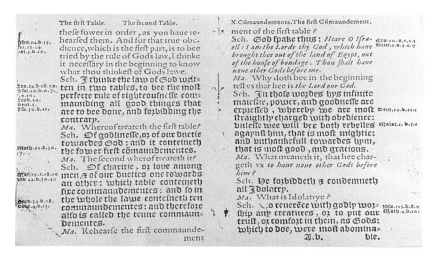

Figure 2.1 Multiple type fonts. *Short Catechism* (London: John Day, 1572), sig. A5ʳ. Image used courtesy of The Newberry Library.

chapter and verse appear in roman type, which is overall more suitably disposed for glossing and making it easier to locate scriptural precedents and cross-references. The latter, consonant with the humanist approach to literary analysis, encouraged attending to the biblical source text (in line with the Protestant watchword of *sola scriptura*), and also, reminiscent of the scholastic tradition, pointed the way toward drawing the acceptable kinds of typological correspondences between and among other books in the Bible—especially across the Old Testament and the New. Before looking at the standard use of biblical typology in this primer, though, we need first to take stock of what can be discerned further about Day's typographical choices instituted in his *Catechism* beginning in 1572.

The most obvious thing to notice about Day's later Elizabethan catechism is that, as a kind of combined visual and oral cue, by way of a composite mnemonic prompt, the Scholar alone now reads—and, as it were, speaks—in black letter. This may be a conscious attempt "by the author and the publisher or printer to reach a kind of inexperienced or slow reader" (Green 2003, p. 7), or perhaps a deliberate decision based on changing fashions in publishing, or even perhaps a financial expedient of the printing house due to a depletion or shortage of black letter font. While these considerations may have had something to do with the streamlining of this unprecedentedly popular text, based on what reasonably can be surmised from Day's characteristic attention to detail in his previous ventures in making his texts distinctive products from his workshop, I maintain that the differing visual registers coming into play between the Edwardian and Elizabethan printing of the catechism reflect his effort to approximate in print a truly dialogic structure in look, tone, and performative possibilities.

Most obviously and formally, a dialogue is supposed to be taking place between the Master and the Scholar. Beyond this however, the Scholar is called on to give voice to—or more properly, to ventriloquize—a very special kind of dialogue between his own studied responses and the words from holy scripture. Just as different kinds of typeface are assigned to each speaker, which marks a difference in the two voices imagined as being heard when such a text is read aloud, the same applies to the catechumen (the person preparing for confirmation in the church), designated as "Scholar," who is called on to speak in two registers designated by two different kinds of type—namely, in both his own voice, printed in black letter, in response to the Master's interrogations, which are printed in roman type, and also in the voice of the Bible, which now are printed in italics. The Scholar thus is directed by the text to read and recite aloud the words placed in these two different typefaces and, in both instances, there is no room for deviation or debate. The typeface thus serves as a recognizable memory cue announcing who is speaking and which voice is to be heard reading which section. The preprepared text quite literally hems in the catechumen by virtue of the dictatorial guidance prompted by the words of the Master; and further, the Scholar is locked into the frame by both the italic passages from the Bible as well as the marginal points of reference. The catechumen's role is to learn how to read and repeat the words as written—both his own "correct" responses, which, as already noted, are rendered in the thick gothic type, and also the aptly quoted words of scripture presented in italics (see again Figure 2.1). There is a doubling of the scholar's voice then, neither of which, of course, is authentically his own *yet* but which will be in time and with proper training owing to the painstaking practice and the dutiful rehearsal of the words before the Master. The Scholar's words therefore betoken two kinds of authoritativeness. On the one hand, they evoke a tone of correctness with his response to the Master that is reinforced by the visual effect of black letter font, which, by the 1570s, already had an antiquated if venerable sentiment attached to it bordering on nostalgia. On the other hand, there is an intimation of authoritative sanctity associated with the italic font in which the Bible now is printed for the catechumen to read. It must be observed that some of the phrasings in this Protestant catechism, obviously, are starkly new when compared to the earlier rehearsals of England's religious dogma that were observed and recited during the reign of Catholic Queen Mary. All of this, I contend, is captured in Day's layout of the *Catechism*, initially under Edward VI and then improved under Elizabeth when his patent was renewed. The latter typographically combines the new wording of Cranmer's expression of acceptable Christian doctrine with the look and tone of an earlier ecclesiastical ethos that now lends to the whole a virtual Protestant imprimatur of newly minted and redoubled authority, both that of the current sovereign and also that which is associated with the timelessness of God's Word made plain to even the dullest scholar.

There is another way still that the dialogic nature of this text as printed by Day calls out for comment. As already suggested, the teacher and student are engaged in a kind of scripted, mock dialogue that resembles play scripts—and here the *dramatis personae* are named "Master" and "Scholar." But it is a dialogue composed out of two interwoven strands of the same thing, with the goal of imparting a coherent narrative that precludes any hesitation or improvisation. As such, the script is itself doubled with respect to what it says and how it says it, with the Scholar taking on the voice of the one who would demonstrate his knowledge to the Master (in Gothic type) while also calling on scripture (in italics) and letting it speak through him as well. The Master's role (in roman type) is intended to prompt the scholar to tell ever more details and to give the appearance of fleshing out the narrative. The whole exercise is geared toward, quite literally, *mastering* the narrative, in every sense of the term. The point is to convey all the necessary information and, in the process, to have it find a place in the theatre of one's mind—to get it by heart—and to do so by way of taking on the role of the character named "Scholar." This form of role-playing is at once a mimetic and mnemotechnical exercise.

The structure of this question and answer format bears a striking resemblance to the tactic of Renaissance English dramatists who supplied the backstory and all that is needed to be known to proceed with the presentation of a play. Rather than relying solely on a long, extended monolog, periodic questions and rejoinders serve to draw forth more of the necessary details. Playwrights often resort to the dialogic pattern as old as theatre itself. The audience will identify most directly with the one who does not know the story and manifestly wants to learn more. In the example presented below then, the theatregoer is aligned vicariously with the character designated "Second Gentleman," while the "First Gentleman" tells all he knows about the situation at court in the opening scene of Shakespeare's *Cymbeline*.[12] His well-placed one-liners, which punctuate and further set up the storytelling speaker to reveal ever more bits of information as the story unfolds, are of the same order as the Master's probing questions posed to the Scholar to elicit more information in what amounts to a playing out of the catechism:

> FIRST GENTLEMAN: But what's the matter? [...] None but the King? [...] And why not [...] You speak him far. [...] What's his name and birth? [...] I honour him
> Even out of your report. But pray you tell me, / Is she sole child to th' King?" [...] How long is this ago? [...] (*Cym* 1.1.3–62)

* * * * *

> MASTER. Why is he called Holy? [...] Proceed [...] Hast any more to say hereof? [...] Now remaineth the fourth part, of the holy Catholic Church, of the which I would hear what thou hast to say. [...] Yea, but I would have it somewhat more plainly and at large. [...] Why is this point put into the Creed? [...] How so? [...]
> (*Catechism*, 1572, sig. E2ʳ–E3ᵛ)

Among other things, such a comparison clarifies the obvious theatricality of the catechistic mode of recitation and the ensuing delivery of information. Moreover, the scholar's interactions with the master are explicitly referred to as a rehearsal: "Rehearse the first commandment of the first table?" (sig. A4ᵛ–A5ʳ; see again Figure 2.1, bottom line of the left page). As with many play texts of the period, the script for the Protestant catechism, as already noted, was the product of many hands. This version being rehearsed by the catechumen unmistakably is different from that used during Mary's reign and indeed from any Catholic version from the continent. This is immediately evident with the reference to the "Articles agreed upon by the bishops ... and published by the king's majesty," and including, for example, the following heading in the catechisms produced by John Day:

> Of Purgatory. The doctrine of school authors concerning purgatory, pardons, worshipping and adoration as well as of images as of relics,

and also invocation of saints, is a fond thing vainly feigned, and grounded upon no warrant of scripture, but rather repugnant to the word of God.

(1553, sig. L6ʳ)

The "Articles" referred to here are those developed mainly by Cranmer with the aim of (as the long title of his *Catechism* indicates) "avoiding of controversy in opinions," and derived from the 1538 Thirteen Articles (based largely on the 1530 Augsburg Confession) by means of which Henry VIII hoped to signal his points of agreement and solidarity with the German princes whose favor he was courting at the time despite having earlier proclaimed in print against Luther (MacCulloch 2005, pp. 201–5).

The reformed content thus conveyed through the black letter register, which, as already observed, was evocative of an earlier time as well as of a visual format of ecclesiastical and religious works, which when first published were presented in a font clearly modeled on and retaining "the characteristics of that same manuscript tradition" (Hellinga and Trapp 1999, pp. 2–4). And the mental—even if unconscious—link to Luther's German black letter *flugschriften* and related reformation pamphlets cannot be overlooked either. To say the words of the catechism, which were written in English and printed in black letter, was to speak with the voice of authoritative knowledge, which now was Protestant knowledge, even if one were merely just sounding out the words and not yet sure what those words meant when strung together. The underlying assumption is that saying them repeatedly—and thus *rehearing* them while rehearsing the catechism aloud—is how to get them by heart and, in time, coming fully and actually to believe the reformed religious ideas thereby conveyed. Hence Day's three main versions of the reformed catechism (usually referred to as short, medium, and full), so one might progress from the basic tenets and continue adding onto that knowledge, filling in more of the prescriptive story and thereby coming to a more comprehensive understanding of the larger message. The *Little Catechism* was designed—and legislated—as a primer for teaching children to read (hence the shorthand title of *The ABC* as already discussed). The expanded title, moreover, in its first incarnation as printed by Day, indicates the seriousness of the larger stakes in this doctrinal enterprise: *A Short Catechism, or plain instruction, containing the sum of Christian learning set forth by the king's majesties' authority, for all schoolmasters to teach* (1553).

In addition to the typographical considerations, there also is a typological component to the *Catechism*, which Day would develop more thoroughly in his later publications, discussed in the ensuing chapters. Built into Nowell's catechism is a way of reading texts that calls on the student to notice correspondences and echoes between episodes in the Old and New Testaments. This assumed that narrative foreshadowing was taken to be both a kind of proleptic proof text for the events described in the New Testament and thus of the divinely ordained fulfillment of prophesy as disclosed in the Old Testament (a theme analyzed further in Chapter 5). And, as mentioned in the Introduction, the anticipation of Christ's resurrection can be found both in Samson carrying away the gates of Gaza locks and all (Judg. 16:3) and Jonah being delivered from the belly of the great fish (Jon. 1:17). These kinds of patterns became part and parcel of the catechizing method and, in learning it, students were being trained to read using this analogical way of thinking with holy scripture as their guide. Protestants tended to favor a notion of *sola scriptura*, wherein everything Godly and needful to be known was contained in the Bible if read aright. For example, Katherine Parr (1547) in *The lamentation of a sinner* explicitly advocates "scripture alone" (sig. A2^v) and "justification by faith" (sig. B7^v), exhorting those who would attain salvation to confess their sins by looking within themselves rather than outward to "this saint or that martyr" (sig. G6^r). All of these points, likewise, are covered specifically in Day's printing of the catechism; for example, "justification by only faith in Jesus Christ" (1553, sig. K8^v). Parr shows special ingenuity in her application of typological thinking in seeing her husband, King Henry VIII (although deceased by the time this work was published), as "our Moses" for having

> delivered us out of the captivity and bondage of Pharaoh … And by Pharaoh, I mean the Bishop of Rome, who has been and is a greater persecutor of all true Christians than ever was Pharaoh of the children of Israel.
>
> (sig. D6^{r-v}).[13]

More usually though, the catechumen was induced simply to see the Pharaoh of Egypt as a type for the Devil. For, insofar as the Ten Commandments were featured prominently in the *ABC with the catechism*, students would be expected to know that its importance for Christians was that "Moses' delivery of the Israelites from bondage in Egypt is a type of Christ's delivery of the faithful Christian from the bondage of sin" (Brink 2019, p. 37).

But there is still another feature about the dialogic structure of the work that lends to it an air of verisimilitude and genuineness true to the form. The way the responses are framed at times sound very much like what an anxiously halting yet earnestly diligent child might say, thus giving to the whole an authentic touch of mimetic performativity:

> MASTER. I hear not yet why almighty God's will was to declare his secret pleasure to one people alone which was the Israelites.
> SCHOLAR. Forsooth, that I had almost forgotten. I suppose it was not done for this intent, as though the law of the ten commandments did not belong generally to all men, for as much as the Lord our God is not only the God of the Jews, but also of the Gentiles, but

rather this was meant thereby that the true Messiah, which is our Christ, might be known at his coming into the world, who must needs have been born of that nation and none other for true performance of the promise.

(1553, sig. C4^v–C5^r)

Just as the "true performance of the promise" of Christ fulfilling the role of the anticipated and scripturally foretold messiah, so too the reader—and all readers—of the words as written will be "rehearsing" the approved teachings of the Elizabethan-reformed Church. The student is both a mouthpiece for and yet also the receptacle of that sanctioned version of redemptive knowledge. It is this knowledge that can bind the nation together with a common religious ideology and thereby inculcate a protocol for applied scriptural hermeneutics so as to create an evangelical community that shared the same beliefs. I make this claim mindful of the subtle critique of Louis Althusser's discussion of "Christian religious ideology" in his exposition of cultural "subject formation" as articulated by Linda Gregerson (1995):

> Ideologies—and the subjects they constitute—are historically contingent. Spenser wrote as and of a subject in whom Christian and monarchic imperatives were deeply (and often contradictorily) inscribed. The Tudor subject was always a crux and an interpellation of power. Subject of, subject to, dependent upon: the concept was relational. [...] If historical analysis yields a single, emphatic lesson, it is that the structures of experience and the practical vocabularies of agency are richer and more varied than any given era can allow or comprehend.
> (p. 82)

Insofar as students learning to read were all using the same prescribed catechism (whether an authorized text printed by Day or a pirated copy), then every one of them would be saying—and taking to heart—the same words, such as the passage about the "Messiah … born of that nation" quoted above, the very fact of which unites the literate in a bond of common experience no less than of shared anxiety. Regarding the latter, Shakespeare's comic foil Speed, always ready with a brace of similes, in his discussion of the "special marks" denoting one who is in love, alludes to the ubiquity and importance of this flimsy book as a work one misplaced at his own peril: "to sigh like a schoolboy that had lost his ABC" (*TGV* 2.1.20).

The anxiety associated with the schoolroom approach to learning the catechism is silently acknowledged and emblematicized on the frontispiece of Day's work from its first appearance during Edward's reign, as is in many more editions over the decades. For pictured here (see Figure 2.2) are bundles of switches on the floor within the master's easy reach, used for beating the child if he falters in his recitation of the assigned passage for the day. In English grammar schools of the 16th century, corporal punishment regularly was used not only as a corrective for behavior but also—and mainly—as the means to promote attentiveness and to induce the student to perform on cue as expected. A notable outlier in this regard was Richard Mulcaster (1581), headmaster of the Merchant Taylors' School:

> For gentleness and curtesy toward children, I do think it more needful then beating, and ever to be wished, because it implyeth a good nature in the child, which is any parent's comfort, any master's delight. And is the nurse to liberal wits, the master's encouragement, the child's ease, the parent's contentment, the banishment of bondage, the triumph over torture, and an allurement to many good attempts in all kind of schools.
>
> (sig. Nn1^v–Nn2^r)[14]

The face-to-face interview, master to student, when both say aloud in sequence the points of doctrine as printed in the catechism, constituted the focal event of daily exercises in the typical Tudor grammar school.[15] The image here (Figure 2.2) is of a well-run classroom with disciplined boys silently reading along with the lesson being recited or perhaps studying parts they still need to con by heart, while the other boys, on the bench in the foreground closet to the viewer, are shown as being patient, well-mannered, gentle, and kind (one child, in a gesture of friendship, has his arm around another).

By contrast, other editions of Day's *Catechism* include a frontispiece that shows what might be considered a more realistic and less idealized *mis en scène* of a Tudor classroom (Figure 2.3). The focal image is the boy's solo recitation of the catechism to the master who follows along in his book; meanwhile, on the periphery, the other students waiting to perform apparently are restless. Several are shown in various states of inattention, including one who assaults the boy sitting next to him. Also, the viewer's attention cannot help but be drawn to the middle of the room where a recumbent dog chews a stick or bone. The decision to include a dog adds a further touch of realism to this depiction of what may be taken as a representation of a typical Tudor grammar school classroom. It might also carry a somewhat deeper allegorical significance given the cultural commonplaces of the day concerning dogs. Not to read too much into it, but the dog is an immemorial emblem of loyal compliance associated with obedience and service to one's master. Robert Burton (1926), speaking as "Democritus Junior" to his reader, alludes to an anecdote by Justus Lipsius and mentions in passing that he "could relate many stories of dogs that have died for grief, and pined away for loss of their masters, but they are common in every author" (p. 87). Burton also offers an analogy that speaks to the first principle of the effective academic enterprise where the stakes are nothing less than the proper development of one's character and indeed—running parallel to the chief aim

Renovating the Catechism *and* Psalms   79

Figure 2.2 Schoolroom scene. *Short Catechism*, frontispiece (London: John Day, 1572). Image used courtesy of The Lambeth Palace Library.

Figure 2.3 Schoolroom scene. *Short Catechism*, frontispiece (London: John Day, 1583). Image used courtesy of The Newberry Library.

of the catechism—the very health and prosperity of one's soul: "An idle dog will be mangy, and how shall an idle person think to escape? Idleness of the mind is much worse than this of the body; wit without employment is a disease … the rust of the soul" (p. 280 [I.2.2.6]). Moreover, as Raymond Klibansky and his Warburg collaborators (2019, pp. 382–3) have conclusively demonstrated, the dog long has been associated with being the faithful companion of solitary scholars and philosophers, as can be seen with the recumbent dog beside the brooding, winged personification of Contemplation in Albrecht Dürer's much studied yet still enigmatic *Melencolia I* (1514) (see Figure 2.4).[16]

Even the simplest of everyday analogies likens the docility of the well-trained dog to the deference and compliance the scholar should show in the presence of his master. This is consistent with what we already have seen with respect to Mulcaster's view that students will behave better and tend to learn more when they are not threatened or physically compelled by the master but rather obey out of their developing sense of what is right and proper (Bushnell 1996, pp. 34–6).

Figure 2.4 Idle Dog. Albrecht Dürer, *Melencolia I* (1514). Image used courtesy of Princeton University Art Museum (object number: x1952–1).

While the catechism was a substantial part of the instruction for students at all levels (which is why, as mentioned above, there were short, medium, and longer versions as well as those in Latin and Greek that served as teaching tools for classical language acquisition especially if a student already knew by rote the meaning of the words in English), there were, of course, other popular works that likewise were staples of the Elizabethan classroom. Most prominent among these standardized texts were *Lily's Grammar* and the extremely well-circulating *Cordier's Colloquies*, which contained hundreds of approved Latin conversations that students were to learn and be able to recite verbatim (Green 2016, pp. 176–81). Typical of this dialogically based approach, John Brinsley (1612), a teacher who promoted the memory arts for pedagogical purposes, used a "mode of daily disputing and opposing," first peer to peer and then pupil to teacher to make sure that knowledge actually was being advanced (sig. Hh1^v–Hh2^r). Another Tudor educator, William Kempe, a devotee of Ramus (whose works he had encountered while a student at Cambridge), was interested in the more practical ways in which memory is connected to pedagogy and behavior (Engel et al. 2016, p. 160). As part of a step-based system conducing ultimately to original compositions, Kempe (1588) developed a lively way to help students memorize precepts and grammar that was consistent with the applied memory arts (sig. E3^r–E4^v). I mention these dialogical and performative exercises because, comparably, the catechism, which likewise was designed to advance literacy skills while inculcating decorous forms of socially sanctioned self-expression, was organized in such a way as to promote the use of mnemonic techniques. The agronomist and miscellany writer Hugh Plat (1594) comments explicitly on the value of mnemonic schemes to help children learn their ABCs (sig. H3^r).[17] The catechism, especially in the piecemeal breakdown of the ten commandments—which was one of the first sections, if not often the very first section of Protestant catechism booklets—lent itself to principles of the applied memory arts based on a "decade" or a composite grouping of two sets of five *loci*, or places (Yates 1978, p. 23). There were many strategies for getting one's assigned text by heart, and the memory arts offered a variety of commonplace approaches (discussed in the Introduction). Further, what Evelyn Tribble (2011) has said of the "cognitive artifacts" and "all aspects of the system" requisite for "any understanding of a cognitive ecology of the theatre" (p. 162) applies as well to the cognitive ecology of an early modern classroom in which the catechism surely was among the most familiar—and persistent—cognitive artifact of all.

The edifying subject matter included in the catechism and considered essential for every English Protestant to know was not, as one might expect, confined exclusively to the classroom. Once the churches had been stripped of railings, the doctrinally offensive saints' images whitewashed over, and other accoutrements associated with the preformed church removed, the interiors of houses of worship often contained "big boards bearing the three texts which all Protestants should know by heart: Nicene or Apostle's Creed, Ten Commandments and Lord's Prayer" such that a church "became a giant scrapbook of the Bible" (MacCulloch 2005, p. 559). All three of these texts just mentioned were included in Day's *Catechism* and are typical of the genre. Posting these passages prominently before the gaze of the congregation made sure that even people who had not attended grammar school or been taught to read at home with approved books would come into contact with and have an opportunity to learn them by heart. By the same token, even should congregants' attention wandered during the sermon, they would be brought back to these essential religious tenets through the posting of these texts, which likewise were enshrined, among other places, in the catechism. Still, catechizing, consistent with the method pioneered by Luther in the 1520s, was deemed the most expedient and immediate means to combat the problem of teaching both children and adults, many of whom "fell asleep during the sermon, misbehaved or failed to get the message" (MacCulloch 2005, p. 587).

There was a brisk and very competitive commercial market for the catechism, with more than a thousand different catechisms produced in England between 1530 and 1740, all or part of over 600 copies that still survive (Green 1996; MacCulloch 2005). This made it all the more important for Day to announce to readers the primacy of his version over any others then found in printers' bookstalls and shops (Neville-Sington 1999, pp. 601–2). The complete wording on the title page of Day's initial 1553 print-run, as already observed in passing, is quite clear about the sovereign's program for a Protestant English catechism and uniformity of belief:

> A short catechism, or plain instruction, contemning the sum of Christian learning set fourth by the king's majesty's authority, for all schoolmasters to teach. To this catechism are adjoined the Articles agreed upon by the bishops [and] other learned and godly men, in the last convocation at London, in the year of our Lorde, 1552, for to root out the discord of opinions, and establish the agreement of true religion: Likewise published by the king's majesty's authority.

This announcement is followed by quite explicit information about Day's monopoly on this approved work: "Imprinted at London by John Day with the king's most gracious license and privilege: Forbidding all other to print the same Catechism." The first pages of the book (the paratext, as discussed in Chapter 1) also reproduce the "Injunction given by the king" to "all schoolmasters and teachers of youth, within all his Grace's realm and dominions for authorizing and establishing the use of this Catechism" (sig. A2r). Following this is "The copy of the king's majesty's letters patents for the printing of this and the Little Catechism," which names John Day three times, as well as including "his factors or assigns" (those to whom he outsourced the production and, for a fee, the sale of the work),[18] as sole proprietor of the work and the king's appointed printer of the same (sig. A6r). The *ABC* was, in the quaint phraseology of Anders (1935), "perhaps the most profitable book on the market ... of which John Day had been the *beatus possidens*" [happy holder] (p. 37).

As was discussed at the end of Chapter 1, when Day wanted his presence in a publication to be known, he advertised it prominently with his *memento mori* printer's mark (see again Figure 1.6), which is the case with his editions of Nowell's *Catechism* after the renewal of his Edwardian patent, such as in the printings of 1570 and 1571 (sig. Y4ᵛ in both editions). And the same applies to his printing of that other of his most coveted licenses which he renewed and was granted once Elizabeth was securely on the throne, four years after her accession, *The Whole Book of Psalms collected into English meter* (1562, sig. Ee7ᵛ).

Instituting aural and somatic memory practices

The precise wording of the title of Day's psalter, as advertised on the title page, warrants careful attention insofar as it makes clear several important aspects of this particular publication with reference to Day's role in the history of the English book trade and also his place in the steady development of a distinctively Protestant Memory Art. The complete title, indicates its origins and aims:

> The Whole Book of Psalms collected into English metre by T. Sternhold, J. Hopkins, and others, conferred with the Hebrew, with apt notes to sing them withal; faithfully perused and allowed according to the order appointed in the Queen's Majesty's injunctions; every meter to be used of all sorts of people privately for their solace and comfort, laying apart all ungodly songs and ballades, which tend only to the nourishing of vice, and corrupting of youth.

Day's monopoly to print all psalms in meter, consistent with what Hannibal Hamlin (2004) has called "the nature of the English publishing business," was among the main factors accounting for the persistence and run-away popularity of the Sternhold-Hopkins version (p. 41). Beth Quitslund (2013) has demonstrated the extent to which it was public congregational singing that "most obviously drove demand for the psalm book," and the frequent reprinting of it "meant that Day could adjust it to fit the ways it was being used, and he did so several times" (pp. 206–8). So important was this patent to sustaining his whole printing business, especially once he was deeply involved with the financing and printing of the expanded edition of the *Acts and Monuments* (the subject of Chapter 3), that John Foxe, in the postscript of a letter to William Cecil in 1569, requested that Day's "Letters Patent" covering the *Psalms* should be explicitly confirmed (Oastler 1975, p. 22).

The *Catechism* and the *Psalms* were so profitable for Day because of the comparatively small outlay, both in term of finance and labor, required for their printing once the form was set and owing to the huge demand and already assured steady sales. Far and away though, it was paper that remained the largest expense Day incurred for a single printing of the metrical psalms, as many as 1,500 copies per print-run (Evenden 2008, p. 51); and, furthermore, "this highly lucrative collection went into at least seventy-three editions published by Day" alone (King 2002, p. 205).[19] The market for such works was so great that, as already observed, they became a target of piratical publishing on the part of risk-averse and would-be cagey competitors seeking a portion of the market share. Day therefore was especially careful to mark these popular bestsellers with his printer's mark, in effect following the lead of other entrepreneurial printers and publishers of the period, most notably Albrecht Dürer (Panofsky 2005, pp. 51, 59). To guard against unauthorized copies of his popular woodcut series of the Apocalypse, Dürer incised each woodcut with what amounted to his trademark monogram "A.D." as was his usual practice and, in the 1511 edition, included a warning which can be translated as "beware all ye thieves and imitators of my work" (MacGregor 2014 p. 304). In both Nuremberg and in Venice, Dürer successfully defended his sole right to publish and sell his works identified as such by his unique monogram, which in effect served as a safeguard to his intellectual property; and, in the process "improvised a new relation between the maker and a global market" (Bartrum 2002, p. 25). And as we already have seen, Day likewise pursued those who sought to violate his patents, taking the matter to the appropriate magistrate or court. He did so both to protect his privilege and to discourage further imitations; and, furthermore, his *memento mori* printer's mark assured the reading public of the authenticity of the book they had purchased. One major addendum to Day's imprinting of his authorial mark of proprietorship in the *Whole Book of Psalms* is that he gave the exact location where one can buy approved copies of this, the royally authorized and properly licensed book—at least for seven years: "Imprinted at London by John Day, dwelling over Aldersgate, beneath Saint Martin's / *Cum gratia et privilegio Regiae Maiestatis per septennium*. / These books are to be sold at his shop under the Gate" (sig. Ee7^v). Day was acutely conscious of the need to retain this monopoly and, through his connections with members of the royal council, most notably William Cecil (1st Baron Burghley and, at the time of Day's patent, Secretary of State to Queen Elizabeth I), was successful in his bid to renew his Edwardian patent in 1559, initially for seven years—and during which time Day produced and sold thousands of copies. An extended second privilege duly was applied for and granted in 1567, and a third on August 1577 which gave the reversion of his patent to his son, Richard.

The work itself is based on the metrical psalms initially undertaken by Thomas Sternhold (formerly Groom of the Robes in the household of Henry VIII and then later Edward VI), which was resumed and augmented after his death by John Hopkins and others. Hopkins apparently had the most at stake, having "contributed the largest number of paraphrases to the completed metrical psalter after Elizabeth's accession" (Quitslund 2008 p. 93). The first collection published during the reign of King Edward and duly dedicated to him by Sternhold was *Certain Psalms* (1548). It was a small octavo volume produced by the evangelical printer Edward Whitchurch (Quitslund and Temperley 2018, p. 510), who also had been responsible for printing Katherine Parr's *Lamentation of a Sinner* (whose active role in the English Reformation previously has been mentioned). Day was ready and able to take over the printing of this volume for we know that by 1552 at the latest, he had assembled "a collection of service music and anthems suitable for the new Protestant rite" (Milson 1999, p. 550).[20] A census of London printing presses, in 1583, reveals that Day had four printing presses which were all in full working order; and moreover, by this time had acquired and was using no fewer than five complete sets of music fonts (Pattison 1939, p. 407).

A sample page (see Figure 2.5), in this case showing the notes for singing Psalm 6 in Day's neatly streamlined version of the metrical psalter, indicates just how far the printing of staves and musical notation had come since the early days of moveable type which used the "two impression" method for mass producing liturgical music on paper. The late fifteenth century pioneering practice for printing musical notes required using a "mask" for the first impression and the whole of the form being inked in red "with which the rubrics and the staves were to be printed"; for the second impression, "when the letterpress and the notes were done, quads replaced the rubrics and the blocks used for the staves, and the whole was inked in black" (Pattison 1939, p. 393). By the time of Day's metrical psalter, the whole process had been fairly well updated and standardized such that the printer could focus more on giving it the look of his own shop's best practices. And in Day's case this including printing the words to be sung in crisp black letter font, thus giving to the whole an ethos of sanctity as well as perhaps a touch of a venerable text's hard-won survival albeit newly translated into English metrical stanzas.

Armed with the requisite and most up-to-date typefonts, then, and having several fully functioning presses and of course the proper licensing, Day was in a position to supply and satisfy a growing public demand for singing psalms. While psalters of course had been around since long before the age of print, the printing press made them available to all kinds of buyers and in a form that especially spoke to the English reformed mentalité. As Elizabeth Evenden (2008) has shown, the singing of psalms became "an essential component of Protestant worship under Elizabeth" (p. 49). Moreover, the psalms—and in particular the Sternhold and Hopkins version as published by Day in ballad meter—were sung in all Protestant services throughout Britain. We will return to the implications and importance of this metrical from shortly, but first it is important to understand that the psalms—as well as the other works printed in metrical form in that volume which included the Ten Commandments, creed, and English versions of other important prayers such as *Te Deum* and *Benedictus*—played a major role in communal domestic piety as well as in private devotion. The singing of psalms was

Figure 2.5 Music notation for Psalm 6. *The Whole Book of Psalms collected into English metre* (London: John Day, 1584), sig. D3^v. Image used courtesy of The Newberry Library.

an activity that universally united Protestants, whether those singing Luther's psalm settings in German lands, Calvinists in central Europe, or followers of the reformed Church in England. MacCulloch (2005) sees the pan-European movement of "mass lay activism" that cut "across all barriers of social status and literacy" as having been inspired by the Psalter, translated from Latin and

> set to music and published in unobtrusive pocket-sized editions which invariably included the musical notation for the tunes [...]. The metrical psalm was the perfect vehicle for turning the Protestant message into a mass movement capable of embracing the illiterate alongside the literate.
>
> (pp. 307–8)

Whether or not the owner of the book could read music, Day's *Whole Book of Psalms* was a book for singing, notwithstanding the fact that, as Quitslund (2013) has shown, "musical literacy was more limited than verbal literacy" (p.210).

Because the metrical psalms in England were aimed at a broad audience, as Hamlin (2004) explains, the vast number were written in "common meter, the simplest meter of the popular ballad"; and, whether "the 'common meter' was made common by psalms or secular ballads, it is clear that its use for English metrical psalms reflected the desire of Reformers to make them both accessible and memorable" (p. 24). This universally recognized mnemotechnical aspect of the metrical psalms was fully mobilized by Day such that by 1562 he had printed no fewer than sixty-five different tunes in *The Whole Book of Psalms* (King 1982, p. 223). Above all however, the ballad form, with its regular rhyming sequence and usual pattern of one word corresponding to one note (or extended over a run of short notes), initially was chosen for its properties of facilitating easy memorization linked to its mimicking of typical English speech patterns (Smith 1946, p. 254). The prolific historian and divine, Thomas Fuller, commented on this directly in his compendious *Church-History of Britain* (1655), correctly assessing the work of Sternhold and Hopkins and their fellow translators in the following terms: "though branched thither, had their root in Geneva" (sig. eee3[v]). He is recalling here Calvin's influence on the reading and singing of psalms among the Marian refugees, many of whom returned to England after Elizabeth's accession with a new and special appreciation of psalms of thanksgiving and also particularly those about bearing up during exile—as exemplified in Golding's (1571) *The Psalms of David and others, with Mr. John Calvin's commentaries.* Fuller comments on this with his characteristic wit,; namely, that their

> piety was better than their poetry; and they had drank more of Jordan, than of Helicon. These Psalms were therefore translated, to make them more portable in people's memories (verses being twice as light, as the self-same bulk in prose) as also to raise men's affections, the better to enable them to practice the Apostles precept: *Is any merry? let him sing Psalms.*
>
> (sig. eee3[v])

He rings further changes on the same mnemotechnical theme in his treatment of the beliefs of pre-Christian Britain, showing an appreciation of versification to inculcate lessons of the state in the hearts and minds of the common sort:

> The bards were next the Druids in regard and played excellently to their songs on their harps; whereby they had great operation on the vulgar, surprising them into civility unawares, they greedily swallowing whatsoever was sweetened with music. These also, to preserve their ancestors from corruption, embalmed their memories in rhyming verses, which looked both backward, in their relations, and forward, in their predictions.
>
> (sig. A1^v)

Like the original psalmist, David, these bards (as Fuller imagines them) played their songs with harp accompaniment, which brings them into closer proximity with the shepherd-king as regards both the visual and aural activation of memory. And by extension, those who take up the *Whole Book of Psalms* and sing the metrical psalms likewise are ingesting what has been sweetened with music. Fuller, it should be recalled, was himself renowned for his capacious memory notwithstanding his criticism of the rhetorical term "*art of memory*" (Patterson 2018, p. 288). In his own day, Fuller was credited with demonstrating in practice all manner of the memory arts (Donaldson 2002, pp. 67–9), using them frequently—at times explicitly—to make his points in the course of table talk, homilies, and published writings (Engel et al. 2016, pp. 211–15). For example, in one of his printed sermons he describes the Eucharist as an artificial memory that imaginatively returns the celebrant to the scene of Christ's sacrifice, "such that the art of memory, opens up the 'heart of memory' so to speak" (Engel et al. 2016, p. 212).

As with Fuller's memory techniques to promote his treatment of the sacraments, Sternhold's meter as published by John Day made use of the English ballad form to activate and prompt one's memory. Indeed, one of the main reasons, according to Hallett Smith (1946), for turning the Psalms into English meter in the first place stems from the ease of memorizing them by such means (p. 254). This was of course a long-standing pedagogical device; and yet, moreover, in *The form of prayers ... used in the English Congregation at Geneva* (1556), it was seen as being all part of the divine plan: "there are no songs more meet, than the psalms of the Prophet David, which the holy ghost hath framed to the same use" such that "the holy ghost by all means sought to help our memory, when he fashioned many psalms according to the letters of the alphabet: so that every verse beginneth with the letters thereof in order" (sig. B2^v). Rather than follow this somewhat intricate pattern evident in the original Hebrew for some of the psalms (especially "the psalm of psalms," 119, an acrostic poem corresponding to the letters of the alphabet, which is the longest chapter in the Psalms and indeed in the whole Bible),[21] Sternhold and Hopkins provided aids to memory by means of English common meter and balladic rhyme.

As they were aware (for they were not the first to use this form), the ballad stanza contained a metrical consistency conducive to the memorization of poems, both because of its cueing rhyme scheme and owing to its emphatic beat—usually in iambic measure, which is to say an unstressed followed by a stressed utterance. Ordinarily, the ballad stanza form consists of alternating lines of four beats and three beats, or a couplet with seven beats per line; hence, the form used with the psalms can be described as a 4–3–4–3 stanza (with the first and third lines in iambic tetrameter and the second four in trimeter)—or, when taken together, a "fourteener" set in iambic heptameter (Attridge 1982, pp. 86–9). This "common meter," so-called after the time of Sternhold, was deemed the most apt verse form for memorizing anything in English, as can be seen in the title of William Samuel's (1569) *An Abridgment of all the canonical books of the Old Testament, written in Sternhold's meter*. He rationalizes and explains his use of "Sternhold's meter" in the following terms:

> I have taken in hand to make in meter the chief and principal matters in the whole Bible, keeping the order of the chapters as they stand, and also beginning the first chapter of every book with A, the first letter of the cross-row, and the second B, the third C, and so to the letter U, the alphabet to last, 20 letters, keeping on twenty chapters.
>
> (sig. A3ᵛ)

This was not the first of Samuel's mnemonic efforts, for he previously had produced a metrical paraphrase of the Pentateuch, *The Abridgment of God's Statutes in Meter* (1551) with the stated goal that all of the people in his nation might be able "to sing the whole contents of the Bible" and "keep them in remembrance of those good things that they have learned" (sig. A2ʳ⁻ᵛ). Among the remarkable features of his *Abridgment* (1569) is his inclusion of an artificial memory system based on an illustrated map of the hand (see Figure 2.6).[22]

This scheme was especially well suited to aid both in the recollection and rehearsal of any given story or parable in the Bible by book and chapter based on his verse paraphrases written in the specifically named "Sternhold's meter" (sig. A5ᵛ). Even the instructions for using this mnemonic device based on the hand are delivered in a version of Sternhold's fourteeners, consisting of internally rhymed couplets within an encompassing balladic rhyme scheme (abcb)—disposed below in a form to help bring out Samuel's mnemonically oriented sing-song verse:

> To every joint, / The finger point,
> In order as they stand:
> The letter then, / To all those men,

Renovating the Catechism and Psalms 91

Figure 2.6 Hand mnemonic. William Samuel, *An Abridgment of ... the Old Testament, written in Sternhold's meter* (London, 1569), sig. A5[v]. Image used courtesy of The Folger Shakespeare Library.

That take this book in hand.
Then shall they know, / And plainly show,
The chapter out of doubt:
Of any thing, / In this writing,
The letter once found out.
From A. to U. / The thing is true,
The Alphabet doth last:
Even twenty just, / From last to first,
So count you must to cast.
If you once find, / The letter in mind,
And know what number it is:
You may be sure, / Of that Scripture
To hit and not to miss.
But perfect must, / You be to trust,
The letter and his sum:

92 *Renovating the* Catechism *and* Psalms

> And then you may, / Withouten nay,
> The story tell to come.
> Also the book, / See that you look,
> How it is called by name:
> And then the text, /And number next,
> Be sure it is the same.
>
> (1569, sig. A6^{r–v})

Such woodcut illustrations of the hand as a mnemonic device, based on a range of available continental models, have long been a familiar and regular feature of manuscript pedagogical manuals for remembering Latin declensions and grammar rules as well as from the earliest days of printing in England. Two versions of such mnemonic hands, for example, each involving different material to be mastered, are illustrated by engravings in John Holt's (1508) *Lac puerorum* [*Milk for Children*] (sig. A3^v and A5^r). Incidentally, and to recall the discussion of the catechizing master's bundle of switches from the previous section (Figure 2.2), the title page of *Lac puerorum* shows three schoolboys with books open at the feet of a school master seated in his chair, *ex cathedra* as it were; in his right hand a prodigious bundle of switches, while with his left hand he points to a rather disconsolate looking boy whose turn it is to speak. The same motif appears as well on the title page of Richard Pynson's 1498 edition of Giovani de Veroli's grammar, which was used at Winchester College to drill students in Latin (Orme 1999, p. 459). The master is shown holding a brace of willow switches in his left hand while pointing with his right to a place in the book where the student, standing in front of the master, is being directed to construe aloud as seven other boys sit anxiously on the floor around him. Getting the rules of grammar by heart would have been made easier by the various rhymes one might devise to sing one's way through the rules and exceptions.

William Samuel uses his singsong fourteeners (usually rhyming abcb) to sum the substance, for example, of Joseph's blessing of his sons immediately prior his death (Gen. 49, in the Bible he was using). His recourse to Sternhold's ballad meter indicates how such an approach might be used to make more memorable every chapter and episode in the Bible.

> Down fell his sons upon their knees
> even twelve of them there was:
> He blest them all and told of things
> that after came to passe.
> Then charg'd he them that they should lay
> his bones in Manebrey field:
> Then pluckt he up his legs to him,
> and up the ghost did yield.
>
> (sig C1v)

Samuel's imitation of the Sternholdian metrical form as found in the *Whole Book of Psalms*, coupled with his exuberant application of an immemorial mnemonic approach to committing biblical texts to memory, can be construed as an homage as well as an obvious effort to cash in on the success of Day's printed psalmodic paradigm. The latter becomes more probable when we consider that Samuel's book was organized, typeset, and seen through the press by Day's former partner and sometime collaborator, William Seres, with whom Day copublished hundreds of religious books and pamphlets, including psalters and biblical texts (as discussed in Chapter 1). Seres, like Day, appreciated the time-tested business practice of going with what had been proven to be successful and repeating it as long as it continued to sell books. At all events, Seres's printing of Samuel's mnemotechnical abridgment of the Old Testament following of Sternhold's ballad meter appeared only a few years after Day's initial printing of his enormously successful *Whole Book of Psalms*. There clearly was a market for books that relied on even the most rudimentary of mnemotechnic practices, especially where scriptural works were concerned, and both Day and Seres took advantage of the vogue for learning by heart parts of the Bible—if not the whole thing, as Samuels suggests his memory system will facilitate.

Banking on the popularity of the ballad form used with metrical versions of biblical poetry under Edward VI (King 1982, pp. 209–10), and the ever-increasing early modern appetite for broadside ballads (Fumerton and Guerrini 2010), *The Whole Book of Psalms* gave a special and renewed life to this poetic form in Elizabethan England owing to its being so ideally suited for the prompt memorization of texts (King 1982, pp. 216–18). Along these lines, a compelling case has been made by Borris and Clark (2011) that the fourteener couplet "argument" for each of Spenser's canto openings in *The Faerie Queene* is modeled on "the Sternholdian psalmic hymnody of the English church, as well as popular ballads" (p. 1149). In the process of substantiating their argument, the authors point out that the canto opening four-line stanzas, most often rhyming abcb, consist of what later was referred to as "common meter," which was a "uniquely English verse form associated with English Protestantism" that regularly "had been used for popular ballads, for Protestant versified translations of the psalms, canticles, and other biblical texts, and for much of the *Whole Book of Psalms* employed for hymn-singing in the Elizabethan English church" (p. 1169). This is consistent with Day's own 1560 psalter, published prior to his *Whole Book of Psalms*, "an opportunistic cobbling-together of previously printed psalms" that, according to Quitslund (2008, pp. 202–3), "must have been actively supported by men who wished to see the English Church adopt the congregational singing that they had shared in exile" in Strasbourg during Mary's reign. Moreover common meter, usually rhyming abcb, was considered "divided meter" or sometimes "broken fourteeners," such that the 8–6–8–6 metrical pattern of common meter, built out of two sets of 4–3–4–3, constitutes the English "ballad stanza." While Hopkins consistently rhymed the four-beat lines with the three-beat lines (abab), one of the other contributors, Thomas Norton, "followed Sternhold in rhyming only the second and fourth lines [abcb]" (Smith 1946, p. 264). There are only two exceptions to Sternhold's using his preferred "abcb quatrains in alternating lines of eight and six syllables," a pattern that Quitslund (2008) remarks was in fact "best known in the mid-sixteenth century as 'Sternhold's meter' "; further, a meticulous survey of the printed verse of the period indicates that "the meter was neither especially common nor associated with psalmody before Sternhold popularized it" (pp. 22, 70–1). At all events, Quitslund and Temperley (2018) reasonably conclude that "the paired, parallel structure of the fourteener couplets could easily reflect the logical organization of the Hebrew psalms; and short units are easiest to assemble into poems of highly variable lengths" (p. 513). With this in mind, the claim made by Borris and Clark (2011) is bolstered further in a way that will return us to a consideration of John Day's self-consciously active role in the fabrication of a Protestant Memory Art by virtue of his polemical activities in the Elizabethan print shop: "Just as common meter or Sternhold's meter was also called 'ballad meter,' *The Faerie Queene*'s arguments somewhat evoke popular ballads as well as Psalmic hymns"; and, furthermore,

> intertextually evoking England's *Whole Booke of Psalmes*, which was often bound together with the English Bible—itself a symbol of English linguistic and religious legitimacy—the seventy-five arguments within Spenser's epic reflect the trials and accomplishments of the English church and nation.
>
> (pp. 1180–1)

Day developed what became standard typographical ways of emphasizing these mnemonic markers in the *Whole Book of Psalms*. The words of the text of the initial stanza are discretely positioned within the space of the printed stave so as to be set below the notes that carried the tune (see again Figure 2.5). Then, at the end of the musical section, clearly laid out in ballad stanza form and continuing to use black letter or Gothic font are the ensuing verses to be sung to that same tune. Day thus provides here another instantiation of how remnants of "humanist scholarship, literacy and the mechanical press combined to facilitate the spread of methods that supplemented aural and oral modes of remembering" (Walsham et al. 2020, p. 5).

The visionary printer as author

The picture that emerges of John Day is of a tenacious and canny printer who took an active role in presenting carefully compiled material in a variety of practical, popular, sometimes cheap, always easy to read, and self-consciously memorable formats. Perhaps the best measure of his success, other than his thriving business, is how frequently his works were pirated and—as was seen in the previous section—how widely they were imitated. Recognizing the strategic need immediately to flood the market with something that would enable him to stake his claim to the metrical psalms, he was willing initially to print only partial versions of his intended *Whole Book of Psalms* while presumably "he waited for his collaborators to versify the rest of the texts" (Quitslund 2008, p. 197). At this stage in his career, Day was committed to giving the texts from his press as pleasing an appearance as possible, making premium use out of the type fonts available to him, on which, as discussed above, he spent considerable time and expense assembling. The aesthetic and visual quality of books from his printshop was important to Day, not only because he had the desire to establish and maintain a reputation as a preeminent printer in Elizabethan London (Evenden 2008, p. 52), but also because he was cognizant of how he might make it easier for readers to keep their minds engaged with a steady flow of "godly" Protestant material. As with the decorum associated with the memory arts, clear and unclutter background mnemonics made for easier recollection.[23] In this case, the recollection involved both attending to the subject matter presented and also recognizing the text itself as being a product of Day's technical—and mnemotechnical—ingenuity. One was reminded of latter by any of the many markers Day left to show he was responsible for the work—on title pages, in prefatory letters attesting to his patent privilege, through his colophon, which is to say his telltale *memento mori* printer's mark as the last thing one saw in his book (Figure 1.6).

Once the easily memorized metrical psalms had been standardized, set in print, and circulated widely by Day, such that the "words of a particular psalm could be associated with a particular melody," as Diarmaid MacCulloch (2005) has thoughtfully conjectured, "even to hum the tune spoke the words of the psalm behind it, and was an act of Protestant subversion," for to sing a psalm "was a liberation—to break away from the mediation of priest or minister and to become a king alongside King David, talking directly to God" (p. 308). While this was true for lay people in general, it held special significance for women because they were prohibited from preaching and only rarely allowed to lead prayer. As a result, the common meter psalms—like secular proverbs in the humanistic tradition as discussed in the Introduction—were common property for all, and even more so once they had been prepackaged for English Protestants by John Day, much in the same way as Luther had done a generation earlier for Germans.[24] It is in this light that Day's achievement with his *Book of Psalms*, as with his *Little Catechism*, can be seen as providing the welcomed mnemonic groundwork for inculcating specific habits of thought. Day directed his efforts to supplying what might be thought of as the mental machinery by means of which an English Protestant Art of Memory was being fabricated, strand by strand, through his active participation in advancing—and mastering—the Elizabethan book trade.

A few parting points need to be expressed before turning to Day's even more emphatic and memorable use of images involving Protestant martyrology, a project made possible by the profits from his valuable monopolies on the *Short Catechism* and *Whole Book of Psalms*. We need to keep in mind the extent to which his innovations in the typographical layout of an essentially dialogic mode of conveying the catechism, as well as the mnemonically charged visual disposition of the metrical psalms, call upon and make use of deep-seated cultural psychograms.[25] Specifically, his carefully conceived and painstakingly rendered panel-like series of visual and aural pathways were designed to stimulate the Protestant viewer's memory and imagination, and hence serve to awaken and activate a new way of understanding one's relation to God's salvific plan for the redemption of the faithful. The two main works discussed in this chapter, each in its own way, subtly trades in mnemotopes, creating sites for communal and, in effect, common memory. Both books involve specific textual materializations of the past valanced in new and dynamic ways and thereby serve as vehicles for personal and cultural memory (cf. Purdy 2002). Mnemotopes play off and recharge that modality of memory that previously had become tied to certain sites, artifacts, or texts, and gave rise to what can be termed a public memory insofar as "the public past is also a collective one" (Trigg 2012, p. 73). Day's *Book of Psalms* thus succeeds in creating a powerful and lasting public—even national—memory, which is to say a fully operational collective cultural memory, for Elizabethan Protestants. For, as with "the individual experience of place memory, the emergence of a public memory is relational, arising against an antecedent context that serves to offset the formation of the event *as* an event" [original emphasis] (Trigg 2012, p. 76).

Since these books were cheaply made and used by their owners to the point of destruction, very few complete versions remain. So much so that a complete version of the *Short Catechism* would need to be reconstructed using parts from a number of different extant editions. The fact that they literally were used up serves further to reinforce the powerful mnemotechnic affect they would have had for their original owners. Once the tunes were set in one's mind's ear, as it were, then one was on the way to having that psalm by heart—and all for which it stood within the wider socioreligious context of the Elizabethan Church of England. Such memories, shared communally and passed on to the younger generation, resulted in the installation and circulation of powerful engrams (those fundamental units of cognitive information accounting for how memories are stored), associated with mnemic energy (the transmission of these discrete bits of stored memory), and tapping into the immemorial reservoir of mythical thought, tunes, and ritual practices. All of this, as will be shown in the next chapter, is taken to the next level of ideational intensity through the well-honed use of affective memory cues—grounded in a

Renovating the Catechism *and* Psalms   97

repackaging, retelling, and refashioning of Protestant history in terms of sacrifice and redemption—in Day's collaboration with John Foxe (1563), *Acts and monuments of these latter and perilous days touching matters of the Church*.

Notes

1 MacCulloch (2016), p. 525; and, on Hooper's going head-to-head with Cranmer, pp. 471–85, 501–5, and 526–9.
2 On Socrates's special use of the Greek rhetorical tactic known as *elenchus* to elicit the truth based on asking and answering questions, see Matthews (2018) and Sebell (2016).
3 See Guggenheimer (2013), *Mishna*, Pesachim 10:4, and cf. Pesachim, 60b; on "The Four Questions," see Guggenheimer (1998, pp. 30–4) for this section of the service traditionally chanted in the cantillation form known as "study mode" associated with learning Talmud.
4 For a breakdown of the main differences between the Catholic and Protestant catechism, including content and language as well as function and technique, see Green (2003, pp. 15–18).
5 On the retention of the Eucharist in the Elizabethan Church of England and the terms conditioning its observance, see Chapter 5, "Patterns of devotional reflection."
6 Cf. Engel et al. 2022, entry II.2: "A revised version of the *Book of Common Prayer* was issued in 1552, which omitted the introit psalms and made significant changes to the communion and burial service."
7 On the importance of this particular work in the transformation of early modern piety in England, see Kao (2018, p. 29); and on Day's receiving the lucrative monopoly to print "the ever-popular writings of Thomas Becon," see King (1982, p. 430).
8 See King (1982, p. 95); and Quitslund (2008), p. 200.
9 See MacCulloch (2016, p. 524). John Dudley, 1st Duke of Northumberland, may be more familiar to those who study Tudor court politics by his earlier stylings: 7th Baron and Viscount Lisle, and 19th Earl of Warwick.
10 On the implications of Day's *carte blanche* to produce this extremely lucrative work see King (1982, pp. 95–6); Bennett (1989, p. 39); Loewenstein (2002, pp. 30–2); and Raven (2007, p. 76).
11 On the terms of the controversy and eventual resolution, see Evenden (2008, pp. 25–6).
12 All references to Shakespeare follow *The New Oxford Shakespeare* (2017).
13 On Parr's place in early English reformation thought and writing, see Coles (2008, pp. 45–62).
14 On Mulcaster's progressive pedagogy, both as regards curricular innovation and behavior modification, see Engel (2018, pp. 11–14).
15 On "new foundation" schools and the spread of grammar schools in early modern England, see Engel et al. (2016, p. 145).
16 For a more detailed iconographic analysis of this aspect of the image, see Panofsky (2005, p. 162).
17 On Plat's place in England's early modern culture of memory, see Engel et al. (2016, pp. 65–9).

18 On John Day's "assigns" and those of his son, Richard, who inherited the patent, see Kirschbaum (1946, p. 45).
19 On the collection and implications of this data, see Davis (1996, pp. 78–93).
20 Additionally, the only known edition of Day's music for church service is dated variously 1560 and 1565 (STC 6418 and 6419, respectively), although the work is referenced as having been in use a decade earlier.
21 The alphabetic acrostic is one of the most easily identifiable poetic forms in the Hebrew Bible; on its use in the book of Psalms especially, see Freedman (1999) and Holm-Nielson (1960).
22 Using the hand as a background mnemonic design, especially for learning and recalling biblical passages, has many early modern precedents; see, Engel (1995, pp. 32–42), Sherman and Lukehart (2001); Engel et al. (2016, pp. 84–90).
23 See, for example, Fulwood (1562), quoted from Engel et al. (2016, p. 63):

> The rule of the places briefly in order is this also: that first there be an invention of the places (whereof it is already spoken), afterwards an ordering, a meditation, a distance, a steadfastness, a solitariness, a mean light, a dissimilitude, a quantity … lest the similitude should cause a confusion.

24 On Luther's translations of the psalms showing his interest in bringing out "the poetic qualities of the biblical text through deliberate use of meter, sound, and imagery," see Chaghafi (2017).
25 On the heuristic value of referring here to psychograms and, in what follows, to mnemotopes, and engrams and mnemic energy, see the Introduction, "Conceptual and analytical coordinates."

Bibliography

Primary Sources

A Catechism, or Institution of Christian Religion, to be learned of all youth next after the Little Catechism: Appointed in the Book of Common Prayer. 1572. London: John Day. STC 18730.
A Short Catechism, or plain instruction. 1553. London: John Day. STC 4812.
Becon, T. 1550. *The Flower of Godly Prayers.* London: John Day. STC 1719.5.
Brinsley, J. 1612. *Ludus literarius: or, the grammar school.* London: H. Lownes. STC 3768.
Burton, R. 1926. *The Anatomy of Melancholy.* London: G. Bell and Sons.
Catechismus. 1548. Preface by T. Cranmer. London: Walter Lynn. STC 5992.5.
Diogenes Laertius. 1929. *Lives of the Eminent Philosophers.* R.D. Hicks, ed. 2 vols. Cambridge, MA: Harvard University Press.
Foxe, J. 1563. *Acts and monuments of these latter and perilous days touching matters of the Church.* London: John Day. STC 11222.
Fuller, T. 1655. *The Church-History of Britain.* London: John Williams. Wing F241.
Fulwood, W. 1562. *The Castle of Memory.* London: Rouland Hall. STC 12191.
Golding, A., trans. 1571. *The Psalms of David and others, with Mr. John Calvin's commentaries.* London: Thomas East and Henry Middelton. STC 4395.

Holt, J. 1508. *Lac puerorum ... Milk for Children*. London: Wynkyn de Worde. STC 13604.
Kempe, W. 1588. *The education of children*. London: Thomas Orwin. STC 14926.
Mulcaster, R. 1581. *Positions ... for the training up of children*. London: Thomas Vautrollie. STC 18253.
Parr, K. 1547. *The Lamentation of a Sinner*. London: Edward Whitchurch. STC 4827.
Plat, H. 1594. *The Jewel House of Art and Nature*. London: Peter Short. STC 19991.
Plutarch [Lucius Mestrius Plutarchus]. 1938–62. *Moralia*. F.C. Babbitt, trans. Cambridge, MA: Harvard University Press.
Samuel, W. 1551. *The Abridgment of God's statutes in meter*. London: Robert Crowley [i.e. R. Grafton]. STC 21690.2.
———. 1569. *An abridgement of all the canonical books of the Old Testament written in Sternhold's meter*. London: William Seres. STC 21690.
Shakespeare, W. 2017. *The New Oxford Shakespeare: Modern Critical Edition*. G. Taylor, J. Jowett, T. Bourus, and G. Egan, gen. eds. Oxford: Oxford University Press.
The form of prayers and ministration of the sacraments ... used in the English Congregation at Geneva and approved by the famous and godly learned man, John Calvin. 1556. Geneva: John Crespin. STC 16561.
The Whole Book of Psalms collected into English meter. 1562. London: John Day. STC 2430.

Secondary Sources

Anders, H. 1935. The Elizabethan ABC with the Catechism. *The Library*. Fourth Series. **16.1**, 32–48.
Appel, C. 2007. Asking, Counting, and Memorizing: Strategies in religious writing and publishing for the common man in 17th century Denmark. In: A. Messerli and R. Chartier, eds. *Scripta volant, verba manent: Schriftkulturen in Europa zwischen 1500 und 1900. Les cultures de l'écrit en Europe entre 1500 et 1900*. Basel: Schwabe Verlag. pp. 191–214.
Attridge, D. 1982. *The Rhythms of English Poetry*. London: Routledge.
Bartrum, G. 2002. *Albrecht Dürer and His Legacy: The Graphic Work of a Renaissance Artist*. Princeton: Princeton University Press.
Bennett, H.S. 1989. *English Book and Readers, 1475 to 1557: Being a study in the History of the Book Trade from Caxton to the Incorporation of the Stationers' Company*. Cambridge: Cambridge University Press.
Borris, K. and Clark, M.D. 2011. Hymnic Epic and *The Faerie Queene*'s Original Printed Format: Canto-Canticles and Psalmic Arguments. *Renaissance Quarterly*. **64.4**, 1148–93.
Brink, J.R. 2019. *The Early Spenser, 1554–80: "Minde on honour fixed."* Manchester: Manchester University Press.
Bushnell, R.W. 1996. *A Culture of Teaching: Early Modern Humanism in Theory and Practice*. Ithaca: Cornell University Press.
Cassirer, E. 1977 [1923]. *The Philosophy of Symbolic Forms*. Vol. 2: *Mythical Thought*. R. Manheim, trans. New Haven: Yale University Press.

Chaghafi, E. 2017. Psalm Translation as Poetic Paraphrase. Unpublished paper presented at the Sixteenth Century Studies Conference, Milwaukee.

Coles, K.A. 2008. *Religion, Reform, and Women's Writing in Early Modern England*. Cambridge: Cambridge University Press.

Cummings, B. 2011. *The Book of Common Prayer: The Texts of 1549, 1559, and 1662*. Oxford: Oxford University Press.

Davis, B.P. 1996. John Day. In: J.K. Bracken and J. Silver, eds. *British Literary Booktrade, 1475–1700*. Detroit, MI: Gale Research. pp. 78–93.

Donaldson, I. 2002. National Biography and the Arts of Memory from Thomas Fuller to Colin Matthew. In: P. France and W. St. Clair, eds. *Mapping Lives: The Uses of Biography*. Oxford: Oxford University Press for the British Academy. pp. 67–82.

Engel, W.E. 1995. *Mapping Mortality: The Persistence of Memory and Melancholy in Early Modern England*. Amherst: University of Massachusetts Press.

———. 2018. The Table of Cebes and Edmund Spenser's Places of Memory. *South Atlantic Review*. **83**.4, 9–29.

Engel, W.E., Loughnane, R., and William, G. 2016. *The Memory Arts in Renaissance England: A Critical Anthology*. Cambridge: Cambridge University Press.

———. 2022. *The Death Arts in Renaissance England: A Critical Anthology*. Cambridge: Cambridge University Press.

Evenden, E. 2008. *Patents, Pictures and Patronage: John Day and the Tudor Book Trade*. Aldershot, UK; Burlington, VT: Ashgate.

Freedman, D.N. 1999. *Psalm 119: The Exaltation of Torah*. University Park: The Pennsylvania State University Press.

Fumerton, P. and Guerrini, A., eds. 2010. *Ballads and Broadsides in Britain, 1500–1800*. Aldershot, UK; Burlington, VT: Ashgate.

Green, I. 1996. *The Christian's ABC: Catechisms and Catechizing in England c.1530–1740*. Oxford: Clarendon Press.

———. 2003. *Print and Protestantism in Early Modern England*. Oxford: Oxford University Press.

———. 2016. *Humanism and Protestantism in Early Modern English Education*. New York: Routledge.

Gregerson, L. 1995. *The Reformation of the Subject: Spenser, Milton and the English Protestant Epic*. Cambridge: Cambridge University Press.

Guggenheimer, H. 1998. *The Scholar's Haggadah: Ashkenazic, Sephardic, and Oriental Versions*. Northvale, NJ and London: Jason Aronson Inc. University Press.

Guggenheimer, H.G., ed. 2013. Jerusalem Talmud: Tractates Pesahim and Yoma. Berlin: De Gruyter.

Hamlin, H. 2004. *Psalm Culture and Early Modern English Literature*. Cambridge: Cambridge University Press.

Hammond, G. 2006. The English Bible. In: D.S. Kastan, ed. *The Oxford Encyclopedia of British Literature*. Vol. 1. Oxford: Oxford University Press. pp. 185–190.

Hellinga, L. and Trapp, J.B. 1999. Introduction. In: L. Hellinga and J.B. Trapp, eds. *The Cambridge History of the Book in Britain, 1400–1557*. Cambridge: Cambridge University Press, pp. 1–30.

Holm-Nielson, S. 1960. The Importance of Late Jewish Psalmody for the Understanding of Old Testament Psalmodic Tradition. *Studia Theologica*. **14**.1, 1–53.

Kao, C. 2018. *Reformation of Prayerbooks: The Humanist Transformation of Early Modern Piety in Germany and England*. Göttingen, DE / Bristol, CT: Vandenhoeck and Ruprecht.

King, J.N. 1982. *English Reformation Literature: The Tudor Origins of the Protestant Tradition*. Princeton: Princeton University Press.

———. 1999. The book trade under Edward VI and Mary I. In: L. Hellinga and J B. Trapp, eds. *The Cambridge History of the Book in Britain, 1400–1557*. Cambridge: Cambridge University Press. pp. 164–78.

———. John Day: 2002. Master Printer of the English Reformation. In: P. Marshall and A. Ryrie, eds. *The Beginnings of English Protestantism*. Cambridge: Cambridge University Press. pp. 180–208.

———. 2011. *Foxe's "Book of Martyrs" and Early Modern Print Culture*. Cambridge: Cambridge University Press.

John Milson, J. 1999. Music. In: L. Hellinga and J.B. Trapp, eds. *The Cambridge History of the Book in Britain, 1400–1557*. Cambridge: Cambridge University Press. pp. 541–54.

Kirschbaum, L. 1946. Author's Copyright in England Before 1640. *The Papers of the Bibliographical Society of America*. **40.1**, 43–80.

Klibansky, R., Panofsky, E., and Saxl, F. 2019. *Saturn and Melancholy: Studies in the History of Natural Philosophy, Religion, and Art*. New Edition. P. Despoix and G. Leroux, eds. Montreal & Kingston: McGill-Queen's University Press.

Lindberg, C. 2010. *The European Reformations*. Second edition. Oxford: Wiley-Blackwell.

Loewenstein, J. 2002. *The Author's Due: Printing and the Prehistory of Copyright*. Chicago: University of Chicago Press.

MacCulloch, D. 2005. *The Reformation: A History*. New York: Penguin.

———. 2016. *Thomas Cranmer: A Life*. Revised edition. New Haven: Yale University Press.

MacGregor, N. 2014. *Germany: Memories of a Nation*. New York: Alfred A. Knopf.

Matthews, G. 2018. Why Plato Lost Interest in the Socratic Method. *Oxford Studies in Ancient Philosophy*. **54**, 27–49.

Neville-Sington, P. 1999. Press, politics and religion. In: *The Cambridge History of the Book in Britain, 1400–1557*. Cambridge: Cambridge University Press. pp. 576–607.

Oastler, C.L. 1975. *John Day, the Elizabethan Printer*. Oxford: Oxford Bibliographical Society.

Orme, N. 1999. Schools and school-books. In: L. Hellinga and J.B. Trapp, eds. *The Cambridge History of the Book in Britain, 1400–1557*. Cambridge: Cambridge University Press. pp. 449–69.

Panofsky, E. 2005 [1943]. *The Life and Art of Albrecht Dürer*. Princeton, NJ: Princeton University Press.

Patterson, W.B. 2018. *Thomas Fuller: Discovering England's Religious Past*. Oxford: Oxford University Press.

Pattison, B. 1939. Notes on Early Music Printing. *The Library*. Fourth Series. **19.4**, 389–421.

Pettegree, A. 2015. *Brand Luther*. New York: Penguin.

Poleg, E. 2020. *A Material History of the Bible: England 1200–1553*. Oxford: Oxford University Press for The British Academy.

Posset, F. 2003. Polyglot Humanism in Germany *circa* 1520 as Luther's Milieu and Matrix. *Renaissance and Reformation / Renaissance et Réforme*. New Series **27.1**, 5–33.

Purdy, A. 2002. The bog body as mnemotope: Nationalist archaeologies in Heaney and Turner. *Style*. **36.1**, 93–110.

Quitslund, B. 2008. *The Reformation in Rhyme: Sternhold, Hopkins and the English Metrical Psalter; 1547–1603*. Aldershot, UK; Burlington, VT: Ashgate.

———. 2013. The Psalm Book. In: A. Kesson and E. Smith, eds. *The Elizabethan Top Ten: Defining Print Popularity in Early Modern England*. Farnham, UK; Burlington, VT: Ashgate. pp. 203–11.

———. 2019. Continuous Sellers and Their Buyers: A Brief Survey of Unknowns. In: A. Marotti, ed. *New Ways of Looking at Old Texts, VI*. Tempe, AZ: Renaissance English Text Society. pp. 149–60.

Quitslund, B. and Temperley, N., eds. 2018. *The Whole Book of Psalms*, 2 vols. Tempe, AZ: Arizona Center for Medieval and Renaissance Studies.

Raven, J. 2007. *The Business of Books: Booksellers and the English Book Trade, 1450–1850*. New Haven: Yale University Press.

Sebell, D. 2016. *The Socratic Turn: Knowledge of Good and Evil in an Age of Science*. Philadelphia: University of Pennsylvania Press.

Sherman, C.R. and Lukehart, P.M. eds. 2001. *Writing on Hands: Memory and Knowledge in Early Modern Europe*. Seattle: University of Washington Press.

Shuger, D.K. 1997. *Habits of Thought in the English Renaissance: Religion, Politics, and the Dominant Culture*. Toronto: University of Toronto Press.

Smith, H. 1946. English Metrical Psalms in the Sixteenth Century and Their Literary Significance. *The Huntington Library Quarterly*. **9.3**, 249–71.

Tribble, E.B. 2011. *Cognition in the Globe: Attention and Memory in Shakespeare's Theatre*. New York: Palgrave Macmillan.

Trigg, D. 2012. *The Memory of Place: A Phenomenology of the Uncanny*. Athens, OH: Ohio University Press.

Walsham, A., Cummings, B., and Law, C. 2020. Introduction: Memory and the English Reformation. In: A. Walsham, B. Wallace, C. Law, and B. Cummings, eds. *Memory and the English Reformation*. Cambridge. Cambridge University Press. pp. 1–45.

Watson, F. 1908. *The English Grammar Schools to 1660: Their Curriculum and Practice*. Cambridge: Cambridge University Press.

Yates, F.A. 1978. *The Art of Memory*. Harmondsworth: Penguin.

3 The grand enterprise of Foxe's *Book of Martyrs* (1563)

> And when he opened the fifth seal, I saw under the altar, the souls of them that were killed for the word of God and for the testimony which they had, and they cried with a loud voice saying: "How long tarriest thou Lord holy and true, to judge and to avenge our blood on them that dwell on the earth?" And long white garments were given unto every of them. And it was said unto them that they should rest for a little season until the number of their fellows and brethren, and of them that should be killed as they were, were fulfilled.
>
> (Rev 6:9–11)

This passage taken from William Tyndale's translation of John the Revelator's vision of the Apocalypse is an especially apt way to introduce the key themes of this chapter. It was a work with which John Day was quite familiar. In connection with his printing the "Matthew Bible" (1551), he would have proofread and corrected Tyndale's New Testament,[1] and, two decades later, print Tyndale's collected writings along with those of two other closely affiliated "worthy martyrs and principal teachers of this Church of England" (Foxe 1573, title page). This work was edited by John Foxe (1563), Day's main mid-career collaborator, with whom he published the *Acts and Monuments*, popularly called the *Book of Martyrs* (King 2001, p. 53). On both of these huge undertakings with Foxe, Day was the printer and publisher. This meant that he was responsible for raising the capital, supplying the presses, hiring skilled artisanal laborers including compositors and engravers, provisioning for and safely storing the requisite paper and ink, supervising and implementing needed corrections, and ultimately handling all aspects of the distribution and sale of finished copies. Then, as the print-run sold, Day would evaluate the need for and subsequently organize a second edition, which (as discussed in Chapter 2) is where the real profits were to be realized. In the case of *Acts and Monuments*, the decision to produce a second edition was made almost immediately,[2] certainly within a year of its first appearance and long before the first edition fully had sold out (Evenden and Freeman 2013, p. 128).

DOI: 10.4324/9780429032431-4

By the 1560s then, Day had shown himself nimble at the marketing and distribution of works that he judged—and, to some extent, gambled—were likely to sell on a large scale. He was the owner and sole proprietor of a prosperous printshop above which he lived—as did others, off and on, affiliated with his business ventures, such as continental typefounders, punchcutters, and printers in his employ (Evenden 2004, p. 76), as well as the occasional traveling humanist or reformed-minded polemicist with whom Day consulted and collaborated. Regarding the latter, during the nearly two years of preparing the material for and printing the first edition of *Acts and Monuments* (Evenden and Freeman 2013, p. 116), Foxe resided with Day (Eisenstein 2011, p. 37), no doubt in the interest of overseeing and expediting the proofreading of freshly printed pages as they came off the press and marking corrections (Simpson 1927, pp. 17–18). At all events, by the early 1560s, Foxe was using Day's Aldersgate address to receive his correspondence and visitors (King 2001, p. 55). As Evenden and Freeman (2002) have pointed out, having "the author present in the printing house while the work was being printed was both a prudent and a common practice" (p. 32). Moreover, Foxe's residing at Day's shop speaks as much to the relatively new English Protestant open-ended network of affiliations associated with religious identity as it does to the continuation of the continental humanist context of sociability among like-minded scholars, especially those involved with book production (Stenner 2019, pp. 114–15).

Day's place of business was well-known as a destination for all manner of people concerned with the dissemination of and trade in Protestant ideas and printed materials. In fact, Day's house is the setting for the meetings and reported conversations in William Baldwin's novel satirizing Roman Catholic observances, *Beware the Cat* (written in 1553, the first year of Mary's reign, but prudently not published until 1561, two years after Elisabeth's coronation), where "Master Streamer" lodges while his theological tract is being prepared for the press.[3] The "force and originality of *Beware the Cat*," with special reference to Day's tutelary if tacit place within the narrative structure, best can be apprehended when focusing "on its status as a *printed* book—and thus as a relatively new kind of cultural object that embodies a distinct mode of communication and a distinct process of producing, storing, and transmitting knowledge" [original emphasis] (Bowers 1991, p. 2). There are thus many moving parts—both seen and unseen—to Day's prosperous and heavily capitalized printshop where (as observed in the Introduction) he maintained three, and later four, fully operational presses (Evenden and Freeman 2002, pp. 24–5). In addition to farming out bit-jobs to his "assigns," Day also leased other properties for the warehousing, binding, and selling of his books around the city.[4] In addition to these daily duties and supervisory tasks, he was actively involved in the preparatory research, collecting texts for print-copy, and ensuring the accuracy of the information that found its way into Foxe's *Book of Martyrs* (Evenden

2008, p. 145). This follows from, as discussed in Chapter 1, Day's usual hands-on policy associated with his printing projects, for example, the many editions of Hugh Latimer's sermons to which he held exclusive rights—Latimer being one of the three "Oxford Martyrs" who would feature significantly in *Acts and Monuments*. As for his other monopolies on a range of voluminous polemical works, beginning in 1552 he received the patent on all works by Thomas Becon. This resulted in, among other lucrative tomes, his publication of *The Sick Man's Salve* (1561), consisting of 545 pages, as well as *The works of Thomas Becon* (1564) which, however, had to be put on hold until he finished with the production of Foxe's *Book of Martyrs* (Evenden 2008, p. 71). *The Sick Man's Salve*, like nearly all of Day's works, bears his proprietary *memento mori* printer's mark (see again Figure 1.6), but this version also carries a motto, in English, printed beneath the colophon—a jaunty couplet summing up the Latin tags found within the emblem: "Although death, doth daily draw near: / Yet (his sting past) virtue shineth clear" (sig. Mm8[v]). And the last leaf announces where the book can be obtained ("dwelling over Aldersgate beneath Saint Martins"), plus, in Latin, a restatement of his regally issued privilege to print the work for seven years ("cum privilegio per septennium," as discussed in Chapter 1). From first to last, then, Day reminds his readers, and potential printing pirates alike, that this is his work.

Throughout his career, Day remained wholly committed to bringing out in print all manner of expressions of the reformed evangelical message for English readers. This is especially evident in his preserving and republishing William Tyndale's writings (King 2001, p. 57). As both an expedient of the standard operating procedures of Tudor-era printing houses, and also as a way to forge an associative link between a range of "godly" Protestant books and his own business, Day again used the architectural title page woodcut from his 1551 Matthew Bible (discussed in Chapter 1; see again Figure 1.2, which includes Day's witty personalized impressa, "Arise for it is Day") for *The whole works of William Tyndale* (1573).[5] He also used it for, among his other books, *Bassus, Certain Notes*, known as "Day's Service Book" (discussed in Chapter 2). As significant as Day's printing of Foxe's collected writings of Tyndale and two other martyrs was for the Protestant cause in England, *Acts and Monuments* is considered one of the most influential books published in England during the 16th and 17th centuries. Part of the reason for its extraordinary popularity is its unflinching singularity of purpose conveyed through and by means of a variety of genres including letters, memoires, spiritual biographies and transcribed autobiographies, prison writings, polemical tracts, speeches, poems, sermons, martyologies, and archived historical and ecclesiastical documents. Andrew Hiscock (2011) does not overstate the case in his conclusion that, by virtue of drawing "upon a multitude of different sources and different generic expectations, Foxe brought to fruition an enormous venture that shaped historical understanding and spiritual experience for generations of readers"; for Foxe offered *The Acts and Monuments* "as a dominant point of contact with the history of the Christian Church for his national audience" (p. 112). The overall effectiveness of the book in accomplishing its aims owes much to the full range of Day's state-of-the-art printing practices including, as King (2011) observes, "the interplay of different type fonts, marginal glosses, woodcuts or engravings, two color printing, cross-references, and indices" (pp. 2–3). As for these technical aspects pertaining to the printer's métier discussed in the previous chapters—including his deluxe engravings in *The Cosmographical Glass*, innovative use of various type fonts in a wide range of licensed printings of the *Short Catechism* and *Whole Book of Psalms*, as well as his user-friendly layout and general apparatus for producing the Bible in whole and in parts—Day gained valuable experience in every one of these areas such that his track record declared his mastery of all aspects of early modern book production. And, as already observed, the ongoing profits from his catechisms and psalms enabled him to devote his available presses full-time, often operating in continuous work shifts, to undertake an enterprise as grand and demanding as Foxe's *Book of Martyrs*. Evenden and Freeman (2013) sensibly have conjectured that it is doubtful the printer fully anticipated how long Foxe would take in researching his martyrology, such that he "lost quite a bit of business, especially his musical works, because of his commitment to printing the *Acts and Monuments*," and, moreover, even before printing was underway, he was "losing money by having to delay or turn down other projects" (p. 113). While he obviously sought to maintain and expand his business interests, ever and always Day was committed to producing works that collectively consolidated and advanced the Protestant agenda in Tudor England (Melnikoff 2018, p. 71).

Remembering martyrs and the consolidation of history

The epigraph to this chapter crystallizes and reinforces the ideational pull of a Protestant politics of memory that motivated and affectively informed John Day's printing enterprise throughout his career. Reform-oriented books, such as *Acts and Monuments* that "enjoined upon Protestants" an incentive to learn to read (Eisenstein 2012, pp. 170–3), reveal the extent of Day's dominant role in the fabrication of an English Protestant Memory Art by means of the printing press as an indispensable agent of change. In the "Preface to the Christian reader" that introduces *The whole works of Tyndale* (1573), Foxe praises Day as being on the front line of advancing the Protestant cause:

> The printer of this book hath diligently collected and in one volume together enclosed the works, I mean of William Tyndall, John Frith, and Robert Barnes: chief ringleaders in these latter times of this Church of England. Wherein as we have much to praise God for

such good books left to the Church, and also for such printers in preserving by their industry and charges such books from perishing.

(sig. A2^r)

Day is praised here for taking up the twin task of preservation and conservation, likewise associated with the traditional memory arts, which "far from waning" with the advent of print culture "entered upon a new and strange lease of life" (Yates 1978, pp. 129–34). Where core beliefs and practices of medieval theology and sacred places were concerned especially, reformers set about reshaping and rebuilding memory and tradition (Walsham 2011, pp. 252–95). But far and away, the most thoroughgoing and successful attempt to recast the religious past in England was the *Book of Martyrs* (Hiscock 2011, pp. 90–112). In addition to creating a "history for English Protestantism, emphasizing its apostolic inheritance and especially its persecution in the sixteenth century, by dramatically retelling the lives and deaths of Protestant martyrs under Queen Mary," Foxe's *Acts and Monuments*, Peter Sherlock (2020) argues, "also celebrated memory itself, as a duty owed by the reader to the maintenance and propagation of true religion," recreating social memory by the "intentional erasure of what they saw as false understandings of the past" (p. 158). Owing to the weaving together of earlier narrative sources of dissenters persecuted for their beliefs in books such as the collected works of Tyndall and the *Acts and Monuments*, Day's contribution to English Reformation memorial practices acquired and tended to normalize what Arcangeli and Tamm (2020) have referred to as the "special dynamics and effect through the specific interfaces of their media transmissions, in which the oral transmission of memory interacted with the written and/or printed memory" (p. 13). Day was not the first to do this, of course. As Alex Ryrie (1999) reminds us, one of the most "distinctive and memorable characteristics of the second generation of Protestantism was the martyrological literature that it produced" (p. 52). Day, however, was the first to undertake the martyrological project on such a grand scale, which no other printers of the period could have matched. For, Foxe's *Book of Martyrs* was, according to John King (2011), "the most physically imposing, complicated, and technically demanding sixteenth-century English book," especially when taking into account Day's numerous state-of-the art woodcuts, which made it "the best illustrated book of the Elizabethan age" (p. 81).[6] Further, Andrew Pettegree (2002) contends that the illustrations in *Acts and Monuments*, from the first edition published in 1563, immediately were recognized as one of the book's most "effective and distinctive features," providing some of "the most familiar images of the English Protestant tradition," which are now

> so much a part of the staple elements of our pictorial heritage that it is hard to remember that in their own day they were exceptional

not only in their power and impact, but in their place in the English illustrative tradition.

(pp. 133–4)

In what follows, I shall be addressing this crucial aspect of the *Book of Martyrs* with special reference to the overarching mnemotechnic value of the images.[7]

The epigraph to this chapter also reflects Tyndall's careful translation of the Book of Revelation as it directly concerns the presence, place, and role of martyrs in Heaven, speculation about which many 16th-century expositors on the Bible studiously avoided. For example, it is the one book in the New Testament that Erasmus did not comment on in his influential biblical *Paraphrase*, doubting whether it even should be considered a canonical book of scripture. Diarmaid MacCulloch (2005b) explains this "uncomfortable silence" about the Book Revelation in terms of the mainstream leaders of the early Reformation being "hurt and surprised by the outburst of radical religion around their own efforts to bring about a controlled godly revolution" (p. 553). And Patrick Gray (2017) affirms that, in this history of the exegetical tradition, it is a universally acknowledged truth that "Revelation is the most bizarre, most difficult to interpret, and thus the most commonly misunderstood book in the New Testament" (p. 217). Any commentary on Revelation during the 16th century inevitably raised potentially incendiary doctrinal issues. This was especially the case since the veneration and adoration of martyrs had been banished from reformed rites and devotional practices. Concomitantly, with the jettisoning of Purgatory from the liturgy as legislated by the Book of Common Prayer and the revised English Church Articles (discussed in Chapter 2), there no longer was a need for intercessionary saints.[8] And yet, clearly, in lieu of charred bones and other such relics involving blood, tears, and scraps of cloth, remembering the sacrifices, stories, and narratives of martyrs still served to unite and bind together a community of believers by giving them a shared history (Freeman 2007). At the time when Foxe first was collecting and publishing in Latin his account of the trials of Christian martyrs, "amid the bitterness of the new struggles of Reformed Protestantism against Counter-Reformation Catholicism from the 1560s," as MacCulloch (2005b) shows, "the Book of Revelation's stock rose accordingly among mainstream Protestants" (p. 553). This was especially the case with Foxe, who clearly borrowed the scheme of Christian eschatological history he found in Heinrich Bullinger's work for "his own influential *Acts and Monuments*," which "was eagerly devoured (not merely by English-speaking readers), producing many new variations on the Last Days theme" (p. 554). In line with this claim, as will be discussed at the end of this chapter, Foxe's final book, published posthumously, was on the Apocalypse.

Martyrs, then, as exemplars of steadfast faith in the face of persecution, were to be admired and duly accorded a special place in England's collective and then gradually emerging Protestant nationalist memory. A few years after the second edition of the *Acts and Monuments*, for example, Meredith Hanmer could use the phrase "Theatre of Martyrs" to tap into the memories so indelibly set up and virtually fixed by the work of Foxe and Day. In his evangelically inflected version of Eusebius's *Ecclesiastical Histories* (1577),[9] Hanmer's evocative details rehearsed in "The Translator unto the Christian Reader" at once draw on the imagery of *The Book of Martyrs* and also situate his exhaustive if vivid catalogue of the trials of the faithful with reference to—and as authorized by—the Book of Revelation, thus returning us once more to this chapter's epigraph (Rev. 6: 9–11).

> If we stand upon the Theatre of Martyrs, and there behold the valiant wrestlers, and invincible champions of Christ Jesus, how can we choose but be ravished with zeal when we see the professors of the truth torn in pieces of wild beasts, crucified, beheaded, stoned, stifled, beaten to death with cudgels, fried to the bones, slain alive, burned to ashes, hanged on gibbets, drowned, brained, scourged, maimed, quartered, their necks broken, their legs sawed of, their tongues cut, their eyes pulled out and the empty place seared with scalding iron, the wrapping of them in ox hides with dogs and snakes and drowned in the sea, the enjoining of them to kill one another, the gelding of Christians, the paring of their flesh with sharp razors, the rending of their sides with the lash of the whip, the pricking of their veins with bodkins, and famishing of them to death in deep and noisome dungeons. It is a wonder to see the zeal of their prayers, their charity towards all men, their constancy in torment, and their confidence in Christ Jesus. These be they whom St. John in his Apocalypse saw in a vision under the altar, that were martyred for the word God and the testimony of Christ Jesus, which cried with a loud voice, saying: "How long tarriest thou Lord, holy and true, to judge and to avenge our blood on them that dwell on the earth…"
>
> (sig. *5ᵛ)

Hanmer's translation was a perennial favorite among evangelical readers (Andreani 2021, pp. 56–82), in large measure owing to its concentrated focus on early martyrs, going through no few than nine editions by the end of the 17th century. For, even though "the Reformations of the sixteenth century split the church, all parties continued to hold the Eusebian model of church history by claiming to be *the* faithful recovery or continuation of the early church" [original emphasis] (Lindberg 2010, p. 5). Martyrs clearly came to occupy very special niches in the Protestant Art of Memory, ready-made images for future use that had been duly revived, sacralized, and stabilized in print by *Acts and Monuments*.

The grand design of Foxe and Day in every respect was geared toward making such memories credible and enduring. Not only did this help strengthen the faith of those already disposed toward evangelical ideas, but it also proved an especially effective approach to sway those who were finding it difficult to cut ties altogether with the images and rituals of the Church of Rome, which until only recently under Queen Mary they had been required to follow. Aston and Ingram (1997) reasonably conclude that, to "think of the pictures in the *Book of Martyrs*"—whether those specifically tailored to events described in the text or the smaller, more generic woodcuts which "were repeated and permutated with great freedom, and sometimes with scant regard to the martyrdom they illustrated"—inevitably is "to think of a body chained to a stake, licked by flames," which were, to be sure, "extremely memorable images," made even more memorable when, "as in the case of the Cambridge 1570 copy, they were hand-colored" (p. 79).[10] It may well be the case, as Roy Strong (1969) claims, that "few periods have been more inimical to the visual arts than the middle years of the sixteenth century" (p. 1), especially when taking into account how many of the Marian exiles returned to England from Calvinist Geneva where scripture alone sufficed and images were suspect. Contemporaneously, however, as the archival sleuthing of Tessa Watt (1996) has shown, Protestants readily turned to other forms of material culture, most notably illustrated psalters, devotionals, and prayers books (pp. 69–70). At all events, by the 1570s, the *Book of Martyrs*, with its state-of-the-art woodcuts, was being used in devotional exercises. Some indication of how the book served in this capacity can be gleaned from Mark Rankin (2010), who points out that, "tracking the direct correspondence of a particular image to a given moment in the text can solidify in the reader's mind the martyrs response to that moment" (p. 88). Moreover, there are also instances when Day strategically includes an image "depicting events other than the moment of death" thereby providing insight into how Day's attentiveness to "illustrations could emphasize the most desirable and convenient moment in the text Foxe supplied" (p. 89).

As a master printer who had acquired a large stock of woodcuts and was well connected with continental craftsmen who could supply him with new ones, Day can take the credit for the compelling illustrations that so immediately endowed the already rhetorically suasive narrative of the *Book of Martyrs* with additional mnemotechnic power. The first iteration of the *Acts and Monuments*, Foxe's *Commentarii rerum* (1554), had no illustrations at all; and his more developed *Rerum in ecclesia gestarum ... Commentarii* (1559) contained only a few woodcuts supplied by his printer (Aston and Ingram 1997, pp. 80–1). While Foxe and Day were drawn together by their shared religious convictions and practical approach to advancing the Protestant cause (Evenden 2008, p. 62), given their differing areas of expertise, it was Day who found, engaged, and paid the illustrators; and, more to the point, it was Day who ultimately determined the content for the woodcuts—namely, which topics, martyrs, and scenes were to be depicted (Evenden and Freeman

2013, pp. 194–5). Rankin (2010) has succinctly stated the case in his examination of the ways in which text and image interact within the *Book of Martyrs* in order to shape interpretation: "Day held the responsibility of overseeing the entire illustration program" (p. 88). Moreover, Rankin's painstaking analysis of the relation of image to text in the *Book of Martyrs* shows that "Day selected narratives that he identified as memorable and then distributed his illustrations as liberally as his finances would allow" (p. 106). Day's management of the images in *Acts and Monuments* thus offers another instance, broadly conceived, of the printer as author exercising his influence and ingenuity in line with the terms of his trade, revealing something quite telling about the fluid liberties pertaining to early modern authorship.

Notwithstanding the relative truth value of the accounts recorded in their book, both Day and Foxe were keen to widen the field of reported experiences so as to accommodate popular tradition, especially when concerning martyrs' dying words as a kind of motto that encapsulated and underscored their sacrifice, conveyed in a way that was easy for readers to remember and then pass along to others by way of their own recounting of the narrative. While a few discredited stories disappeared between the first and second editions, 1563 and 1570, respectively (Loades 2005, p. 48), others, such as Latimer's famous last words spoken to Ridley from atop the soon-to-be-lit pyre, were not in the first edition at all. The authenticity of the remark thus is cast in doubt (Freeman 1999, p. 44). Even though it did not survive the first round of judicious editing, it still somehow found its way into the second edition: "Play the man, Master Ridley; we shall this day light such a candle, by God's grace, in England, as I trust shall never be put out" (King 1997, p. 23). It is also in the second edition that short rehearsals of events from the first edition were fleshed out in more detail, new material added—such as Latimer's affectively memorable quip destined to become a kind of ubiquitous motto for English Protestants thereafter. Further, later editions show a pronounced proliferation of margin glosses designed specifically to call attention to the ideological, political, and figurative nature of the interpolated words. There was no need for a detailed allegorical exegesis here, both because that was not the tenor of the original commentary and also because the margin notes—reminiscent of those peppering the Geneva Bible—tell the reader all that needs to be known about how it applies to the evangelical message. Further, these indexical notations double as topical headings summing the substance of an episode seen through a Protestant lens. For example, in the section on Anne Askew's trial and execution, the following marginal notes appear in succession: "The Mass an abominable idol," "Anne Askew brought unto the stake," and (in reference to her being tied to a chair and carried to the pyre) "Anne Askew lamed upon the rack" (Foxe 1576, sig. PPP4^r).[11] The asides are memory triggers in every sense of the term making double sure that readers knew exactly where they stood with respect to the narrative at

112 *Grand enterprise of the* Book of Martyrs

hand, clarifying what was required to be taken away from the reported event, and also making it easy to find one's way back to and recover that same information at a glance upon future readings and consultation of the book. Day's typographical expertise with and subtle insight into the mnemotechnical value of such margin markers was a characteristic feature of his printing practices (as discussed at length in Chapter 2). In some cases, the memory of a story in the *Book of Martyrs* is strengthened further by a vivid illustration provided by Day, as with the burning of Anne Askew (Foxe 1576, sig. PPP3^v)—and, as famously, with the immolation of Hugh Latimer and Nicolas Ridley (see Figure 3.1).

This combination of a stirring image and textual banners operate according to the same mnemotechnically oriented principles as did popular emblems of the day (Engel 1999). As such, it brings home the politics and theology of the episode to the viewers, making it all the more likely such symbolically encoded images (the *imagines agentes* of the classical memory arts) will find a secure place in what might be called the Memory Theatre of the English Reformation, the principles of which already can be seen at work in Hanmer's apt evocation of the "Theatre of Martyrs."

This oversized woodcut tipped in separately from the page gatherings, like Day's map of Cunningham's Norwich in *The Cosmographical Glass* discussed in Chapter 1, although consistent with his usual house style, stands out from the rest of the images both because of its status as a foldout picture and also because of how it is positioned in the volume (Rankin 2022, pp. 26–8). Given his characteristic proactive planning for such contingencies, Day would have commissioned this woodcut long before they got around to printing this section of *Acts and Monuments*. Most likely, since there are only two such fold-out pages of illustrations in the first edition, he clearly foresaw its prominent place in the overall program of illustrations relative to the nearly 50 standard and quarter-sized woodcut blocks, the overall content of which was still being determined. Also typical of Day's process are the empty speech bubbles of the woodcut, or banderoles as they were called—an inheritance from earlier English printed hagiographic works such as *The Golden Legend* (1483)—which a compositor has filled in using a smaller font to fit the specific size of the drop in typesetting (King 2011, p. 207). Such banderoles, which in some cases are left blank to be filled in by various owners according to their own responses to the stirring images depicted (p. 202), and in others appear as truncated passages from the Bible, serve as mnemonic triggers for the recollection of words imprinted in the memory of the reformed Christian reader (p. 200). This approach to multimodal expression in such illustrations supplied by Day, moreover, provided readers with a system for learning how to cross-reference for themselves what they encountered in the *Acts and Monuments* with the Bible, thus further bolstering the reformed Protestant application of *sola scriptura* (scripture

Grand enterprise of the Book of Martyrs 113

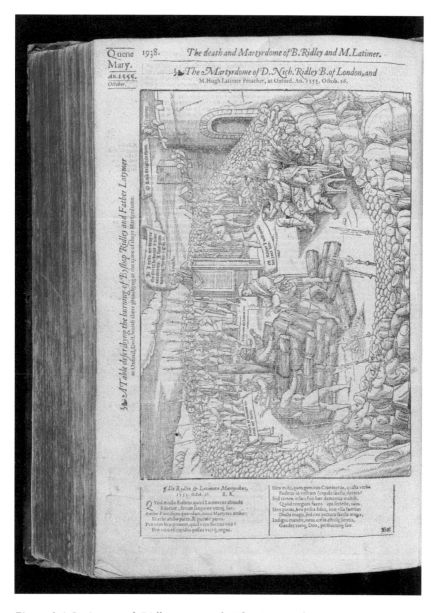

Figure 3.1 Latimer and Ridley executed. *The Acts and Monuments* (London: John Day, 1563), f. 1938. Image used courtesy of The Lambeth Palace Library.

114 *Grand enterprise of the* Book of Martyrs

alone), as was discussed in Chapter 2 with reference to Katherine Parr's *The Lamentation of a Sinner* (1547).[12]

In this particular illustration (Figure 3.1), which may well be, according to King (2001), "the best remembered depiction of martyrdom in the whole of the *Book of Martyrs*" (p. 207), there are three such allusive scriptural mnemonic cues. Hugh Latimer's "Father of heaven receive my soul" follows closely the words of the first martyr, Stephen, immediately before his death (Acts 7:59),[13] leaving the reader to fill in the rest of Stephen's pronouncement and prayer, which in the Matthew Bible reads: "Lord, lay not this sin to their charge." And Ridley is depicted as uttering, in Latin, Christ's final words on the cross beginning "In manus tuas domine" ["Into your hands, O Lord…"] which in the Vulgate concludes "commendo spiritum meum" ["I commend my spirit"] (Luke 23:46). The comparison of these two Oxford Martyrs to St. Stephen and to Christ respectively cannot be lost on anyone familiar with scripture, such that all that needs to be dropped into the word bubble is enough to activate the mnemonic trigger. In both cases, users of the book, taking in the whole of the represented scene of the martyrs' imminent death by fire, are left to fill in the rest on their own. A third scriptural reference is set in train by the abbreviated Latin opening of 1 Corinthians 13:3, proclaimed by Richard Smith who stands at the portable pulpit brought in for the occasion of the public execution. The large banderole situated centrally at the top of the woodcut would have been easily identified and recognized by Protestants, both because this is recorded as having been the Pauline text on which Smith preached that fateful day and also because the text already had become a powerful and prominent passage for the persecuted nonconformist community: "I may dole out all I possess, or even, give my body to be burnt, but if I have no love, I am none the better." Similarly, drop in typesetting also is used to label key individuals and, as it were, quote their words, thus serving to guide the viewer's proper affective response to the tableau. For example, at the top right, Thomas Cranmer, overlooking the scene from his captivity in the Bocardo prison says: "O Lord strengthen them." Viewers are lifted up from the crowd, as it were, and allowed to take it all in at a single glance. They apprehend the whole episode in its more encompassing divinely overseen context, which is at once transtemporal and inscribed in the historical record. The whole scene offers itself to be read as a step in the steady providential march toward the ultimate victory of Protestantism as the one True Church. The illustration thus consolidates all that conditioned this memorable moment culminating in the burning of Latimer and Ridley, in effect giving viewers a privileged glimpse back in time so as to be vicariously and virtually present to see the main actors and hear their words. They are thus provided with a framework for comprehending the carefully staged scene from its proper—which is to say Protestant—perspective. Luborsky and Ingram (1998, p. 366) describe the experiential effect of engaging the images in terms of the reader being cast "in the role of an involved spectator like the spectators themselves who watch the martyrs in the narrative scenes." By such means, Day succeeds in creating a series of especially resonant mnemonic *loci* (or places) that, in retrospect, can be seen to function as so many focal nodes in a mnemotechnical network, thereby participating in and at the same time helping to constitute a distinctively Protestant Memory Art in early modern Britain.

Making new memories and supplanting the old

Day and Foxe recognized and sought to capitalize on the obvious polemical and mnemonic value of representing specific people who had suffered for the evangelical reformed cause owing to Queen Mary's promotion of Roman Catholicism as the official state religion. Such martyrs—newly named and identified as such—were accorded a prominent place in the writings and collective memory of the emerging Elizabethan English nation–state. Foxe and Day were committed and well-equipped to evoke and give a rich textual form to those martyrs now being remembered and duly memorialized, and, in the process, to reform and shape the very memories survivors had of recent events by providing a providential context for making sense of it all. From its inception, the *Book of Martyrs* was directed toward a clearly delineated and prefigured end that was ideologically consistent with the gathering momentum of the reformed, evangelical movement in England. Typical of their generation, Day and Foxe had experienced firsthand the perilous and uncertain times of the Marian persecutions. As will be discussed further in the final section of this chapter, Day himself was imprisoned and, upon his release, sought to ply his trade without drawing any unnecessary attention to his printshop activities.. Foxe was among the exiles who fled initially to Strasbourg and ended up in Basel. Thus, their personal experiences both authenticated and validated the drive to produce a *Book of Martyrs* and also mirrored the experiences of the nonconforming British intelligentsia, clerics, and members of the creative and pedagogical classes who survived the years of religious uncertainty and cultural trauma. Their timely book project tapped into the sense of urgency associated with collecting and telling martyrs' stories in the aftermath of Mary's five-year reign, during the final years of which her Spanish consort, Philip II, impatiently urged her to institute a more rapid and complete return of England to Roman Catholicism. With the accession of her evangelically leaning stepsister, Elizabeth I, Mary's state religious policies incrementally were rolled back (albeit not quickly enough for some of the more vocal Protestant preachers). In line with the tenor of the changing times, Foxe and Day decided to provide an engaging way to reunite reform minded Christians of all stripes by showcasing their own martyrs, both from earlier times and also those of recent memory. They set about recovering and repackaging—with the aim of memorializing and textually enshrining—the special place of their martyrs in the history of the True Church.

Although Foxe's understanding of martyrs and martyrdom necessarily drew on and had something in common with earlier Catholic models (Monta 2009, pp. 65–6), and especially with Eusebius as already mentioned, he had absolutely no truck with relics. Like later Protestants under Archbishop Laud, Foxe made no allowance for the veneration of bones (Schwyzer 2022. The full title of Day and Foxe's grand enterprise indicates what kinds of "monuments" are being set up, what remnants of the dead recollected and resituated in their book—which can be figured as a kind of textual sepulchre retaining memorable traces of the martyred (King 1997, pp. 21–2). In addition to transcripts from inquisitorial examinations of early evangelicals and letters written during their incarceration that had been carefully preserved in manuscript, there were many other writings that formed what has been called a "scribal culture of Marian martyrs" (Freeman 2004), much of which found its way into the *Book of Martyrs*. As Alexandra Walsham (2012) has shown, such writings came to be seen as "precious remnants of the martyrs" (p. 913). The full title of the first edition (1563) clarifies the specific field of memory from which the records pertaining to Britain's martyrs are being recovered and to what end, such that texts themselves—rather than relics and body parts, as with the earlier Catholic martyrological tradition—became valued as valid and powerfully suasive witnesses of faith.

> Acts and monuments of these latter and perilous days touching matters of the Church, wherein are comprehended and described the great persecutions [and] horrible troubles, that have bene wrought and practiced by the Romish prelates, [e]specially in this realm of England and Scotland, from the year of our Lord a thousand, unto the time now present. Gathered and collected according to the true copies [and] writings certificatory, as well of the parties themselves that suffered, as also out of the bishops' registers, which were the doers thereof.

The emphasis is on both "true copies" and "writings certificatory," by which are meant royal as well as state records including the last-mentioned ecclesiastical registers, in effect setting up something of an early modern truth-telling commission making room for personal accounts of those who were witnesses in every sense of the term. While striving to evoke the persuasive discourse of historical facticity in titling the work *Acts and Monuments*, Foxe also appreciated what Thomas Betteridge (2002) has analyzed in terms of "the invisible of worldly history, those who have been denied a voice, who have lacked historical presence" because "it is in their testimony that the universal Word of God can be heard" (p. 147). Moreover, Day's woodcuts make this invisible history palpably visible through graphic representations designed to bring out and augment the psychograms and mnemic energy already associated with the Marian martyrs.

Day's images therefore convey a signification beyond what simply pertains to the particular person or group, whether engulfed by flames or resolutely standing on scaffold. Set within the framework as being "acts" as well as "monuments," these illustrations, in and of themselves, guaranteed the sanctified status of the martyrs' testimonies and witnessing of God's Word. A superadded symbolic value thus accrues to the woodcuts beyond their specific iconography; though admittedly some have involved programs that the narrative often unpacks and interprets. There are also instances of "mutually validating and authorizing relations between image and word expressed" which relates directly to "an unease over the ability of words *or* images to produce the 'truth' of the martyr's suffering on their own" (Betteridge 2002, p. 155). The imagery and overall persecutorial situatedness of many of the illustrations in the *Book of Martyrs*, of course, "was attached to a long tradition of Continental iconography," both from the Catholic tradition (as will be discussed further in what follows), as well as "at some points visibly positioned between Lutheran and Calvinist image-making" (Aston and Ingram 1997, p. 137).[14] Many of the woodcuts are stylized in such a way as to avoid the inclusion of overly gruesome visual details, thereby steering viewers away from becoming too invested in the abject horror of such tortures and, instead, encouraging a cultivation of pathos such that images of immolated martyrs "appear jubilant and frequently barely scorched," making "the relationship between woodcut illustrations and the narrative accounts of violent immolation" at times rather "complex and sometimes paradoxical in the *Book of Martyrs*" (Rankin 2010, p. 97). Day was at pains to make sure the universality of martyrdom, which over time and due to repetition can tend to fade into a kind of trope of redundancy, was properly imbued with an evangelically oriented character so that each image received and was assured a secure and singular place in his wide-ranging Protestant Memory Art.

Earlier medieval hagiographical and martyrological precedents, of which Day and Foxe were keenly aware, can be found among other popular works Jacobus de Voragine's (1483) 13th-century *Golden Legend*. This compendium famously was translated into English and printed by William Caxton in 1483, and many times thereafter.[15] It offered a viable genre, albeit one steeped in the Catholic tradition, that provided a formal structure for organizing and presenting the ultimate sacrifice of the steadfast in their faith that was readily co-opted for the Protestant cause. Foxe himself, in the preface to the first edition of *Acts and Monuments* (1563), mentions the *Legenda Aurea* explicitly with reference to how others, longing to see his work at last in print, have spoken of his forthcoming monumental martyrology (sig. B3[r]). While Foxe may want to put some distance between his project and *The*

Golden Legend, the allusion to Foxe's repurposing of old forms for new Protestant ends likewise and comparably characterizes Day's printing career during the reign of Queen Elizabethan (explored further in what follows and, more particularly still, in Chapters 4 and 5). A good case in point is Day's addition of a Protestant calendar of martyrs inserted at the beginning of the first edition (Evenden and Freeman 2013, p. 126). It is not simply a one-for-one substitution of the focal figures from the pre-Reformation times with those of "these latter and perilous days," but well and truly a subversion of the Catholic way of reckoning the Church year and hence ritual observance. Consequently, it also subverts and replaces the Roman Catholic view of teleology and eschatology, which is to say the all-important End Times (returning us once more to the epigraph of this chapter). The supplanting of Catholic sainted martyrs with Protestant ones had the effect of reinforcing a hagiographic division of the year into distinct mnemonic loci, which inflected that slate of interlinked psychograms and mnemotopes with a Reformation view of God's sacred order for the whole of human history. This was, of course, intolerable to Catholic polemicists and critics of *Acts and Monuments*; most notably, the English Jesuit, Robert Parsons, whose *Treatise of Three Conversations* (1603–04), published after Foxe's death, systematically counters point by point and martyr by martyr, the events and people chronicled in the *Book of Martyrs*. That there was a well-publicized and ongoing dialectical exchange between Catholics and Protestants in the form of competing martyrologies indicates that, as John King (2011) observed, "methodological reading of calendric entries was a widespread practice" (p. 263). Given Day's inclusion of the rubricated grid calendar of Protestant martyrs with the first edition of 1563, and Foxe's ensuing chronological approach to recounting the history of the True Church from a reformed perspective, there can be no doubt they wanted *Acts and Monuments* to become a viable and sweeping replacement for "Catholic devotional works in popular consciousness" with the aim of "creating a Protestant culture" in Britain (Ford 2020, p. 167).

Insofar as the term "culture" is not an uncontested idea, it is appropriate to take a moment to qualify what might be meant both here and in what follows by "a Protestant culture," because something along these lines is precisely what Day was devoted to establishing and stabilizing, the printer as author. Briefly then, and with deference to the history of the social sciences, a long-held classic textbook definition of "culture" reads as follows:

> Culture consists of patterns of and for behavior acquired and transmitted by symbols, constituting the distinctive achievements of human groups, including their embodiments in artifacts; the essential core of culture consists of traditional (= historically derived and selected) ideas and especially their attached values.
> (Kroeber and Kluckhohn 1952, p. 35)

E.P. Thompson (1993) fleshed out this concept further, and in a way that has direct bearing on Foxe and Day's intervention in the processes leading to an English national Protestant culture:

> [A] culture is also a pool of diverse resources, in which traffic passes between the literate and the oral, the superordinate and the subordinate, the village and the metropolis; it is an arena of conflictual elements, which requires some compelling pressure—as, for example, nationalism or prevalent religious orthodoxy or class consciousness—to take form as a "system." And, indeed, the very term "culture," with its cozy invocation of consensus, may serve to distract attention from social and cultural contradictions, from the fractures and oppositions within the whole.
>
> (p. 6)

These conceptual elements brought forward in Thompson's characterization of culture from a social historical perspective reemerge in important ways in studies concerning "the history of the book" as carried out by Lucien Febvre and Henri-Jean Martin (2010). They treat the early modern book first and foremost as a commodity:

> the book was a piece of merchandise ... [t]hus it was vitally necessary from the outset to find enough capital to start work and then to print only those titles which would satisfy clientele, and that at a price which would withstand competition. The marketing of books was similar to that of other products [where] finance and costing were the key problems.
>
> (p. 109)

David Hall (1996) contends in this regard that the "significance of book history was that it forced a recognition of culture not as something uniform or imposed from above" (p. 5).

With such considerations in mind, we can tease out further the strands of Foxe's editorial process that fully supported, reinforced, and helped further shape Day's goal to create through print so as to promote a proper, seemingly self-evident and self-consistent, reformist expression of Protestant culture. For Foxe, in his chronicling of the sweep of Christian history by focusing on the persecution of those who dissented from papal authority, was meticulous in his depictions of each of the martyr's unique situations, the specific charges brought against them, and their final hours. Insofar as the history of each martyr is a story in and of itself and also, at the same time, implicitly accorded specific symbolic value within a larger cultural system of political exchanges, it is not far from the mark to see his martyrological enterprise as the production of an early modern mythology with a definitive reformist valance in the service of revisionist nation-building. A comparable claim as regards the place of myth in English Renaissance cultural production has been made with reference to Francis Bacon by Clark Hulse (1988), which resonates as well with Foxe's literary craft, namely, that

> he seeks to purify myth of the taint of its origins and to mystify the operations and exercise of power, suggesting that command of the state lies within those who command statecraft through their grasp of the significance of examples and their capacity to apply them to the present situation.
>
> (p. 338)

For in Foxe's telling of the histories of individual persecutions, seen as a mode of witnessing the True Word of God, he tended to "occlude the diversity of their opinions in the interests of presenting these victims of persecutions as a united and homogenous group," in effect airbrushing out "the bitter divisions that racked the early Protestant community" (Walsham et al. 2020, pp. 37–8). This frequent eliding of doctrinal differences among the Marian martyrs enables Foxe and Day to focus on setting up a less complicated and thus more indelible slate of new memories—of mnemotopes, enabling a visual interpretation of the past that makes public memory accessible, and thus creating meaning for the community and for individuals. D.R. Woolf (1995) argues that Day's "celebrated woodcuts further support Foxe's simplification of narrative action and his suppression of historical difference" (p. 265). The *Book of Martyrs* therefore provides, Woolf contends, an easily navigable "channel between the oral tales of martyrdom" and a digest of universal church history rendered in a "popular form," drawing heavily on the tropes of romance narrative, "that could be read by the literate but also comprehended by the vulgar" (p. 251). Fundamentally mnemonic in its structure, reception, and reliance on repetition, the traditional form of the romance story is especially useful in accounting for how *Acts and Monuments* ends up being "more than just a mere series of discontinuous lives laid end to end," by telling a story "the *object* of which is the eventual triumph of the saints" [original emphasis] (p. 251). The restorative and re-creative power of myth can be seen to come into play in *Acts and Monuments* in terms of—and as—the telling and retelling of a community's history through individual stories, including and taking into account all of the occlusions and additions that tend to accrue in their many repetitions and iterations, and especially by means of Foxe's well-intentioned if monological curation of the many and diverse voices represented in the *Book of Martyrs*.

This notion of the importance of attending to the revival of orality as found in Foxe's scripting of the foundational stories given to and taken up by a community—or culture—likewise preoccupied Ernst Cassirer (1977b) in his analysis of mythical thought as part of his philosophy of symbolic forms, discussed preliminarily in the Introduction. Cassirer contends that each of the major areas of culture, especially with reference to the power of myth, represents a different type of knowledge and has its own self-consistent kind of logic, consisting of what he terms "symbolic forms." What differentiates myth from other forms of experience, for Cassirer, "is to be found in the particular way in which the general structure of experience is actualized in it" (Verene 1966, p. 557). Cassirer treats myth as two moments (in a Hegelian sense) in the evolution of a culture's history, namely, first as the form of immemorial even atavistic or "primitive" thought, which, inevitably later, second, reemerges as a force in modern political life (Cassirer 1977a, pp. 73–85). Cassirer was quick to see, however, that myth was not merely a trope in the attempted reconstruction of some coherent narrative of a culture's origins. Instead, he treated myth as no longer being confined exclusively to the thought of so-called "primitive" cultures and communities. Rather, his realization of the potency of myth in social life and history involved analyzing it as a present and even quite pressing concern: "The problem is not the material content of mythology but the intensity with which it is experienced, with which it is *believed*—and only something endowed with objective reality can be believed" [original emphasis] (Cassirer 1944, p. 79). Hence, such believable if extraordinary stories of martyrs retold by Foxe, especially within the context of narrative details aimed at humanizing and particularizing the victims as protagonists so as to make them seem less singular and therefore easier to identify with, are thereby (as with a romance story format) more easily remembered, recounted, and retold. Foxe's overarching plan consisted of incorporating these mini-narratives into a larger epic scope of higher, sacred purpose. And the framework itself owed much to earlier forms, for Foxe and Day essentially engaged in recuperating and overwriting older Catholic forms in the process of creating a new phalanx of everyday heroes that were, in Woolf's (1995) characterization, "reformed countersaints, purified of false, romish miracles" (p. 247).

Such a practice and overall strategy for developing the *Book of Martyrs* was well within their purview—and the terms of their license, sanctioned as it was by royal privilege and financially supported in part by court patronage. Day and Foxe's grand enterprise thus differs considerably from those of polemicists who comparably were engaged in promoting their versions of evangelical ideology. Foxe's mini-narratives, in tandem with Day's images, simplified and in effect translated the salient information into graphic accounts calculated to capture the reader's attention and set in place new memories. Many of the woodcuts individually function in ways startlingly reminiscent of religious icons from an earlier era of Christian history, which reinforce through visual means the suasive power of the tales, trials, and tests of faith associated with a particular saint or martyr (see Figure 3.2).

Harnessing this affective power of the religious icon for the reform movement was an essential part of Day's strand by strand fabrication of

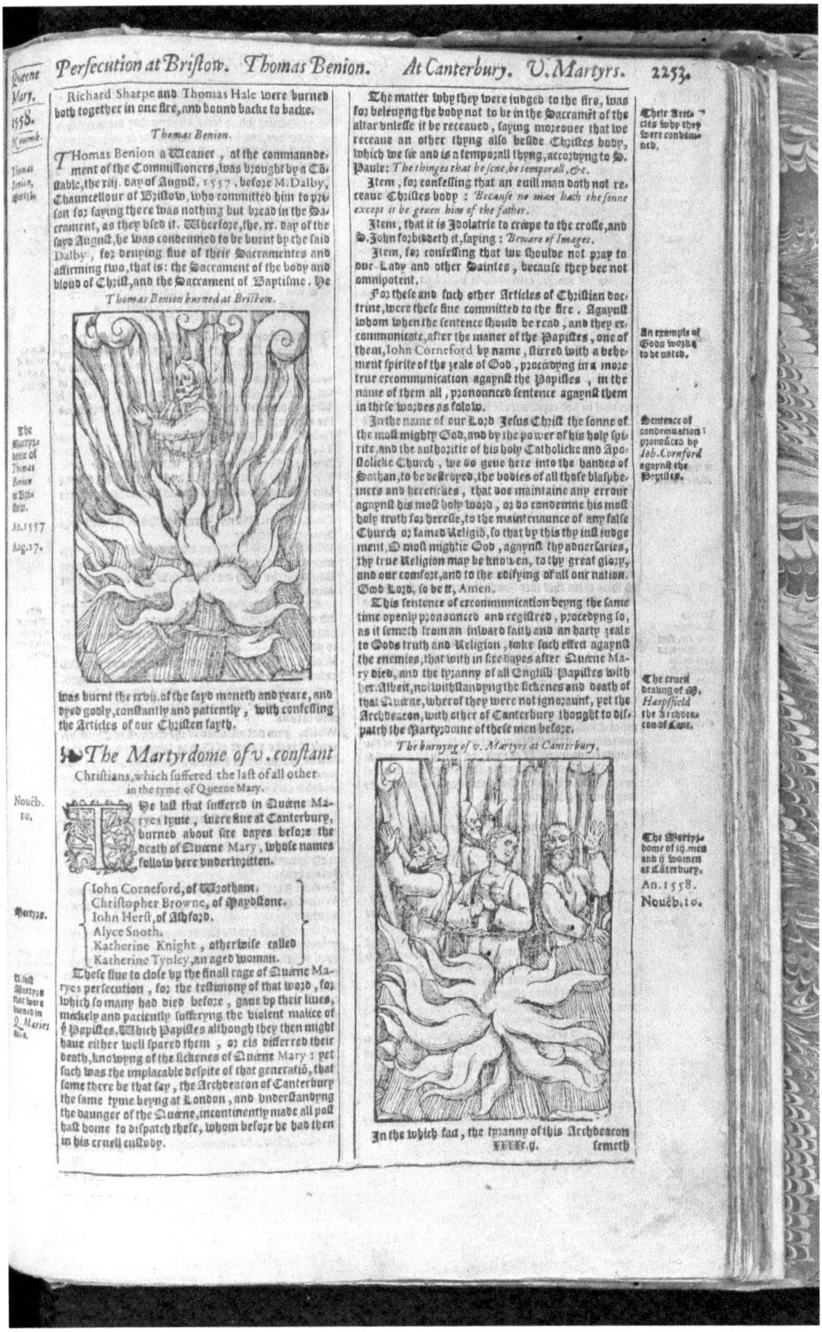

Figure 3.2 Burning martyrs. *The Acts and Monuments* (London: John Day, 1563), f. 2253. Image used courtesy of The Lambeth Palace Library.

a Protestant Memory Art. This is especially the case "when martyrs are depicted in isolation, apart from any social context, and, printed within the columns of the text, the images of anonymous martyrs burning at the stake become cumulatively affective as semi-icons" (Luborsky and Ingram 1998, p. 366). Based on the evidence of surviving copies of the *Book Martyrs*, the larger of these arresting pictures, especially the foldouts—most notably the "Table of 10 Persecutions of the primitive church"— and full page illustrations, like any mnemotopic artifact made to serve as a vehicle for personal and cultural memory, were frequently cut out of the book, colored, and tacked on walls (Collinson 1988, p. 117; Watt 1996, p. 158). During this period, households, inns, and also alehouses, many of which were adjacent to if not directly connected to churchyards (Cressy 2002, pp. 164–72), rapidly were becoming sites for the promotion of a new brand of visual culture (Watt 1996, pp. 69–70).[16] In line with this, pages from the *Book of Martyrs*, whether hand-colored or not, would have been quite at home in such venues, thereby making these stirring images available to an even wider audience, appealing especially to the illiterate as well as to new readers. For, much in the same way portable icons served to bring the religious past into one's immediate presence and present moment, turning an ordinary domestic space into a vital site of history remembered and pious reflection, illustrated pages from the *Book of Martyrs* (whether in the book or detached from it and, as it were, standing on their own) served the function as viable devotional mnemonics for people of all social degrees. Whatever the many and various uses of this book by a wide range of readers, hearers, and viewers, the traditional principles of the Renaissance memory arts are bound up with and help account for the popularity and rich afterlife of *Acts and Monuments*.

In a culture in which "the art of remembering was primarily an art of mental visualization," as Alexandra Walsham (2012) has shown, "the reformers recognized that removing physical reminders of popish error was vital to the task of transforming mentalities" (p. 907). More specifically, as pertains to extoling the new martyrs of Mary's persecution of evangelicals and nonconformists now fully accommodated in Elizabeth's 1559 parliamentary Church settlement (MacCulloch 2005a, p. 87), Day and Foxe knew what had to be done. The presentation of their grandly conceived bimedial enterprise involves stirring narratives of persecutions with accompanying eye-catching woodcuts. Day was committed to making sure the illustrations were well executed and stood out in bold relief. The result was a series of remarkably memorable images. During the Renaissance, it was generally understood that the most effective and enduring mnemotechnical schemes followed specific time-tested principles. The gist of how to go about inventing suitable images for a well-appointed memory theatre is covered by William Fulwood in his *Castle of Memory*, dedicated to Robert Dudley (mentioned in Chapter 1, with respect to his championing Day's printing projects, and also earlier in this chapter, for his patronage of Hanmer's Eusebian history of early martyrs):

> Again you shall not forget that in placing or setting of the images or figures in their places the thing is always to be placed with a merry, a marvelous, or cruel act, or some other unaccustomed manner: for merry, cruel, injurious, marvelous, excellently fair, or exceedingly foul things, do change and move the senses and better stir up the Memory, when the mind is much occupied about such things.[17]

The cruel and the merry meet in the persecuted bodies of faithful martyrs who, after enduring horrible injurious torment, will joyfully find their place in Heaven (again recalling the chapter's epigraph). This is a marvelous transformation for a reader to imagine indeed, making for a vivid image that lends itself to easy recall according to the terms of a decorously designed artificial memory scheme. Keeping with the orderly and sequential arrangement of such memory images (as discussed in the Introduction), Foxe situates these martyrs specifically in terms of the story, stage by stage, of the history of the Church. Consonant with this approach, as already mentioned, Day had set up and printed eye-catching grid-tables at the beginning of the book with a calendar of martyrs' anniversaries "clearly intended to provide an alternative list of Protestant saints" (Dryness 2004 p. 101). By such means, coupled with Foxe's orderly presentation of the history of the Church in terms of the persecutions visited upon the true followers of Christ, Day succeeded in discouraging any competitors in the field by cornering the market on the large-scale publication of contemporary martyr literature in Britain. Thus, in line with Febvre and Martin's analysis of "The Book as Commodity" (2010), *Acts and Monuments* effectively "smothered the competition, putting an end to a flourishing business in small, ephemeral English martyrological works" and furthermore, according to Evenden and Freeman (2002), was "immediately received as authoritative and indispensable, creating its own market" (p. 36).

The material conditions for propagating new memories

Although their martyrology was announced as being underway as early as 1559 in Foxe's preface to the literary remains of Marian martyr extraordinaire, Nicholas Ridley (1559), incidentally a work also printed by Day, it wasn't until five years after Elizabeth's accession that *Acts and Monuments* first appeared.[18] The delay involved, in part, Foxe's staying in Strasbourg to wrap up his publication projects (including *Rerum ecclesia gestarum … Commentarii* (1559), the second of his Latin martyologies), the content of which ultimately would provide the groundwork for his larger plan of *Acts and Monuments* (Evenden and Freeman 2013, p. 52). Also, as his son later claimed, Foxe was too strapped for cash to move his household back to London unless funds could be sent to him by sympathetic patrons (Greenberg 2005, p. 702). Of the approximately 800 Marian exiles (Garrett 1938, pp. 41–2), most returned in the first half of 1559, the same year that Edmund Grindal become Bishop of London, readily taking the Oath of Supremacy and thus signaling a new dawn for English religious reform. Changes in both state and church government were now being rung in a distinctively Protestant key. Old alliances were renewed, cultural obligations were remembered, and offices had to be filled. Grindal, in fact, ordained Foxe and continued to convey to him words of encouragement, as he had done earlier during the years of exile, writing that he intended "to promote your undertaking, that you may be able to bring to such an end as we desire the history of this English persecution" (Nicholson 1858, p. 229). Likewise, William Cecil, the newly appointed Principal Secretary to Elizabeth, made overtures to Foxe as well reassuring him and seeking to persuade him to convince the English people that a Protestant Church was both the desire of the Queen and the will of God (Loades 2005, p. 46). And Day's most important patron, Matthew Parker (as discussed in Chapter 1 and featured further in Chapter 5), was installed as the Archbishop of Canterbury in what we now think of as the Church of England. Fox and Day thus were well positioned to take up and realize their grand enterprise.

The resulting first edition of *Acts and Monuments* (1563) ended up becoming an event that far exceeded Foxe and Day's original expectations and goals, eventuating in four ever-expanded versions during their lifetime. For, in addition to the documents already assembled, some of which Foxe already had edited and published although in Latin, relatives of Marian martyrs inundated Foxe and Day with material for a second edition. As Evenden and Freeman (2013) descriptively put it, the first edition "had opened the floodgates for torrents of personal testimony" as actual participants "in the events described in the book," or their friends and families, sent material to Foxe or to Day, presenting their versions of what had happened (p. 143). Within months of the publication of the first edition, Day and Foxe correctly assessed that there needed to be a second, both so they could get in the rest of the material they had to leave out due to limitations of time and a dwindling supply of good paper, and also because of the overwhelming demand for the book both for private purchase and also for use in parishes and other venues of public worship. The effect was that by the 1570s the *Book of Martyrs* was a staple in homes for devotional exercises; and, after 1571, in accordance with an action of the Bishops of the Church, copies were to be "chained" in every cathedral church. In real terms, this meant that, as Luborsky and Ingram (1998) explain, excepting images found in illustrated Bibles, "Day's images in *Acts and Monuments* were most probably seen more often and by more people than any others" (p. 366). Along these same lines, William Dryness (2004, p. 101) concludes that this book "probably did more than any other book to develop the notion of England and its people being specially chosen by God." From its opening pages then, with a Reformation inflected calendar of martyrs and saints, the anti-papal evangelically reformed message of *Acts and Monuments* is duly conveyed throughout—irrespective of the printing errors inevitably to be expected with a book of its length and complex page layout.

Despite the careful proofreading process used in Day's shop, evidence of which can be found in the many stop press corrections, some egregious omissions and not a few compositor's mistakes can still be detected. In proofreading the second edition, however, Day, Foxe, and others on hand to mark corrections on recently printed pages undoubtedly became aware that some compelling additions of reported martyrological events contained inaccuracies, namely, in the material originally deemed unverifiable and hence omitted from the first edition. Regarding the later, as already noted (with reference to Figure 3.1), and as discussed in terms of Cassirer's understanding of the importance of myth in the shaping of political life in a culture (as one of a number of ways by means of which cultural experience is structured), Latimer's "last words" did not appear in 1563 first edition. On the other hand, some discredited stories that appeared in the first edition were not picked up in the second, and much of the non-English material was developed to fill the space. In fact, so much new material was interpolated during the printing process that, in order to finish the book with Day's available paper supply, the last part of the second edition required smaller margins as well as smaller type font for both the text and headings. As Julian Roberts (1997, p. 44) explains, this required a revised "casting off of copy," that is marking of the manuscript, leaf by leaf, to enable compositors to set the type and judge which font and size to use to accommodate the remaining paper supply.[19]

The latter consideration is a fundamental aspect of Elizabethan printing that is often overlooked, namely, *all book-quality paper had to be imported*. For example, among the many other trading vessels carrying sundry cargo, two boats (*The Greyhound* of Ipswich for Miles Mason, and *The Julian* of Rochester for Thomas Usher) brought in their hulls from a voyage from Rouen, renowned for its paper mills, a total of 1,346 reams of papers for specifically named London merchants who then dealt with publishers and printers directly (Dietz 1972). Since paper was not manufactured in England at the time, and given the burgeoning book trade in London, there always was a need for it, accounting for why nearly every merchant ship mentioned in the London Port Book (fol. 62b–63) lists some quantity of paper on its return manifest. Day dealt directly with merchants who had connections to the paper trade in the Low Countries and in France (Evenden 2008, p. 61). And the amount of paper required for a colossal project like the *Acts and Monuments* meant that Day had to plan carefully, calculating as accurately as possible how much paper would be required. He had to put aside sufficient reserve capital earmarked for paper and get his orders registered in a timely way or else find himself running behind in his already tight printing schedule.

Toward the end of the production of the second edition (1570), the physical and textual evidence indicates that Day experienced a shortage of good and full-length paper, in all likelihood owing to Foxe's many interpolations requiring Day to make occasional stop press corrections already mentioned. Also, the extensive use of woodcuts, some of which were repeated, probably complicated somewhat Day's original casting off of copy perhaps resulting in his miscalculating how much paper was actually required to finish the volume. At all events, short-length paper leaves were pasted together to make folio-size sheets for the final gatherings in some extant versions of the first volume of the much expanded 1570 edition.[20]

The apparent exuberance of the first edition, evidenced by the many things that were added and from the newly commissioned images inserted into the book a year into the production process, is as much a result of the scrupulous nature of Foxe's work habits, editorial intuitions, and scholarly training as it is the sense of victory and liberation portended by the return of state-sanctioned reformed prayer book and devotional practices in England under Elizabeth. The time for production on the second edition took longer than ordinarily would have been the case, even with a book as voluminous and complicated to produce as this one, both because of Day's disposition toward using a wide variety of typefaces (as discussed in Chapter 2); and also because, during the extended periods when Day needed to recalculate the casting off of a section, Foxe appears to have introduced new material and sometimes excised existing passages all of which then needed to be set anew—for example, removing the Latimer quotation from the first edition (1563) before it went to press because of suspected spurious attribution and then, for the second edition (1570), including it along with an array of similar human-interest features brought to Foxe's attention by new sources and eyewitness accounts.

Such firsthand accounts also appear in the first edition, of course, most remarkably, one involving the printer himself. After the episode about the imprisonment in 1553 of John Rogers (1563, sig. Aaa2^v), Tyndale's close associate and the first Marian martyr (mentioned in the first note of this chapter), and following a half-page woodcut of the burning of Rogers, Foxe reports on Day's incarceration.

> Amongst others being then in prison, this he spake to the printer of this book, who then also was laid up for like cause of religion: thou said he, shalt live to see the alteration of this religion, and the Gospel freely to be preached again. And therefore have me commended to my brethren, as well in exile, as others, and bid them be circumspect in displacing the Papists, and putting good ministers into churches, or else their end will be worse than ours: and for lack of good ministers to furnish churches, his devise was, Hooper also agreeing to the same, that for every ten churches someone good and learned superintendent, should be appointed, which should have under him faithful

readers, such as might well be got: so that popish priests should be put out, and the bishop once a year to oversee the profiting of the parishes. This was his counsel and request. At the stake his pardon was brought, if he would have returned, but he utterly refused. And so constantly gave the first conflict with the fire for the love and testimony of Christ and his Word, (1563, sig. Aaa3ʳ)

This statement about what Rogers said prior to his execution makes Day a very significant witness in every respect of that term. Readers, if they had not already made the connection, suddenly realize that the printer himself can authenticate the very words they are reading, thus lending a kind of immediacy and intimacy to the reading experience as well as a sense of being (albeit vicariously) in the company of the famous first Marian martyr.

Day's singularity is also expressed in another way as well. Foxe implies that his printer's encounter with godly martyrs in prison while undergoing his own trials is all part of God's larger plan—namely, Rogers, providentially had been ordained, as it were, through his body's immolation, to be witness of God's Word and the soundness of *sola scriptura*; and Day, by God's special grace, had been so placed to bear witness to all of this. His life was spared so he might be delivered to a time when later he might publish this very book celebrating the Marian martyrs in furtherance of the reformed cause in England.

Day also stood out from the other printers in London in that he alone was in a position to get the patent for and be in a position financially and professionally to undertake such a monumental project—one that tied up his presses for years without a payout on that effort. Of course, as already mentioned, he had made a fortune from his several book monopolies without which the production of *Acts and Monuments* would have been unthinkable (Evenden and Freeman 2002, p. 30). Further, he still maintained his several assigns authorized to print his works that later would be sold in his shop and other designated London locations. Court records put Day's annual earnings from these monopolies between at least £200 and as much as £500 (Evenden and Freeman 2002, pp. 27 and 50n26), which far exceeds the average Tudor gentleman's yearly income from land which "was around £17, and a knight's around £200" (MacCulloch 2018, p. 6). Elizabeth Evenden (2008) surmises that in deciding to risk printing the *Acts and Monuments*, Day "was making long term career choices on the basis of one, albeit significant, book" (p. 73). Day's confidence in his capacities to make this book a reality, coupled with Foxe's resolve (along with his accumulated Latin martyrological material), and bolstered by the backing of those close to the Queen, most notably William Cecil (Evenden and Freeman 2002, p. 30), made this speculative adventure truly something of a grand enterprise. Initial sales were excellent such that, as already observed, *Acts and Monuments* was "received as the authoritative and indispensable work on the English martyrs; it not only dominated the market, but also expanded it" as demand steadily grew (Evenden 2008, p. 70). Owing to the wording of a previous privilege granted to him for the publication of any new books printed at his own expense (discussed in Chapter 1), Day was set to undertake more editions—and the work grew from 1,800 to 2,300 folio pages with triple the number of woodcuts, from 53 to over 150.[21]

In order to secure enough skilled artisans to repair some of the old woodcuts (bits of the carved block tended to crack or break off due to the wear and tear of the press process) and to make many new ones, requiring a level of technical expertise beyond most native English sculptors, Day sought a waiver from the Stationers' Company to hire more foreign workers than the maximum of four alien-residents allowed to be employed by any single London business concern (Evenden 2004, pp. 76–7), which suggests he already had that number hard at work in his shop. Again, few if any printers, or even a consortium of publishers in the 1570s, could have pulled off what Day accomplished with the first two editions of *Acts and Monuments*. And few if any could afford to undertake a project that kept all of one's presses dedicated to a single book for the better part of six years. It is quite telling that after Day's death, his son, Richard, released the patent of *Acts and Monuments* to the Stationer's Company, which continued to issue later editions and involved many printers and shops (Evenden 2008, p. 176). With the *Book of Martyrs*, Day established himself as the preeminent printer of the age, especially when taking into account that the illustrations he added to the second edition created what justifiably has been characterized by Evenden (2008, p. 100) as "a new standard in book illustration" in England. It was a standard that Day himself maintained and ended up exceeding with the ever-improved four editions of *Acts and Monuments* during his lifetime (Evenden and Freeman 2013, pp. 186–231), and with (as will be discussed in the two remaining chapters) works like Jan Van der Noot's emblem book, *A Theatre for Voluptuous Worldlings*, and *The Book of Christian Prayers* popularly known as *Queen Elizabeth's Prayer Book*.

Surveying the material aspects of Day's output provides coordinates for reckoning the horizon of possibilities with respect to the unconscious life of memory images associated with the wider cultural impact of his lifework as a printer and publisher—and author. Day was at the forefront of a larger movement that involved setting up an English book production industry instrumental in what Richard McCabe (2016) refers to as "creating a native sense of literary history, promoting the development of contemporary vernacular literature, and establishing the importance of the author as both creative agent and marketable product" (p. 167). Foxe, in association with Day, became just such a marketable product in and of himself—one that Day was wholly committed to capitalizing on. Basically, he wagered all that he had gained up to that point in terms of accumulated wealth and also his reputation as a printer and major patent holder of Protestant books. He staked everything on the prospective and sustained success of *Acts and Monuments*, going so far as to borrow hundreds of pounds from his brother-in-law and other well-to-do Protestant neighbors in order to pay for the paper and other printing supplies to bring this grand enterprise to fruition (Oastler 1975, p. 28). If ever there was a case to be made about the rise of capitalism and Protestantism going hand in hand, then it is John Day.[22]

Although Foxe assuredly was less fiscally driven than his collaborator, he likewise saw the evangelical Reformation as divinely ordained. His writings reveal that he believed God's plan for thwarting the Pope and overcoming the Antichrist went hand in hand with the invention of printing. In the first edition of *Acts and Monuments*, he speaks allusively about God having foreordained printing to appear in Europe when it did, coincident with the rise of an evangelical commitment to reject Rome and rely on scripture alone, a theme he will resume with fervor in the second edition, along with a much more detailed treatment of the sacralized nature of printing. In the first edition, he only briefly touches on the theme of printing having been prophesied from mythopoetic, classical times—by the Sybils, who divined and foretold the future through writing their visions on leaves. The link between their prophetic pronouncements being conveyed through writing and early modern printing on pages, or leaves, of books, should not be overlooked. The significant point of difference is that books like the *Acts and Monuments* will endure long enough for people to read and remember the divine message it contains. The words written by a sybil on leaves were usually placed at the entrance to her cave "and it required particular care in such as consulted her to take up these leaves before they were dispersed by the wind, as their meaning then became incomprehensible" (Lemprière 1984, p. 627). A closer look at Foxe's meta-critical reflection on the very process by which his evangelically suffused book was produced will serve to resume and conclude this chapter's guiding concern with the material conditions underlying the early modern English book trade and also, more particularly, Day's decisive and intentional role in the development and promotion of a Protestant Memory Art.

Under the chronologically headed section labeled "1440" in the first edition of *Acts and Monuments* (1563, Foxe isolates the invention of printing as another instantiation of God's foreknown and foreordained master plan, providentially predestined to usher in the advent of a pan-European and ultimately global Protestant movement. He sees printing as a means by which the Reformation was facilitated as if on divine cue to come at its appointed time. No doubt Day, who conscientiously devoted his life to bringing out Protestant writings and practical primers, shared this view, but did not write about it. He was too busy raising capital and providing for the production of this book in which printing itself is thematized and extolled as part of God's will in the world. He was preoccupied with the casting off of copy, supervising the inking of his state-of-the-art matrices, and making sure that printed pages were being hung out to dry in their proper order to accommodate easier proofreading, correction, and collation.

> This art and science, how profitable it hath been unto all the whole world, these our days do sufficiently declare, if that we diligently weigh and consider, how that thereby ignorance is utterly banished, and truth manifested and declared, and finally the Pope and Antichrist there by utterly subverted, which could never have come to pass if this most worthy science had not been found out. For so much as otherwise, books were so scarse, and there with all of such excessive price, that few men could thereby attain to knowledge or understanding, which now by this means, is made easy unto all men. Here in also appeareth the prophecy of the Sybils to be fulfilled, who long time before had prophesied, that flax and linen, should subvert and overthrow Antichrist, God's enemy. Wherefore as God by his marvelous providence, for the advancement of his glory, gave the understanding of this art or science, for the abolishing of ignorance and idolatry. So as in these our days, we may well perceive and see how that the pope, that great Antichrist of Rome could never have be suppressed and, being suppressed, could not have been kept under except this most excellent science of printing had bene maintained, whereby the shameful hypocrisy of the papists is detected and discovered unto the whole world, and God's truth and glory manifestly set forth and advanced.
>
> (Foxe 1563, sig. Ll1^v–Ll2^r)

Foxe unwaveringly saw the invention of printing as a milestone in the unfolding of human history conducing to the End Times.[23] Aided by the printing press, and indeed perhaps *because* of printing, he believes that evangelical Christian opposition to the papal reign at last can be realized and sustained. The implication is that printing will, like the widely circulating products of the printing press, continue this sanctified work by rolling out a steady stream of refutations that will open evermore eyes to the truth of the message of the reformed faith. Although his disquision on printing is much longer in the second edition (1570), and the Sybils are not mentioned, Foxe still takes a long view of Christian teleology and the Apocalypse such that he sees the advent of printing quite literally as a Godsend. In fact, the last work Foxe (1587) wrote prior to his death, *Eicasmi seu meditationes in sacram Apocalypsim* (published posthumously), is a critical expostulation on the Book Revelation—which brings us once more back to the epigraph of this chapter. The sybils are replaced by John who prophesied on the island of Patmos. The Revelator's prophesies likewise involve writing, and Foxe sees John as foretelling the coming of the printing press to promote God's true Word, which is to say a doctrine consonant with Reformation theology (sig. I6^r). The providential steps along the way to discerning the truth of the history of Christianity are clear to Foxe: John Faustus made the first type, Gutenberg perfected the mechanism by which the Bible could be printed, thereby making possible future evangelical publications—such as his own *Book of Martyrs*, in which his printer, John Day, features as a witness. It is fitting that printing, a "divine and miraculous invention," should be singled out as a "famous and memorable" event worthy of inclusion of *Acts and Monuments*.

> In following the course and order of years, we find this foresaid year of our Lord 1450 to be famous and memorable, for the divine and miraculous invention of printing. [...] Printing came of God. Notwithstanding what man soever was the instrument, without all doubt God Himself was the ordainer and disposer thereof. [...] Now to consider to what end and purpose the Lord hath given this gift of printing to the earth, and to what great utility and necessity it serveth, it is not hard to judge [...]. God of His secret judgment, seeing time to help His church, hath found a way by this faculty of printing, not only to confound his life and conversation, which before he could not abide to be touched, but also to cast down the foundation of his standing, that is, to examine, confute, and detect his doctrine, laws, and institution most detestable, in such sort, that though his life were never so pure: yet his doctrine standing, as it doth, no man is so blind, but may see, that either the Pope is Antichrist, or else that Antichrist is near cousin to the Pope: And all this doth, and will hereafter more and more appear, by printing.
>
> The reason whereof is this: for that hereby tongues are known, knowledge groweth, judgment increaseth, books are dispersed, the Scripture is seen, the doctors be read, stories be opened, times compared, truth discerned, falsehood detected, and with finger pointed, and all (as I said) through the benefit of printing. Wherefore I suppose that either the Pope must abolish printing, or he must seek a new world to reign over: for else, as this world standeth, printing, doubtless, will abolish him. Both the Pope, and all his College of Cardinals, must this understand, that through the light of printing, the world beginneth now to have eyes to see, and heads to judge. [...] So that either the Pope must abolish knowledge and printing, or printing at length will root him out. By reason whereof, as printing of books ministered matter of reading: so reading brought learning: learning showed light, by the brightness whereof blind ignorance was suppressed, error detected, and finally God's glory, with truth of His word, advanced.
>
> (Foxe 1570, sig. DD5^{r-v})

This same intimation of providential predestination animates and informs Day's Protestant emblem book, Jan Van der Noot's *A Theatre of Voluptuous Worldlings* (the subject of Chapter 4), in which he used "the divine and miraculous invention of printing" to do what he did best: advance the Protestant cause and turn a tidy profit along the way. Day's ongoing work-product, beyond the four editions of the *Book of Martyrs* on which he collaborated so intimately with Foxe, reveals the extent to which early modern literacy (and, as will be stressed further in what follows, visual literacy) was vivified anew by print technology. In this sense, then, Day's ongoing printing projects can be seen as "agents of change," in line with the touchstone argument propounded by Elizabeth Eisenstein (1979).[24] Moreover, at the same time, they can be seen in terms of what Tessa Watt (1996) has called early modern "forces for cultural continuity" (p. 330). The interplay between the visual and the verbal, facilitated by the early modern English book trade in which Day was a key player, inevitably gave rise to a proliferation of hybrid literary and religious forms. Chief among these expressive forms is the ubiquitous emblem, which met, fostered, and moreover generated the needs of an audience learning to "read" images in this new configuration of words allusively combined with pictures. The *Book of Martyrs*, among other things, attests to how adroitly and readily Day made use of image and text to make a book that set a new standard for printing in England. The ensuing chapter therefore takes up what he was able to accomplish next with a book that begins by sporting a picture at every turn of the page.

Notes

1 As discussed in Chapter 1 concerning the so-called "Matthew Bible" (Figure 1.3), the New Testament principally was the work of William Tyndale along with Miles Coverdale. Matthias Crom, using the pseudonym "Thomas Matthew," published the whole in Antwerp in 1537, which had been edited and added to by John Rogers, Tyndale's close associate and the first martyr under Mary I, resulting in a work that "appealed to the reformed faction in Henry's court" (Poleg 2020, p. 118).
2 On the records relating to the publication history of the Foxe's *Book of Martyrs*, see Evenden and Freeman (2002, p. 35 and 2013, p. 52, n49).
3 On any contemporary Elizabethan reader recognizing "the house at Saint Martin's Lane end as the premises of the Reformation printer John Day," see Ringler (1979, p. 114); and, on Day's house, as the place where Protestants, especially those associated with the London book trade, were known to congregate, see Bonahue (1994, p. 289).
4 On Day's home and printing office, off-site warehouse, various leaseholds, and other places where his books were sold, see Oastler (1975, pp. 29–32); for a helpful caveat about "book stalls" as permanent structures, especially those in and around Paul's Cross Churchyard, see Blayney (2000, pp. 323–42), and cf. Evenden (2008, pp. 180–1).
5 See King (2001, p. 73) on the architectural title page with the central area reserved for the descriptive information about *The whole works of W. Tyndale* (1573).
6 See also in this regard King (2001, pp. 69–70); and, on the origin and nature of the woodcuts, Luborsky (2018, pp. 67–84).

134 *Grand enterprise of the* Book of Martyrs

7   For a complete list with brief descriptions of the images in the order in which they appear in *Acts and Monuments*, including the famous initial letter "C" with Queen Elizabeth as the Emperor Constantine, see Luborsky and Ingram (1998, pp. 367–82).
8   On the rejection of Purgatory in English reformed practices and its impact on daily life, see Gittings (1984), Duffy (1992), Gordon and Marshall (2000), Cressy (2002), Marshall (2002), and Engel et al. (2022).
9   The second edition (1585) was dedicated to Robert Dudley, by then 1st Earl of Leicester, a long-time champion of the pro-Protestant cause who had been William Cunningham's patron, as acknowledged publicly with a full-page coat of arms and dedication in the paratext of Day's printing of *The Cosmological Glass* (1559, sig. A1^v–A2^v); see Chapter 1.
10 For a detailed breakdown of the patterns of illustrations in the first four editions of the *Acts and Monuments* and of the woodcuts reused from other books, see Luborsky (2018, pp. 69–70).
11 For a more detailed treatment of Askew's martyrdom and the shaping of her narrative by Foxe and others, see Freeman and Wall (2001, pp. 1165–96) and Engel et al. (2022, entry II.4)
12 Additionally, with special reference to the polemical concerns of this chapter, on Parr's having "assimilated the dynamics of Tyndalian style," evident in her "profuse citations" from "the Pauline epistles," which "reveal a systematic likeness to Tyndale's," see Mueller (1988, p. 23).
13 For an account of Thomas Cranmer's last words echoing those of the earlier two Oxford Martyrs, Latimer and Ridley, who had suffered six months before at the same place, see MacCulloch (2016, p. 603): "Lord Jesus receive my spirit …"
14 On the origins and early trends in the Protestant illustrative tradition, see Pettegree (2002).
15 On the extremely high demand for reprintings of this popular book in Tudor England, initially by Caxton and later by others including Wynkyn de Worde, see Ford (2020, pp. 105–65).
16 Apropos of which, see Watt (1996, p. 194): "wall paintings with moral sayings or figure subjects were a common feature of inns and taverns" such that even "mean alehouses were expected to provide decoration for their customers."
17 This modernized excerpt from Fulwood's treatise quoted from Engel et al. (2016, p. 64). It should be noted that this work already was well within the purview of English Tudor court circles for some time (and, along with it, continental ideas about place system mnemonics) insofar as Fulwood's *Castle of Memory* (1562) is a translation of Guglielmo Gratarolo's *De Memoria* (Zurich, 1553), which had been dedicated and presented to young King Edward VI.
18 Cf. Evenden (2008, p. 63) and Evenden and Freeman (2013, p. 100).
19 On copy preparation and casting off, which "helped the overseer to allot work on the book, and informed final decisions to be made about the typographical details so that, for instance, the text would not overrun the last whole sheet by a page or two," see Gaskell (2015, p. 41); and, on casting off protocol in the early modern print shop, see Moore (1992, p. 11).
20 For a more detailed account of this aspect of the publication process, see Evenden and Freeman (2002, pp. 37–42) and King (2011, p. 114).

21 On the rationale behind these statistics, see Aston and Ingram (1997, p. 79); regarding the exact image count of the 1563 edition, "fifty-three cuts in fifty-seven occurrences," see Luborsky and Ingram (1998, p. 367); and, cf. Rankin (2010, p. 89): "Counts for the total number of illustrations differ, but all attempts cite over 100 designs that recur over 150 times in the 1583 edition, the last on which Day and Foxe collaborated."
22 For the *locus classicus* of this early 20th-century argument, see Weber (2002), in which Luther's notion of "calling" and the Calvinist belief in predestination both prepare the groundwork for the emergence of "the capitalist spirit."
23 On this aspect of Foxe's later career, to which my own analysis in what follows is indebted, see Freeman (2011), note on the text, "The Invention of Printing."
24 The main argument of Eisenstein (1979) can be distilled as follows: fundamentally, the most significant effects of print reside not in the ways in which it transmits information but in how it fixes and secures tradition; such that, much of what is deemed new in the Renaissance and Reformation is a product of the ability of typographical culture to secure and, quite literally, to re-represent what is old, thereby opening it up for further scrutiny and questioning.

Bibliography

Primary Sources

Becon, T. 1561. *The Sick Man's Salve*. London: John Day. STC 1757.
Foxe, J. 1554. *Commentarii rerum in ecclesia gestarum*. Strasbourg: Wendelin Richelieus.
———. 1559. *Rerum in ecclesia gestarum ... Commentarii*. Basel: Johannes Oporinus.
———. 1563. *Acts and monuments of these latter and perilous days touching matters of the Church, wherein are comprehended and described the great persecutions and horrible troubles that have been wrought and practiced by the Romish prelates, specially in the realm of England and Scotland....* London: John Day. STC 11222.
———. 1570. *[...] Acts and monuments of things passed in every king's time in this realm, especially in the Church of England principally to be noted, with a full discourse of such persecutions, horrible troubles, the sufferyng of Martyrs....* London: John Day. STC 11223.
———. 1573. *The whole works of W[illiam] Tyndall, John Frith, and Doct[o]r Barnes, three worthy martyrs, and principal teachers of this Church of England*. London: John Day. SCT 24436.
———. 1576. *[...] Acts and monuments*. London: John Day. STC 11224.
———. 1587. *Eicasmi seu meditationes in sacram Apocalypsim [Sacred reflections on the holy Revelation]*. London: Thomas Dawson. STC 11237.
Fulwood. W. 1562. *The Castle of Memory*. London: R. Hall. STC 12191.
Gratarolo, G. 1553. *De memoria reparanda*. Zurich: Andreas Gesner and Rudolf Wyssenbach.
Jacobus de Voragine. 1483. *The Golden Legend*. Westminster: William Caxton. STC 24873.

Parsons, R. 1603–04. *A treatise of three conversations of England from Paganism to Christian religion*. St. Omer: François Bellet.
Parr, K. 1547. *The Lamentation of a Sinner*. London: Edward Whitchurch. STC 4827.
Ridley, N. 1559. *A Friendly Farewell*. London: John Day. STC 21051.
The Ancient Ecclesiastical Histories. 1577. M. Hanmer, trans. London: Abraham Miller. STC 10573.
The Bible. 1551. London: John Day. STC 2088.

Secondary Sources

Andreani, A. 2021. *Meredith Hanmer and the Elizabethan Church: A Clergyman's Career in 16th Century England and Ireland*. New York and London: Routledge.
Arcangeli. A. and Tamm, M. 2020. Introduction: Early Modern Memory Cultures. In: A. Arcangeli and M. Tamm, eds. *A Cultural History of Memory in the Early Modern Age*. Vol 3. London: Bloomsbury. pp. 1–18.
Aston, M. and Ingram, E. 1997. The Iconography of the *Acts and Monuments*. In: D. Loades, ed. *John Foxe and the English Reformation*. Aldershot, UK: Scolar Press. pp. 66–142.
Betteridge, T. 2002. Truth and History in Foxe's *Acts and Monuments*. In: C. Highly and J.N. King, eds. *John Foxe and his World*. Aldershot, UK; Burlington, VT: Ashgate. pp. 45–159.
Blayney, P.W.M. 2000. John Day and the Bookshop That Never Was. In: L.C. Orlin, ed. *Material London, ca. 1600*. Philadelphia: University of Pennsylvania Press. pp. 322–43.
Bonahue, E.T. 1994. "I Know the Place and the Persons": The Play of Textual Frames in Baldwin's *Beware the Cat*. *Studies in Philology*. **91.**3, 283–300.
Bowers, T.N. 1991. The Production and Communication of Knowledge in William Baldwin's *Beware the Cat*: Toward a Typographic Culture. *English Renaissance Literature*. **33.**1, 1–29.
Cassirer, E. 1944. *An Essay on Man: An Introduction to a Philosophy of Human Culture*. New Haven: Yale University Press.
———. 1977a [1923]. *The Philosophy of Symbolic Forms*. Vol. 1: Language. R. Manheim, trans. New Haven: Yale University Press.
———. 1977b [1923]. *The Philosophy of Symbolic Forms*. Vol. 2: Mythical Thought. R. Manheim, trans. New Haven: Yale University Press.
Collinson, P. 1988. *The Birthpangs of Protestant England: Religious and Cultural Change in the Sixteenth and Seventeenth Centuries*. New York: Palgrave Macmillan.
Cressy, D. 2002. *Birth, Marriage, and Death: Ritual, Religion, and the Life-Cycle in Tudor and Stuart England*. Oxford: Oxford University Press.
Dietz, B., ed. 1972. *The Port and Trade of Early Elizabethan London: Documents*: London Port Book, 1567–8, Nos. 200–99 (Dec 1567–Jan 1568). London: London Record Society Publication.
Dryness, W.A. 2004. *Reformed Theology and Visual Culture: The Protestant Imagination from Calvin to Edwards*. Cambridge: Cambridge University Press.
Duffy, E. 1992. *The Stripping of the Altars: Traditional Religion in England 1400–1580*. New Haven: Yale University Press.

Eisenstein, E.L. 1979. *The Printing Press as an Agent of Change: Communications and Cultural Transformations in Early-Modern Europe*, 2 vols. Cambridge: Cambridge University Press.

———. 2011. *Divine Art, Infernal Machine: The Reception of Printing in the West from First Impressions to the Sense of an Ending*. Philadelphia: University of Pennsylvania Press.

———. 2012. *The Printing Revolution in Early Modern Europe*. Cambridge: Cambridge University Press.

Engel, W.E. 1999. Mnemonic Emblems and the Humanist Discourse of Knowledge. In: P. Daly and J. Manning, eds. *Aspects of Renaissance and Baroque Symbol Theory, 1500–1700*. New York: AMS Press. pp. 125–42.

Engel, W.E., Loughnane, R., and Williams, G. 2016. *The Memory Arts in Renaissance England: A Critical Anthology*. Cambridge: Cambridge University Press.

——— 2022. *The Death Arts in Renaissance England: A Critical Anthology*. Cambridge: Cambridge University Press.

Evenden, E. 2004. The Fleeing Dutchmen? The Influence of Dutch Immigrants upon the Print Shop of John Day. In: D. Loades, ed. *John Foxe at Home and Abroad*. Aldershot, UK; Burlington, VT: Ashgate. pp. 63–77.

———. 2008. *Patents, Pictures and Patronage: John Day and the Tudor Book Trade*. Aldershot, UK; Burlington, VT: Ashgate.

Evenden, E. and Freeman, T.S. 2002. John Foxe, John Day and the Printing of the "Book of Martyrs." In: R. Myers, M. Harris, and G. Mandelbrote, eds. *Lives in Print: Biography and the Book Trade from the Middle Ages to the 21st Century*. New Castle, DE and London: Oak Knoll Press and The British Library. pp. 23–54.

———. 2013. *Religion and the Book in Early Modern England: The Making of John Foxe's "Book of Martyrs."* Cambridge: Cambridge University Press.

Febvre, L. and H.-J. Martin. 2010; repr. 1958. *The Coming of the Book: The Impact of Printing, 1450–1800*. D. Gerard, trans. and G. Nowell-Smith and D. Wootton, eds. London: Verso.

Ford, J.A. 2020. *English Readers of Catholic Saints: The Printing History of William Caxton's "Golden Legend."* London and New York: Routledge.

Freeman, T.S. 1999. Text, Lies and Microfilm: Reading and Misreading in Foxe's *Book of Martyrs*. *Sixteenth Century Journal*. 30.1, 23–46.

———. 2004. Publish and Perish: The Scribal Culture of the Marian Martyrs. In: J. Crick and A. Walsham, eds. *The Uses of Script and Print, 1300–1700*. Cambridge: Cambridge University Press. pp. 235–54.

———. 2007. Over Their Dead Bodies: Concepts of Martyrdom in Late Medieval and Early Modern England. In: T. Freeman and T. Mayer, eds. *Martyrs and Martyrdom in England, 1400–1700*. Woodbridge: Boydell. pp. 1–34.

———. 2011. Invention of Printing: Commentary on the Text. *The Unabridged "Acts and Monuments" Online*. Sheffield: The Digital Humanities Institute. www.dhi.ac.uk/foxe/index.php?realm=text&gototype=&edition=1563&pageid=414#C166.1.

Freeman, T.S. and Wall, S.E. 2001. Racking the Body, Shaping the Text: The Account of Anne Askew in Foxe's *Book of Martyrs*. *Renaissance Quarterly*. 54.4, 1165–96.

Garrett, C.H. 1938. *The Marian Exiles: A Study in the Origins of Elizabethan Puritanism*. Cambridge: Cambridge University Press.

Gaskell, P. 2015. *A New Introduction to Bibliography*. New Castle, DE: Oak Knoll Press.

Gittings, C. 1984. *Death, Burial and the Individual in Early Modern England*. London: Croom Helm.

Gordon, B. and Marshall, P., eds. 2000. *The Place of the Dead: Death and Remembrance in Late Medieval and Early Modern Europe*. Cambridge: Cambridge University Press.

Gray, P. 2017. *The Routledge Guidebook to the New Testament*. London: Routledge.

Greenberg, D. 2005. Community of the Texts: Producing the First and Second Editions of *Acts and Monuments*. *Sixteenth Century Journal*. **36.3**, 695–715.

Hall, D.D. 1996. *Cultures of Print: Essays in the History of the Book*. Amherst: University of Massachusetts Press.

Hiscock, A. 2011. *Reading Memory in Early Modern Literature*. Cambridge: Cambridge University Press.

Hulse, C. 1988. Spenser, Bacon, and the Myth of Power. In: H. Dubrow and R. Strier, eds. *The Historical Renaissance: New Essays on Tudor and Stuart Literature and Culture*. Chicago: University of Chicago Press. pp. 315–46.

King, J.N. 1997. Fiction and fact in Foxe's *Book of Martyrs*. In: D. Loades, ed. *John Foxe and the English Reformation*. Aldershot, UK: Scolar Press. pp. 12–35.

———. 2001. "The Light of Printing": William Tyndale, John Foxe, John Day, and Early Modern Print Culture. *Renaissance Quarterly*. **54.1**, 52–85.

———. 2011. *Foxe's "Book of Martyrs" and Early Modern Print Culture*. Cambridge: Cambridge University Press.

Kroeber, A.L. and Kluckhohn, C. 1952. *Culture: A Critical Review of Concepts and Definitions*. Papers of the Peabody Museum of American Archaeology and Ethnology, 47. Cambridge, MA: The Museum.

Lemprière, J. 1984. *Lemprière's Classical Dictionary*. Facsimile of 1865 edition. London: Bracken Books.

Lindberg, C. 2010. *The European Reformations*. Second edition. Oxford: Wiley-Blackwell.

Loades, D. 2005. Foxe's *Book of Martyrs* and the face of England," *History Today*. Dec. pp. 40–9.

Luborsky, R.S. 2018. The Illustrations: Their Pattern and Plan. In: D. Loades. *John Foxe: An Historical Perspective*. London: Routledge. pp. 67–84.

Luborsky, R.S. and Ingram, E.M. 1998. *A Guide to English Illustrated Books, 1536–1603*. Tempe: ACMRS.

MacCulloch, D. 2005a. Putting the English Reformation on the Map. *Transactions of the Royal Historical Society*. **15**, 75–95.

———. 2005b. *The Reformation: A History*. New York: Penguin.

———. 2016. *Thomas Cranmer*. New Haven and London: Yale University Press.

———. 2018. *Thomas Cromwell: A Revolutionary Life*. New York: Viking.

Marshall, P. 2002. *Beliefs and the Dead in Reformation England*. Oxford: Oxford University Press.

McCabe, R. 2016. *"Ungainfull Arte": Poetry, Patronage, and Print in the Early Modern Era*. Oxford: Oxford University Press.

Melnikoff, K. 2018. *Elizabethan Publishing and the Makings of Literary Culture*. Toronto: University of Toronto Press.

Monta, S.B. 2009. *Martyrdom and Literature in Early Modern England*. Cambridge: Cambridge University Press.
Moore, J.K. 1992. *Primary Materials Relating to Copy and Print in English Books of the Sixteenth and Seventeenth Centuries*. Oxford: Oxford Bibliographical Society.
Mueller, J. 1988. A Tudor Queen Finds Voice: Katherine Parr's *Lamentation of a Sinner*. In H. Dubrow and R. Strier, eds. *The Historical Renaissance: New Essays on Tudor and Stuart Literature and Culture*. Chicago: University of Chicago Press. pp. 15–47.
Nicholson, W. ed. 1858. *Remains of Edmund Grindal*. Cambridge: Cambridge University Press.
Oastler, C.L. 1975. *John Day, the Elizabethan Printer*. Oxford: Oxford Bibliographical Society.
Pettegree, A. 2002. Illustrating the Book: A Protestant Dilemma. In: C. Highly and J.N. King, eds. *John Foxe and his World*. Aldershot, UK; Burlington, VT: Ashgate. pp. 133–44.
Poleg, E. 2020. *A Material History of the Bible: England 1200–1553*. Oxford: Oxford University Press for The British Academy.
Pollard, A. 1912. *Fine Books*. New York: G. P. Putnam's Sons.
Rankin, M. 2010. The Pattern of Illustration in Foxe's *Book of Martyrs*: Problems and Opportunities. In: T.P. Anderson and R. Netzley, eds. *Acts of Reading: Interpretation, Reading Practices, and the Idea of the Book in John Foxe's "Actes and Monuments."* Newark: University of Delaware Press. pp. 87–115.
———. 2022. John Day's Production of Woodcut Prints from John Foxe's *Acts and Monuments*. *The Library*, Seventh Series, **23.1**, 25-46.
Ringler, W.A. 1979. *Beware the Cat* and the Beginnings of English Fiction. *Novel*. **12.2**, 113–26.
Roberts, J. 1997. Bibliographical Aspects: John Foxe. In: D. Loades, ed. *John Foxe and the English Reformation*. Aldershot, UK: Scolar Press. pp. 36–51.
Ryrie, A. 1999. The Unsteady Beginnings of English Protestant Martyrology. In: D. Loades, ed. *John Foxe: An Historical Perspective*. Aldershot, UK; Brookfield, VT: Ashgate. pp. 52–66.
Schwyzer, P. 2022. Scattered Bones, Martyrs, Materiality, and Memory in Drayton and Milton. In: W.E. Engel, R. Loughnane, and G. Williams, eds. *Memory and Mortality in Renaissance England*. Cambridge: Cambridge University Press.
Sherlock, P. 2020. Remembering and Forgetting. In: A. Arcangeli and M. Tamm, eds. *A Cultural History of Memory in the Early Modern Age*. Vol. 3. London: Bloomsbury. pp. 151–68.
Simpson, P. 1927. Proof-Reading by English Authors of the Sixteenth and Seventeenth Centuries. *Oxford Bibliographical Society*. **2.1**, 5–24.
Stenner, R. 2019. *The Typographic Imaginary in Early Modern English Literature*. London: Routledge.
Strong, R. 1969. *The English Icon: Elizabethan and Jacobean Portraiture*. New York: Pantheon.
Thompson, E.P. 1993. *Customs in Common: Studies in Traditional Popular Culture*. New York: The New Press.
Verene, D. 1966. Cassirer's View of Myth and Symbol. *The Monist*. **50.4**, 553–64.
Walsham, A. 2011. *The Reformation of the Landscape: Religion, Identity, and Memory in Early Modern Britain and Ireland*. Oxford: Oxford University Press.

———. 2012. History, Memory, and the English Reformation. *The Historical Journal.* **55.4**, 899–938.
Walsham, A., Cummings, B., and Law, C. 2020. Introduction: Memory and the English Reformation. In: A. Walsham, B. Wallace, C. Law, and B. Cummings, eds. *Memory and the English Reformation.* Cambridge. Cambridge University Press. pp. 1–45.
Watt, T. 1996. *Cheap Print and Popular Piety, 1550–1640.* Cambridge: Cambridge University Press.
Weber, M. 2002. *The Protestant Ethic and the Spirit of Capitalism.* P. Baehr, ed., and trans. London: Penguin.
Woolf, D.R. 1995. The Rhetoric of Martyrdom: Generic Contradiction and Narrative Strategy in John Foxe's *Acts and Monuments.* In: T. Mayer and D.R. Woolf, eds. *The Rhetorics of Life-Writing in Early Modern Europe: Forms of Biography from Cassandra Fedele to Louis XIV.* Ann Arbor: University of Michigan Press. pp. 243–82.
Yates, F.A. 1978. *The Art of Memory.* Harmondsworth: Penguin.

4 Underwriting England's first Protestant emblem book (1568)

> The first kind of compound ideas is of them which consist partly of a direct idea, partly of a scriptile. Of this sort are an history painted in a fair table with verses underneath explaining it; a libel or epigram made upon something done, supposed to be written in a paper and pasted upon the opposite wall, and the thing done expressed in action upon the stage: an armored knight bearing a scutcheon and imprese written therein, and the like. The second kind of compound idea is of them which consist partly of a relative idea and partly a scriptile. Of this sort are innumerable examples in emblems written by Beza, Alciato, Peacham, and others. For in all emblems, the picture occupying the upper part of the table is a relative idea, and that which is written underneath, a scriptile.
> —John Willis, *The Art of Memory* (1621, sig. C5^v)[1]

John Willis's advice to aspiring practitioners of the memory arts is to avail themselves of the emblems collected and commented on by conscientious humanists, such as the French religious reformer Théodore de Beza, Italian jurist Andrea Alciato, and English miscellany writer Henry Peacham. Along with proverbs and adages (as discussed in the Introduction), emblems were a staple in the early modern transmission of knowledge from antiquity into Renaissance Europe (Enekel 2019, p. xiv). Emblems offered a bimedial approach for tapping into and making good use of the immemorial reservoir of mnemotechnic cultural commonplaces.

The previous chapter explored how the interplay of text and image in the *Book of Martyrs* served affectively to convey and implicitly to forge connections "between physical and spiritual vision, key to the emblematic mentalities" of the day (Howe 2017, p. 309). Foxe and Day treated the world and human history as a theatre of God's judgment within which the invention and benefits of printing were accorded special importance. Such a model for the realization of the divine will working in the world through book traffic was fundamental to their effort to advance the construction of England's national memory. Through graphic images and a wide range of descriptive narrative strategies, as well as at-a-glance indoctrinational features such as a calendar of martyrs and saints with special relevance to the reformed cause, Foxe and Day systematically consolidated and bolstered the resolve of evangelical Christians, inspiring and goading them to continue the important cultural work of overcoming—and indeed of drawing strength and a sense of purpose from—the historical trauma of persecution.[2]

Such a perception of the world as a stage was a dominant feature of late medieval and especially Tudor historiography (Woolf 2000, pp. 11–78). God, through His supernal wisdom, provides the script, divinely foreknown—and, depending on one's view of "unconditional election," also foreordained.[3] Add to this Day's innovative and engaging use of typography and page layout, coupled with his concern for how image and word mutually might reinforce one another to bring out more intense meanings than either could elicit on its own, and we can discern in the *Book of Martyrs* "the beginning of a Protestant iconography" (Dryness 2004, p. 101).

These same cultural elements—the metaphor of the world as theatre of God's judgment, the reemergence of a reformed Church projected as triumphing over Catholic oppression, and the affective value of emblems and related memory images mobilized in the interest of promoting intra-national comity—likewise coalesce and come more tightly into focus in England's first Protestant emblem book, *A Theatre for Worldings*. This work, as Rebeca Helfer (2012) convincingly has argued, "participates in the early modern reception of the art of memory tradition" and produces—and exemplarily models—an "emblematic memory theatre" (pp. 59, 161). Written by the continental humanist, Jan Van der Noot, residing in London at the time and hospitably entertained by his publisher, John Day, it was printed first in Dutch.[4] Although no printer is given on the title page, Day signed off as such in the dedication to Queen Elizabeth in his nearly simultaneous publication of a French edition (Stein 1934, p. 111; Brink 2019, p. 44). Both the guiding conceit and overall aesthetic impact of these emblematic images and accompanying sonnets—whether in the Dutch and French editions by Day, or in the later English and German versions—depend on an operational analogy between dramatic spectacle and the construction of memory images.[5] Correlatively and more particularly, *A Theatre for Voluptuous Worldlings* "offers important insights into early modern uses of the art of memory" and is itself a "mnemonic space, and an edifice intended to edify" (Helfer 2012, pp. 21–2).

Conditions of trade and the emblematic context

Alert to the steadily growing market occasioned by London's "Stranger communities," whose homes and churches were not far from Day's shop, it made good business sense to bring this book out simultaneously in Dutch and in French (Evenden 2008, pp. 95–7). The illustrations most likely were provided by Marcus Gheeraerts (Hodnett 1971, p. 41), some of which most likely he executed before fleeing the Netherlands in 1568, or by another eminent Dutch refugee artist, Lucas de Heere, also then working in London (Friedlander 1956, pp. 107–20). As discussed in the opening of Chapter 1, Day readily and cannily catered to the religiously oriented reading needs of foreigners, many of whom had sought religious refuge and gainful employment in Britain. He printed both a psalter and the reformed catechism in Dutch, copies of which also would have been eagerly if surreptitiously welcomed in the Spanish Hapsburg–occupied Netherlands. By the end of the 1560s then, Day could count on his books—no less than his name as a publisher of Protestant material— being well known to evangelically minded readers at home and abroad. Recognized and sought out by recently arrived artisans and journeymen, Day had access to "the very best foreign illustrators and typographers arriving in London early in Elizabeth's reign" (Evenden 2008, p. 96).

Day's preliminary market research on Van der Noot's emblem book paid off, and he turned a sufficient profit such that no additional capital expenditures were devoted to the project. In part, this was a result of his being otherwise preoccupied in 1568 with preparing for press the second, much expanded two-volume edition of *Acts and Monuments* (discussed in Chapter 3). And just a few months after the release of his foreign language emblem book, Day brought out a comparable work in English, Stephen Bateman's *A christall glasse of christian reformation, wherein the godly may behold the coloured abuses used in this our present time* (1569),[6] that made use of 37 pictures (also probably by Marcus Gheeraerts),[7] which is 17 more than appear in *A Theatre for Voluptuous Worldings*. Thus, preoccupied with his other lucrative reformation-oriented illustrated book projects, Day did not look back to *A Theatre* once it had been published. Instead, he let others press on with this popular emblem book, which would, no matter who took it up next, bear the signs of having originated from his shop. Neither did he publicly advance rights to it; there are no records of charges being brought against those who copied his emblem book outright. And even if he was only to make money on the Dutch and French editions now part of his saleable stock, he could derive satisfaction from knowing that his reformed polemical message was continuing to be spread to English and German readers.

While Day showed no signs of wanting to pursue the production of an English version, Van der Noot was eager to see one in print and turned to Henry Bynneman (Waterschoot 1997, p. 38). Bynneman was well known to the Day family—at one point surreptitiously obtaining an illustration from Day's son, Richard, for his own use.[8] Somewhat new to the London printing game, having only recently completed his apprenticeship, Bynneman opened his own shop no earlier than 1566.[9] Van der Noot apparently became impatient with Bynneman's production process (a frustration heightened probably because he wanted to deliver presentation copies of his emblem book to prospective English patrons before his scheduled departure for Germany), and may well have appealed to

Day "to print the last quires," which "would make exceptionally fast progress" (Waterschoot 1997, p. 46). Although Bynneman was getting patents and taking on large projects (some involving complete registers of Hebrew and Greek type font), his plodding pace seems to have been characteristic of his work ethic throughout his career as a printer. For example, on more than one occasion, he received a license for a work that, for one reason or another, he was unable to complete and hence needed another printer to step in and finish the book—as was the case, for example, with his version of Beza's Greek New Testament (Trapp 1999, p. 289). At all events, to make good on Van der Noot's business arrangement, Bynneman set about obtaining his own set of woodcuts—based directly on Day's emblems—as well as contracting with a translator. And so it came about that in 1569 Edmund Spenser, at most 17 years old (Brink 2019, p. 44), and yet who appears already to have been "familiar with major European poets, Petrarch, Du Bellay, and Marot" (Hadfield 2011, p. 150), "translated the apocalyptic, visionary poems facing the woodcuts in the English version of Van der Noot's *A Theatre for Worldings*" (Howe 2017, p. 309).

Spenser most likely was enlisted because of his "great facility for languages" (Hadfield 2011, p. 150), including Dutch and French, and owing to the recommendation of his schoolmaster, Richard Mulcaster, who was friendly with Van der Noot's cousin, Emanuel van Meteren, and otherwise well-connected in London's Dutch émigré community (Forster 1967, p. 33; Hadfield 2012, pp. 38–44). Experts in the comparison of the different versions of this Protestant emblem book concur that the Dutch sonnets remain closest to the pictures (Waterschoot 1997, p. 57), and that Spenser, most likely using the French version for his translation,[10] tends to rely on the passive rather than active voice in his renderings of the poems (Melehy 2010, pp. 103–8). Tom MacFaul (2014, p. 152) states in no uncertain terms what more forgiving admirers of Spenser are perhaps reticent to express: "As one might expect from a poet who was only fifteen to seventeen years old, the 'epigrams' and 'sonnets' are not particularly impressive work" (cf. Stein 1934, pp. 126–35). And yet, whatever else might be said about Spenser's early career as a translator of French poetry (Prescott 1978, p. 14), his first step on the ladder leading to *The Fairie Queene*—both in terms of Protestant patronage and the development of his poetic craft—began with the work of John Day whose initial and successful orchestration of *A Theatre* warrants closer scrutiny.

Day's production of Van der Noot's *Theatre* is the first English book to be illustrated with etchings, and the first Renaissance emblem book published in England.[11] And yet, as Karel Bostoen (1997) demonstrates, the important issue here is not whether the apocalyptic visions of *A Theatre* are emblems properly speaking, but in recognizing the extent to which "our perception of the text and picture is sharpened by an emblematical approach to these visions" (p. 60). Indeed, Day's considered attention to visual elements, no less than taking a chance on publishing a work featuring lyric poetry that was somewhat outside the usual range of his books associated with the reformed evangelical agenda, marks him once again as being an innovator in English printing practices. The 20 full-page illustrations in Day's Dutch and French versions are etched copperplate engravings (Friedlander 1956, p. 108); whereas Bynneman's English version to which Spenser contributed the sonnets facing the images uses woodcut copies, which also is the case with the German editions printed in Cologne (Waterschoot 2012). Most of the images in the woodcuts appear "reversed" (Daly 1988, p. 5), suggesting a direct-copy process from the engravings, and possibly some were modeled on watercolor illustrations then in circulation (Bath 1988).

Notwithstanding the Calvinist complexion of *A Theatre*, the decision to include images is justified on the basis of sound pedagogical principles and rationalized further in terms of the moral value ascribed to commonplace mnemotechnical designs.

In the section entitled "A Brief Declaration of the Author upon his visions," Van der Noot explains:

> And to set the vanity and inconstancy of worldly and transitory things, livelier before your eyes, I have brought in here twenty sights or visions, and caused them to be graven, to the end all men may see that with their eyes, which I go about to express by writing, to the delight and pleasure of the eye and ears, according unto the saying of Horace.
>
> Omne tulit punctum, qui miscuit utile dulci.
> That is to say,
> He that teacheth pleasantly and well,
> Doth in each point all others excel.
>
> (1569, sig. F2ᵛ–F3ʳ)

In what amounts to a Protestant apology for using images—a devotional practice traditionally associated with Roman Catholic piety—readers here are given license to enjoy the pictures and, moreover, enjoined to allow the emblems' moral sense to lead them to a higher purpose. After all, printed emblem books originated with Andrea Alciato in 1531, coincident with the early years of the Protestant reform movement, and managed to flourish abundantly throughout Europe.[12] The plates were added by his publisher "as a guide for the less educated reader, where the learned understood just as well without an illustration" (Miedema 1968, p. 243). Pictures—perhaps paradoxically—reminded viewers of what they cannot see. Huston Diehl (1986, p. 66) clarifies that "the emblematic image points away from itself" for when readers see the image and use it properly, they are seeing "through or beyond the material image" and remembering "another world," substituting "spiritual for physical sight." In this way, Protestant emblem books rehabilitate and, in effect, "reform the inherited images of medieval Catholicism, internalizing and personalizing them, altering forever the person's relation to them" (p. 66). Additionally, as Rebeca Helfer (2012, p. 22) points out, "emblem books illuminate how locational memory (as poetry or painting) speaks to the human psyche: even in print, we learn and remember best when given vivid pictures and place markers for them." John Day obviously had no issue with using pictures, as place-marked memory images, to enhance the appeal of his Protestant publications—and was, in fact, a trendsetter in this area of the English book trade.

The reference to Calvinist "unconditional election" mentioned earlier also has a role to play in *A Theatre* owing to the polemical slant of the emblems' sequentially delivered composite message. In addition to the final four specifically apocalyptic-themed images in the collection, an anti-Catholic view is evident in and reinforced by 200 pages of prose commentary. The "Brief Declaration of the author" (1569, sig. D7r), expounding upon "the fall of the City of Man and the rise of the City of God" (Helfer 2012, p. 22), is based for the most part on John Bale's *The image of both churches*, a work that Day printed in 1550 when he was expanding his business prospects and just prior to parting ways with William Seres (see Chapter 1, n.16). The other main source is *A Hundred sermons upon the Apocalypse* (1561) by the Swiss reformer Heinrich Bullinger, also printed by Day and advertised on the title page as being "newly set forth and allowed, according to the order appointed in the Queen's majesty's injunctions." Copies of both texts, especially the latter, would have been accessible and available for distribution, whether still being sold at his Aldersgate shop "over the gate" or warehoused nearby (Oastler 1975, pp. 30–1).

Comparable to Foxe's identification of the Antichrist with the Pope in Rome, against whom reformed publications can and must ceaselessly combat in print (as explained in Chapter 3), Van der Noot's emblematic project expresses explicitly in the commentary the theme of a New Jerusalem prepared for the faithful and waiting just on the other side of the Apocalypse. In a pastiche of biblical quotations inflected with reformed tenets of faith, the text resonates with a certitude that bespeaks a belief in the one true—which is to say Reformed—Church.

> I shall make a pleasant Jerusalem... From that time forward shall there be heard within her, no more sorrow nor pain, neither shall there be any death, for death shall be destroyed for evermore. The conscience of man shall not then be subject to any mistrustfulness or other infirmity, but shall have joy in the holy Ghost. They shall through sin, not die any more, but shall live through faith in God. That cruel whore shall drink no more in the blood of the martyrs, for she with all her adherents, and wicked tyrants, shall be kept in that filthy lake which burneth with fire and brimstone for evermore: So that no kind of trouble, persecution, slander, hatred, malice, anguish or pain, or any kind of adversity, cruelty, or wretchedness, which

could be devised, can hurt or hinder them: for sorrows, wailing, and weeping, shall be put far from them.

(1569, sig. O6ᵛ)

This recurring eschatological New Testament theme—and compelling mnemotechnical image—of the "cruel whore" of Babylon holding a chalice for drinking "in the blood of the martyrs," which figures frequently in the anti-papal rhetoric and imagery of the pan-European evangelical movement, is the focal subject of one of the engravings in *A Theatre* (Figure 4.1).[13]

As with the *Acts and Monuments*, there is a steady focus in *A Theatre* on interpreting John's vision as prophesying the fall of the Antichrist (Rev 8:4 and 17:3–7), who delights in deception and drinking "in the blood of Martyrs" (1569, sig. O6ᵛ), and duly is emblematized by the luxurious "Woman sitting on a beast" with seven heads and "ten horns also the stately beast did bare" (1569, sig. D3ʳ).

Apocalyptic mythography

The epigrams and sonnets in *Theatre for Worldings* clarify, guide, and constrain the viewer's interpretation of the symbolic images presented in the 20 illustrations. Each emblem is like a stand-alone stage in a series of linked performative tableaux conducing to a new and more encompassing—and dynamic—understanding of the End Time of Christian teleology. As such, the sequence can be seen as consisting of two "decades" (or sets of ten) in a traditional memory theatre as discussed in the Introduction.[14] This pattern of presenting sequential allegorical tableaux recalls religious processions and civic pageants or "triumphs," as they were designated during the Renaissance. Their humanist literary precedent derives from Petrarch's celebrated *Trionfi* (c. 1351–74), which had been part of the applied emblematic tradition in England at least as early as 1500 (Coogan 1970, p. 310). Petrarch, moreover, is an instrumental component in the foundation of *A Theatre* insofar as the first group of poems follows Clément Marot's translation of Petrarch's *Rime* 323 (Rasmussen 1980, pp. 3–8), which Spenser translates into English, followed by Joachim Du Bellay's *Songe* for the second sequence in the emblem book (Erikson 2014, p. 116).[15] The third sequence, consisting of four sonnets, is Van der Noot's versification of John the Revelator's vision of the Apocalypse (treated in Chapter 3), which "constitutes the most significant part of the book, since nearly three-fourths of the prose commentary is dedicated to it" (Bostoen 1997, p. 52; cf. Rasmussen 1980, p. 14).

With this in mind, the person who takes up *A Theatre for Worldlings* is confronted by three groupings of dream vision sonnets making up a total of 20 discrete vignettes or mnemonic tableuax. The 17th emblem with accompanying sonnet, the third-to-the-last in the sequence (Figure 4.1), proves exemplary for bringing together the various cultural stands and

148 *Underwriting England's first emblem book*

Figure 4.1 Whore of Babylon. *A Theatre for Worldlings* (London: Henry Bynneman, 1569), sig. D4ʳ. Image used courtesy of The Folger Shakespeare Library.

symbolic forms mentioned at the outset of this chapter. In it we find the following familiar themes: the world as a theatre of God's judgment, the reemergence of a reformed Church projected as triumphing over Catholic oppression, and the affective use of moral emblems in setting up self-referential places, or *loci*, that constitute—and indeed motivate—an overarching Protestant Theatre of Memory.

> I saw a *Woman* sitting on a beast
> Before mine eyes, of *Orange* color hue:
> Horror and dreadful name of blasphemy
> Filled her with pride. And seven heads I saw.
> Ten horns also the stately beast did bear.
> She seemed with glory of the scarlet faire,
> And with fine pearl and gold puffed up in heart.
> The wine of whoredom in a cup she bear.
> The name of *Mystery* writ in her face.
> The blood of *Martyrs* dear were her delight.
> Most fierce and fell[16] this woman seemed to me.
> An *Angel* then descending down from *Heaven*.
> With thundering voice cried out aloud, and said:
> Now for a truth great *Babylon* is fallen. [emphasis added]

While it is my editorial policy to modernize early modern printed materials for the sake of clarity, in this case I have retained the mid-sentence capital letters as they appear in the English version of the poem (and emphasized the words in italics) owing to their mnemotechnic value for readers in the late 1560s.[17] These seven tagged words, when taken together, provide readers with a sequential précis of the overall allegorical meaning of key concepts represented in the emblem. By means of an encoded at-a-glance mnemonic itinerary, the key stops along the way are highlighted with reference to the emblem's special approach to disclosing the evangelically inflected content. Specifically, the mnemotechnical cue words are: Woman, Orange, Mystery, Martyr, Angel, Heaven, and Babylon. As such, they resemble headwords in a thematically organized commonplace book, under each of which a wide range of ruminations and parallel references from other works might be entered and corresponding scriptural passages alleged.

First, the word "Woman" signals—and stands out as—the focal image in this retelling of the relevant passage from the book of Revelation, with the other capitalized words serving further to reinforce attention to what is said to have been seen: "a Woman sitting on a beast." She represents the Whore of Babylon, traditionally linked to the Antichrist (Rev. 17:3–9); and the poem initially follows the biblical passage fairly closely. Additionally, the translator of the prose section of *A Theatre*, Theodore Roest, unpacks the symbolism of the beast as signifying "the congregation of the wicked and proud hypocrites ... they are whelps and generations of the devil" and its heads "the outrageous bishops, spiritual lawyers, priests, hypocrites, and false magistrates" (1569, sig. G2v).[18] This woman sitting on a seven-headed beast with ten horns is a memory image to which Spenser later will return and likewise infuse with Protestant

150 *Underwriting England's first emblem book*

meaning in his portrait of the duplicitous Duessa in *The Faerie Queene*—the episode in which her protector, Orgoglio, who allegorizes that form of Pride associated with the world's would-be usurper, and broadly standing for the biblical Satan (*FQ* I.vii.16–18). James Nohrnberg (1976, p. 222), with characteristic acuity, sums up the meaning of the defeat of Orgoglio and the rest of the legend as allegorically suggesting "the consolidation of the reform Church under Elizabeth." Apropos of which, a compelling case can be made that Spenser's contribution in translating the "Epigrams" and "Sonnets" of this "vigorously Protestant volume prefigures his career as the poet of a nation in (mostly beleaguered) opposition to Rome," and that, although "Van der Noot's ideas and images are mostly very common for his time (in the Reformed camp at least)," still we can find "almost all of Spenser's later preoccupations in embryo in the *Theatre*" (MacFaul 2014, p. 149).[19]

The second capitalized word, "Orange," thus provides a mnemonic backdrop against which the key terms—as *loci*—are to be read, situated, and understood. This word in particular, "Orange," gives readers a way to color the black-and-white image within their mind's eye. It thereby stands out, so to speak, as being significant within this allegorical tableau designed to find a place in and be retained within the reader's own private Memory Theatre—one which will be shared with the larger community of readers who likewise are doing the same. So named and colored, the panel is clearly differentiated from the others, which is to say different from the other 19 engraved emblems. Imagining a distinctive color associated with each new slate of ten images of a Memory Theatre is one of the main practices advocated by mnemonists. John Willis (1661) discusses the enhanced mnemotechnical value of assigning colors to the same template of the empty stage (as a background mnemonic on which to place the next set of symbolic images) so as to accommodate, in sequence, and later to revisit and retrieve the encoded devices thus placed within each separate differently colored *mise en scènes* (sig. E8^v–F2^v). Further associative logic is in play here for orange had specific symbolic resonances in the Renaissance. It was linked to brass, deemed not as worthy as gold or silver, and hence signals less than noble values and virtues. Further, since orange was the fabric dye color cheaper to produce than the more pure and rich colors, it came to signify the pale imitation of the proverbial real thing.

Readers thus are invited to understand and to puzzle out the rest of the key words capitalized in the sonnet along the lines discussed above. As a parting example, let us consider "The name of Mystery writ in her face." The wording of this segment of John's vision (Rev. 17: 5–6) is as follows in the Geneva Bible, the New Testament of which was published in 1557:

> And in her forehead was a name written, A Mystery, great Babylon, the mother of whoredom, and abominations of the earth. / And I saw

the woman drunken with the blood of Saints, and with the blood of the Martyrs of Iesus.

(sig. Gg8ʳ)

The forehead in question of course is part and parcel of the iconic image of the Whore of Babylon from Revelation; and yet like all true mysteries in the theological register, it remains open to several interpretations, which, given the sequencing of the 20 emblems, resolves quietly and simply into what can be thought of as a "muted apocalypse."[20] The overarching narrative of the visions in *A Theatre,* staged emblem by emblem as it were, all the while self-consciously mirroring the grander vision of John the Revelator, is resolved quite literally as and by means of the theatrical convention of *dues ex machina*.[21] It is ultimately God's doing. This dramaturgical metaphor, taken together with Van der Noot's preemptive redirection of Du Bellay's poetic traces, opens the way toward seeing *A Theatre* as "pointing toward a realm of divinity that may never fully be known on earth" (Melehy 2010, p. 102). For to think that it can be known—let alone by "worldlings"—is yet another instantiation of the same kind of vanity that *A Theatre* militates against in its presentation of 20 mnemonic tableaux for readers to keep in mind and take to heart as they go out into the world once the book itself is closed.

Van Der Noot's goal, and one that substantially is enabled by the engravings Day arranged originally to accompany the text, is to guide the reader, step-by-step, image by image, from being steeped in worldly vanity and move closer toward spiritual knowledge. In this regard, Carl J. Rasmussen (1980) argues convincingly that the descriptive poems are dramatic monologues that explore a range of spiritual states, such that the speakers of the first two groups of poems (modeled on, respectively, Petrarch "Epigrams" and Du Bellay "Sonets") show "worldlings" caught up in the stultifying illusion of earthly matters; whereas the speaker of the final four apocalyptic "Sonets" provides an allegory of conversion (pp. 22–7). Seen in this light, Rome becomes yet another allegory (albeit a powerful and major one) of vanity, which is to be overcome by God's Word alone, not by armed conflict, religious battles, and sectarian contention. Such is the revelation that is being expressed in the final three lines of the sonnet quoted above. *A Theatre* thereby urges conciliation by promoting a broader understanding of divergent approaches to the truth of Christianity in terms of God's love for the world, which is also to say for "worldlings," as declared in John 3:16: "For God so loveth the world, that he hath given his only begotten Son, that whosoever believeth in him, should not perish, but have everlasting life" (Geneva Bible).

So even though *A Theatre* clearly is critical of Roman Catholic doctrine and observances, it is "more than just an antipapal track" (Prescott 1978, p. 45). The images and poems present a composite mnemonic spectacle of earthly vanity, even as it offers itself as a mirror in which readers can see themselves reflected and, at the same time, take stock of the mechanisms of the book's own signifying features (cf. Melehy 2010, p. 103 and Crewe 1986, p. 101). But above all else, and with direct relevance to the book's importance as a product issuing initially from Day's technical ingenuity, *A Theatre for Worldlings* "is, or means to be," as Anne Lake Prescott (1978) astutely observes, "a mnemonic image of a world in which the spirit moves mysteriously behind the literal and material surface of things" (p. 45).

Contextualizing the circulation of memory images

That this emblem book came out in Dutch and French simultaneously also speaks to Day's sense of reaching out to a more international audience both in London and abroad. At this stage in his career (as disclosed at the outset of this chapter), he had access to and solid working relationships with a number of continental artisans who enabled him, in the 1560s, to take his work to the next level in his program to advance Protestant visual literacy through his prominent role in England's book trade. And, as was made clear in Chapter 3, it was also at this time when Day saw, made, and seized opportunities to enhance the visual elements—and hence augment the mnemotechnical possibilities—of the *Book of Martyrs*, with the number of woodcuts nearly tripling from 53 in the first edition (1563) to over 150 in subsequent editions during his lifetime.

In Renaissance book production, illustrators and engravers time and again express in their work an appreciation of connections between the emblem book and the memory theatre (Sider 1979, p. 2). The epigraph to this chapter speaks to how early modern emblem books were enlisted to become part of one's own individualized Memory Theatre, and this chapter has clarified the extent to which England's first printed emblem book drew on and made use of mnemotechnical principles in the service of its overarching evangelical vision. Along these same lines, Francis Bacon (1605) systematically describes the place of emblems as an aspect of the memory arts:

> This art of memory is but built upon two intentions; the one prenotion, the other emblem. Prenotion dischargeth the indefinite seeking of that we would remember, and directeth us to seek in a narrow compass, that is, somewhat that hath congruity with our place of memory. Emblem reduceth conceits intellectual to images sensible, which strike the memory more; out of which axioms may be drawn much better practice than that in use; and besides which axioms, there are divers more touching help of memory not inferior to them. But I did in the beginning distinguish, not to report those things deficient, which are but only ill managed.
>
> (sig. Pp2^v)

The same may be said of Day's program to underwrite and set in circulation key images–quite literally, emblems—within a larger Protestant

Memory Art. He was in many respects a silent partner initially in *A Theatre*, willing to assume a hidden and nearly anonymous role. As already observed, his name does not even appear on the Dutch version as having been the printer. Clearly though, he did not do this out of concern for his personal safety over printing a work that promoted Protestant ideology and was critical of Catholic devotional practices, which might have been the case had he sought to bring out such a work during the reign of Queen Mary. Rather, he did it as a way to take a backseat and let Van der Noot's work proceed as planned and make its own way in the world. Also as discussed at the beginning of this chapter, for whatever his reasons, Day was content to let another printer bring out the English translation. What mattered to him was that the images associated with this particular emblem book (as with his other illustrated Protestant books now steadily coming from his presses around the same time) continued to circulate and thereby become a vital part of the visual vocabulary of the day. Much in the same way that works by Luther, Calvin, and Bullinger were quickly translated from their original languages, Day—the printer as author, as discussed in Chapter 1—brought out an emblem book that in short order made the rounds in Dutch, French, English, and German.

As the underwriter of *A Theatre for Worldings*, Day again was reprising his role as witness and propagator of God's truth in the world along the lines discussed in Chapter 3. We will recall that he had heard and seen firsthand and had himself been imprisoned with martyrs whose stories fill the pages of *Acts and Monuments*. His authority to address such matters was in fact enhanced by his decision—and ability—to publish their words rather than relating and making much of his own. As a printer devoted to providing others with viable memory places out of which to build and consolidate their faith, his touch here is subtle and light, nearly invisible. In bringing forward Van der Noot's humanistically inflected vision of reform in *A Theatre*, Day succeeded in setting up and expanding the contemporary evangelically informed vocabulary at once involving politics and religion, visuality and poetics, and of course the memory arts. By such means, he conveyed and added strength to the muted apocalypse associated with Van der Noot's visionary call to action. Day's continuation and further development of this aspect of his ongoing fabrication of a Protestant Memory Art is explored further in the next chapter with respect to the rather more involved and sustained forms of visuality marking his production of *Queen Elizabeth's Prayer Book*, which was to become the go-to handbook of domestic piety in Tudor-Stuart England.

Notes

1 Willis here refers to the memory images of a painted shield ("scutcheon") and tournament devices ("imprese"), consisting of an image and motto collectively disclosing some secret intention or aspiration of the bearer. On this

passage in particular and Willis's contribution to the mnemotechnical tradition in Renaissance England, see Engel et al. (2016, pp. 73–84).
2 See Anderson (2006) on the notion of "a traumatic past that insistently presses its claim on the present" (p. 1), and, more particularly, on early modern theatrical spectacles' capacity to compensate for "even as they repeat, the traumatic loss of the place of the dead" (p. 127).
3 On predestination and "God's elect," see Calvin (1561, sig. Hh6^v–Ii2^v), as translated by Thomas Norton (discussed in Chapter 2 with reference to his contribution to the English metrical psalms).
4 Although some literary historians have treated Van der Noot as a "Flemish" or "Netherlandish" poet, insofar as he fled Spanish forces and authorities in 1567 along with thousands of other Protestant refugees during the Hapsburg ascendency in the Low Countries, I refer to his emblem book as being printed in "Dutch" consistent with how it was described in Elizabethan England. On the complexities associated with designations of the various regions and languages appertaining to "The Eighty Years War," see Van der Lem (2019, pp. 35–68).
5 On this aesthetic and epistemological affinity between stage plays and memory images as it is being referenced here, see Bolzoni (2001, p. 173), Engel (2002, pp. 52–3), and Wilder (2010, p. 54).
6 Diverging in this instance from my usual editorial procedure, I give the original spelling of the full title here to highlight the pun on "crystal" and "Christ-all," and also to highlight the extended allegory of the looking glass as a mirror of manners, comparable to his emblem book being figured as a theatre in which one can see played out the errors in spiritual conduct among people too enamored with things of this world. Also, whether a compositor's accident or perhaps taken directly from the manuscript used as the guide for setting the type, the word "reformation" is not capitalized suggesting the sense of a spiritual process that each person must undertake individually (rather than intending to signify a widespread, politicized religious movement).
7 On the extensive illustration of *A christall glasse of christian reformation*, see Luborsky and Ingram (1998, pp. 57–61). On Bateman's subtle view of "imagined gods," which maintained "the ancients were better than the Catholics, who were also damned, and on top of that brought licentiousness and discord," see Hartmann (2018, p. 71).
8 Evenden (2008, p. 120); and, on Richard Day's plans with Bynneman "to bring in an income by pirating his father's key texts," see pp. 162–3.
9 By all accounts, Bynneman was a Protestant printer originally from the continent who was "trusted by Parker, Leicester, and Cecil," but whose business "had neither the capacity nor capability to produce books for them on a regular basis" (Evenden 2008, pp. 129–30).
10 Cf. MacFaul (2014, p. 152): "The translations of the apocalyptic 'sonets' are particularly weak, slavishly following the word order of the French (they make no use of the Dutch at all)."
11 To be sure, bibliographical purists historically have maintained that emblems consist of three parts, *pictura* (icon, imago), *inscriptio* (motto, lemma), and *subscriptio* (Miedema 1968, p. 234), and the emblems in *A Theatre for Worldings* possess "only two of the conventional emblem's three elements" (Howe 2017, p. 309). Quite sensibly, Peter Daly (2014) has opined that "it is notoriously difficult to hit upon any description that will account for the

various manifestations of the emblem even in emblem books" (p. 17). It must also be noted in this regard that the earliest English emblem book, properly speaking, is Thomas Palmer's *Two Hundred Poosees*, which "like several of its successors, was not a printed book, but a manuscript which remained unpublished in its own day" (Bath 1994, p. 57); it predates Day's printing of Van der Noot's *A Theatre* by two years. It is written in a neat secretary hand and dedicated to Robert Dudley, Earl of Leicester, whose patronage role for Day and Hanmer has been discussed in Chapters 1 and 3, respectively. John Manning (1988) meticulously traces Palmer's debt to continental sources, most notably, Alciato, Aneau, Coustau, Paradin, and Valeriano, as well as the *Adages* of Erasmus (regarding the latter, see the Introduction, "Mnemotechnic cultural commonplaces"); and Michael Bath (1994, pp. 57–69) instructively situates Palmer's place in the larger context of the English emblem book tradition.

12 The first edition of Alciato's *Emblematum liber* (Augsburg: Heinrich Steyner, 1531), of which 97 of the 104 emblems are illustrated with small woodcuts attributed to Hans Schäufelein after the Augsburg painter Jörg Breu, apparently was unauthorized and some of the images inaccurate or otherwise not corresponding to the epigrams, such that Alciato prepared a second edition (Paris 1534); see Scholz (1991, pp. 213–25). On the "irony that the popularity of emblems coincides with the advent of Protestantism" thus placing the movement's "iconoclastic strain into a very different perspective," see Strong (2019, p. 86); cf. Gilman (1980, pp. 389, 409).

13 The illustration of this figure, one deeply rooted in the Christian eschatological imaginary, in the 1545 edition of Luther's Bible shows the Whore wearing the triple-tiered papal tiara thus linking her to the Roman Catholic Church, which would make the beast upon which she rides the Antichrist of the final battle heralding the End Times.

14 See, for example, Plat (1594, sig. N1^r): "In every one of these rooms you must place ten several subjects at a reasonable distance one from the other, lest the nearness of their placing should happen to confound your memory. Your subjects must consist of decades." On Plat's place in the early modern English mnemotechnical tradition, as well as for helpful glosses on this passage with reference to relevant classical sources, see Engel et al. (2016, pp. 65–6).

15 On Spenser's continuing engagement with Du Bellay's poetic sequence, in his "*Complaints* (1591) as the *Visions of Bellay*, now unillustrated but rhyming," see Prescott (2017, p. 264).

16 The early modern meaning of "fell," derived from Old English, was cruel or ruthless; see, for example, Shakespeare's Macduff's "at one fell swoop" (*Mac.* 4.3.220).

17 Insofar as capitalizing words at the beginning of each line was standard typographical convention for the printing of verse forms such as a sonnet, these line-opening words are not included in the gathering of the key words, which clearly stand out (by virtue of being mid-sentence capitalized words) and can serve here as viable mnemonic *loci* in this Tablet of Memory corresponding to the seven key terms for recalling and reflecting on the larger allegory.

18 For a detailed iconographic interpretation of the first of the apocalyptic sonnets, its picture and prose commentary, which has direct relevance to the 17th engraving under discussion here, see Bostoen (1997, pp. 53–61).

19 Also in this regard, see Helfer (2012, p. 23) on the *Complaints* emulating "the mnemonic devices found in the *Theatre*, which clearly influence Spenser's work throughout his career"; and Wallace (2017, p. 10), "much of what is most dynamic in Spenser's poetry—early, middle, and late—flows directly from the blend of daring and dependence that is already on view in his contributions to *A Theatre*."
20 Michael Bath (1994, p. 109), following Charles Roger Davis, uses this apt term to refer to Van der Noot's approach to "the transitional or disappearing vision."
21 On this theatrical mechanism used originally in Greek tragedy, whereby a god is presented as intervening in the action of the play to chart a course beyond the otherwise irresolvable socio-political dilemma presented, see Sommerstein (2009, pp. 166–7).

Bibliography

Primary Sources

Bacon, F. 1605. *Of the Advancement and Proficience of Learning*. London: T. Purfoot and T. Creede. STC 1164.

Bale, J. 1550. *The image of both churches after the most wonderful and heavenly Revelation of Saint John the Evangelist*. London: John Day and William Seres. STC 1298.

Bateman, S. 1569. *A christall glasse of christian reformation, wherein the godly may behold the coloured abuses used in this our present time*. London: John Day. STC 1581.

Bullinger, H. 1561. *A Hundred Sermons Upon the Apocalypse*. London: John Day. STC 4061.

Calvin, J. 1561. *The Institution of Christian Religion, written in Latin by master John Calvin, and translated into English … by Thomas Norton*. London: R. Wolfe and R. Harrison. STC 4415.

Foxe, J. 1563. *Acts and monuments of these latter and perilous days touching matters of the Church, wherein are comprehended and described the great persecutions and horrible troubles that have been wrought and practiced by the Romish prelates, specially in the realm of England and Scotland …*. London: John Day. STC 11222.

Plat, H. 1594. *The Jewel House of Art and Nature*. London: P. Short. STC 19991.5.

Shakespeare, W. 2016. *The New Oxford Shakespeare: Modern Critical Edition*. G. Taylor, J. Jowett, T. Bourus, and G. Egan, gen. eds. Oxford: Oxford University Press.

Spenser, E. 2007. *The Faerie Queene*. Second edition. A. C. Hamilton, ed. Harlow: Pearson Education.

The New Testament. 1557. Geneva: C. Badius. STC 2871.

Van der Noot, J. 1568a. *Het theatre*. London: John Day. STC 18601.

———. 1568b. *Le theatre*. London: John Day. STC 18603.

———. 1569. *A theatre wherein be represented as well the miseries and calamities that follow the voluptuous worldlings*. London: Henry Bynneman. STC 18602.

Willis, J. 1621. *The art of memory, so far forth as it dependeth upon Places and Ideas*. London: W. Jones. STC 25749.
———. 1661. *Mnemonica, or, The art of memory*. London: Leonard Sowersby. Wing W2812.

Secondary Sources

Anderson, T.P. 2006. *Performing Early Modern Trauma from Shakespeare to Milton*. Aldershot, UK: Ashgate.
Bath, M. 1988. Verse Form and Pictorial Space in Van der Noot's *Theatre for Worldlings*. In: K.J. Höltgen, P.M. Daly, and W. Lottes, eds. *Word and Visual Imagination: Studies in the Interaction of English Literature and the Visual Arts*. Erlangen: Universitätsbund Erlangen-Nürnberg. pp. 73–105.
———. 1994. *Speaking Pictures: English Emblem Books and Renaissance Culture*. London: Longman.
Bolzoni, L. 2001. *The Gallery of Memory: Literary and Iconographic Models in the Age of the Printing Press*. J. Parzen, trans. Toronto: University of Toronto Press.
Bostoen, K. 1997. Van der Noot's Apocalyptic Visions: Do you "see" what you read?. In: B. Westerweel, ed. *Anglo-Dutch Relations in the Field of the Emblem*. Leiden: Brill. pp. 49–61.
Brink, J.R. 2019. *The Early Spenser, 1554–80: "Minde on honour fixed."* Manchester: Manchester University Press.
Coogan, R. 1970. Petrarch's *Trionfi* and the English Renaissance. *Studies in Philology*. **67.3**, 306–27.
Crewe, J. 1986. *Hidden Designs: The Critical Profession and Renaissance Literature*. New York: Methuen.
Daly, P. ed. 1988. *The English Emblem Tradition (Index emblematicus)*, vol. 1. Toronto: University of Toronto Press.
———. 2014. *The Emblem in Early Modern Europe: Contributions to the Theory of the Emblem*. Farnham: Ashgate.
Diehl, H. 1986. Graven Images: Protestant Emblem Books in England. *Renaissance Quarterly*. **39.1**, 49–66.
Dryness, W.A. 2004. *Reformed Theology and Visual Culture: The Protestant Imagination from Calvin to Edwards*. Cambridge: Cambridge University Press.
Enekel, K.A.E. 2019. *The Invention of the Emblem Book and the Transmission of Knowledge, ca. 1510–1610*. Leiden: Brill.
Engel, W.E. 2002. *Death and Drama in Renaissance England: Shades of Memory*. Oxford: Oxford University Press.
Engel, W.E., Loughnane, R., and Williams, G. 2016. *The Memory Arts in Renaissance England: A Critical Anthology*. Cambridge: Cambridge University Press.
Erikson, W. 2014. Spenser's patrons and publishers. In: R.A. McCabe, ed. *The Oxford Handbook of Edmund Spenser*. Oxford: Oxford University Press. pp. 106–24.
Evenden, E. 2008. *Patents, Pictures and Patronage: John Day and the Tudor Book Trade*. Aldershot, UK: Ashgate.
Forster, L. 1967. The Translator of the *Theatre for Worldlings*. *English Studies*. **48.1**, 27–34.

Friedlander, L.S. 1956. The Illustrations in *The Theatre for Worldings*. *Huntington Library Quarterly*. **19**.2, 107–20.
Gilman, E.B. 1980. Word and Image in Quarles's *Emblemes*. *Critical Inquiry*. **6**.3, 385–411.
Hadfield, A. 2011. Edmund Spenser's Translation of Du Bellay in Jan van der Noot's *A Theatre for Worldings*. In: F. Schurink, ed. *Tudor Translation*. Basingstoke: Palgrave Macmillan. pp. 143–60.
———. 2012. *Edmund Spenser: A Life*. Oxford: Oxford University Press.
Hartmann, A.-M. 2018. *English Mythography in its European Context, 1500–1650*. Oxford: Oxford University Press.
Helfer, R. 2012. *Spenser's Ruins and the Art of Recollection*. Toronto: University of Toronto Press.
Hodnett, E. 1971. *Marcus Gheeraerts the Elder of Bruges, London, and Antwerp*. Utrecht: Haentjens Dekker & Gumbert.
Howe, S. 2017. Emblem and Iconography. In: A. Escobedo, ed. *Edmund Spenser in Context*. Cambridge: Cambridge University Press. pp. 301–12.
Luborsky, R.S. and Ingram, E.M. 1998. *A Guide to English Illustrated Books, 1536–1603*. 2 vols. Tempe: ACMRS.
MacFaul, T. 2014. *A Theatre for Worldings* (1569). In: R.A. McCabe, ed. *The Oxford Handbook of Edmund Spenser*. Oxford: Oxford University Press. pp. 149–59.
Manning, J., ed. 1988. *The Emblems of Thomas Palmer: "Two Hundred Poosees"/Sloane MS 3794*. New York: AMS.
Melehy, H. 2010. *The Poetics of Literary Transfer in Early Modern France and England*. Farnham, UK: Ashgate.
Miedema, H. 1968. The Term *Emblema* in Alciati. *Journal of the Warburg and Courtauld Institutes*. **31**, 234–50.
Nohrnberg, J. 1976. *The Analogy of "The Faerie Queene."* Princeton: Princeton University Press.
Oastler, C.L. 1975. *John Day, the Elizabethan Printer*. Oxford: Oxford Bibliographical Society.
Prescott, A.L. 1978. *French Poets and the English Renaissance: Studies in Form and Transformation*. New Have: Yale University Press.
———. 2017. Spenser's French Connection. In: A. Escobedo, ed. *Edmund Spenser in Context*. Cambridge: Cambridge University Press. pp. 264–72.
Rasmussen, C.J. 1980. "Quietnesse of Minde": *A Theatre for Worldings* as a Protestant Poetics. *Spenser Studies*. **1**, 3–27.
Scholz, B.F. 1991. The 1531 Augsburg Edition of Alciato's *Emblemata*: A Survey of Research. *Emblematica*. **5**.2, 213–54.
Sider, S. ed. 1979. *Cebes' Tablet: Facsimiles of the Greek Text, and of Selected Latin, French, English, Spanish, Italian, German, Dutch, and Polish Translations*. New York: Renaissance Society of America.
Sommerstein, A.H. 2009. Tragedy and Myth. In: R. Bushnell, ed. *A Companion to Tragedy*. Malden, MA; Oxford: Blackwell Publishing. pp. 168–80.
Stein, H. 1934. *Studies in Spenser's "Complaints."* New York: Oxford University Press.
Strong, R. 2019. *The Elizabethan Image: An Introduction to English Portraiture, 1558–1603*. New Haven: Yale University Press.
Trapp, J.B. 1999. The Humanist Book. In: L. Hellinga and J.B. Trapp, eds. *The Cambridge History of the Book in Britain, 1400–1557*. Cambridge: Cambridge University Press. pp. 285–315.

Van der Lem, A. 2019. *Revolt in the Netherlands: The Eighty Years War, 1568–1648*. A. Brown, trans. London: Reaktion Books.

Wallace, A. 2017. Pedegogy, Education, and Early Career. In: A. Escobedo, ed. *Edmund Spenser in Context*. Cambridge: Cambridge University Press. pp. 7–13.

Waterschoot, W. 1997. An Author's Strategy: Jan Van Der Noot's *Het Theatre*. In: B. Westerweel, ed. *Anglo-Dutch Relations in the Field of the Emblem*. Leiden: Brill. pp. 35–48.

———. 2012. Jan van der Noot among English and German Printers. *Quaerendo*. **42.3–4**, 316–21.

Wilder, L.P. 2010. *Shakespeare's Memory Theatre: Recollection, Properties, and Characters*. Cambridge: Cambridge University Press.

Woolf, D.R. 2000. *Reading History in Early Modern England*. Cambridge: Cambridge University Press.

5 The compelling visuality of *Queen Elizabeth's Prayer Book* (1569)

> Like the phonetic image the mythical image serves not solely to designate already existing differences but also to fixate them for consciousness, to make them visible as such: it does not merely reproduce existing distinctions but in the strict sense of the word *evokes* distinctions [original emphasis].
>
> —Ernst Cassirer (1977b, p. 203)

This epigraph provides a way to approach the compelling visuality of the specific kinds of mnemonic images Day sets to work in *Queen Elizabeth's Prayer Book*. It also brings us full circle, back to the long passage quoted from Cassirer's *Mythical Thought* in the opening pages of the Introduction. Further, this epigraph anticipates the concern in Chapter 5 with "building up of the divine world from the particular impulses and directions of human activity" to attribute supernal oversight to all manner of temporal events (Cassirer 1977b, p. 203). As was discussed in Chapters 3 and 4, for Protestants especially, this implied God's providential staging of human history.[1] Cassirer argues that this "building up of the divine world" discloses "the same form of objectivization ... found in language" (1977b, p. 203).[2] The following excerpt will clarify how this insight pertains to our present discussion of mythical thought tacitly encoded in the visual format of the enormously influential Protestant prayer book produced by John Day:

> Language seems fully definable as a system of phonetic symbols—the worlds of art and myth seem to consist entirely in the particular, sensuously tangible forms that they set before us. Here we have in fact an all-embracing medium in which the most diverse cultural forms meet. The content of the spirit is disclosed only in its manifestations; the ideal form is known only by and in the aggregate of the sensible signs which it uses for its expression.
>
> (Cassirer 1977a, p. 86)

More specifically, and apropos of the aims and formal considerations that go into the production of a domestic prayer book sanctioned by

DOI: 10.4324/9780429032431-6

Elizabethan state authorities including the sovereign herself, "consciousness arrives at a clear division between the different spheres of activity and between their divergent objective and subjective conditions only by referring each of these spheres to a fixed center, to one particular mythical figure" (Cassirer 1977b, p. 203).[3] And the "one particular mythical figure" in Christianity, of course, is Jesus Christ.[4] He is the fixed center around which all the germinal activities in the ensuing providential and foreordained teleology of Christian history and lore cluster and to whom they ultimately refer, the scriptural pericope of which is the retelling of Christ's crucifixion and resurrection conducing to the plan by which Christians might be redeemed. The exact interpretations and implications of such salvific redemption, however, differ sometimes widely between the various confessions of Christian faith, whether Protestant or Catholic, and as well as among the main denominations of these dominant religious movements. And yet in all cases, the savior figure, as Cassirer (1977b) explains, is regarded not as produced by believers but as received by them in a state of completion, such that they understand this activity only by removing it from themselves and projecting it outward, "and from this projection arises the figure of the god, no longer as a mere power of nature but as a culture-hero, a bringer of light and salvation" (p. 204). It is important to keep in mind as we proceed in our investigation of Day's role in the fabrication of a Protestant Memory Art that, as Cassirer (1977b) stresses throughout in his exposition of mythical thought, "the philosophy of Symbolic Forms is concerned with the totality of spiritual expressive functions" in which they are regarded, "not as copies of being but as trends and modes of formation, as 'organs' less of mastery than of signification" (p. 217). It is toward these "trends and modes of formation," concerned less with mastery and more with signification, that we now turn in *Queen Elizabeth's Prayer Book*.

The previous four chapters have showcased and explored the principal ways in which memory "is transformed from imagined, mental spaces to material physical spaces" (Reid 2019, p. 63). The material, spatial, and structural elements of early modern books, as has been shown to be the case with the major works of John Day, operate essentially as *loci* and *imagines agentes*, as so many predetermined places animated by vivid images associated with classical mnemotechnical commonplaces (as discussed in the Introduction). And, more particularly, Chapters 3 and 4 treated how and the extent to which Day "established his dominance over the trade in English martyrologies and cemented a reputation for brazen Protestant polemics packaged in richly illustrated books" (Epstein 2021, p. 361). In so doing, Day plays into and makes much of what Rachel Stenner (2019) has called "the typographic imaginary" in early modern English literature and print culture. The typographic imaginary is to be understood "as both an authorial strategy and a critical tool" (p. 1). In *Queen Elizabeth's Prayer Book*, Day once again can be seen to arrogate the role of the printer as author as described Chapter 1 with *The*

162 *Compelling visuality of the* Prayer Book

Cosmographical Glass, and as demonstrated in Chapter 2 with respect to the catechism and metrical psalms, in Chapter 3 with the *Book of Martyrs*, and in Chapter 4 with England's first printed emblem book, which, like his earlier polemical works, holds close to and promotes a decidedly reformed religious agenda.

Chapter 5, by way of rounding out and augmenting this presentation of Day's place in the fabrication of a Protestant Memory Art in Tudor England, brings together elements of the preceding chapters to indicate more fully how he engages strategies of the typographic imaginary. This comes into view best against the backdrop of his incremental development of a mnemonically puissant Protestant iconography made possible by virtue of his indefatigable pursuit of perfecting and promulgating principles of accepted evangelical visuality. As with his adept repurposing of Catholic martyrological charts, stories, and imagery to set up a new register of essentially Protestant mnemonic thought in the *Book of Martyrs*,[5] Day likewise draws directly from and refashions time-tested Catholic models in *Queen Elizabeth's Prayer Book* (Figure 5.1).

This exemplary page from Day's prayer book, with the outer margin border panels addressing the scriptural theme of resurrection, conveys at a glance his obvious debt to Catholic works such as the Book of Hours in its layout and overall visual format. The *mise-en-page* includes, on the inner margin, classical acanthus designs as well as subtly inserted satyr-like grotesque foliated heads, here recalling the pre-Christian Western European "Green Man" symbolic of rebirth and regeneration,[6] in keeping with the stylized vertical vase motif signaling abundant efflorescence.

Before moving on to examine the focal images of these prayer book pages, however, it must be observed in passing that the visual *sprezzatura* of the sportive and seemingly insignificant depictions of natural and pagan elements serving what appears to be a purely decorative function in early modern books—including those with sacred and devotional aims—warrants much more critical attention than can be undertaken here. Suffice it to remark of the ubiquity of such grotesques interleaved with vegetative border designs, a typical and expected feature of Renaissance book production indebted both to manuscript illumination and also fueled by a long tradition of decorating transitional architectural spaces that was revivified in large measure owing to the rediscovery of Nero's *Domus Aurea* at the end of the 15th century, only that

> the gradual progress of grotesques, their evolution and censorship, and their defence and transformation within Renaissance art and thought acquires new potential perspectives through which to read this global artistic phenomenon that contributed to paving the way for a new phase of modernity.
>
> (Acciarino 2021, p. 51)

Compelling visuality of the Prayer Book 163

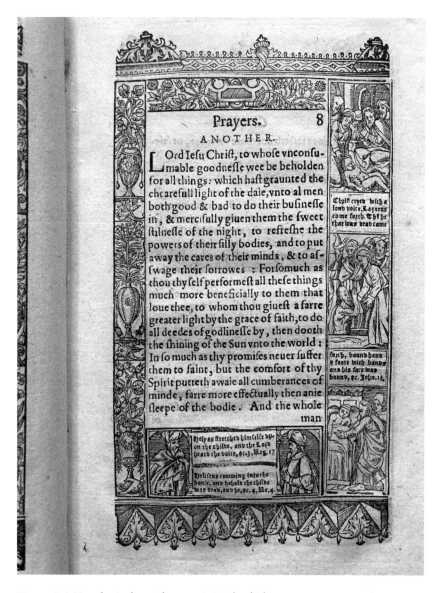

Figure 5.1 Typological page layout. *A Book of Christian Prayers* (London, 1608), sig. C4ʳ. Private collection. Photo credit © William E. Engel.

The central image of the religious iconographic program on this particular page (Figure 5.1) depicts Christ raising Lazarus from the dead (John 11:1-44), which, informed by the foreknown teleology of Christ's life-narrative, foreshadows his own glorious resurrection after being crucified and placed in the tomb (following a standard method of typological reading and biblical hermeneutics already discussed both in the Introduction and in Chapter 2 with reference to the catechism).[7] The subsidiary and complementary images from the Old Testament, above and below respectively, refer to Elijah's bringing back to life the widow's son (1 Kings 17:17-24) and Elisha's restoring life to the child whose birth he previously had prophesied (2 Kings 4:21-23). Both events prefigure Christ's resurrection in the New Testament and are tagged textually as such (in the bottom panel) so as to leave no doubt that these two Old Testament episodes are being singled out as proleptic memory images.[8]

Further typological and typographic analysis of just such groupings of biblical passages, as well as scripturally and doctrinally related mnemonic images represented as surrounding—or hemming in—the text, will be the primary focus of this chapter. The words and images Day selectively repurposed from his inherited brand of allegorical and tropological interpretation will be shown to relate always in some way to the basic issue—and problem—of redemption, and thus

> to the historical reality of the redeemer as its fixed center. All temporal change, all natural events and human action, obtain their light from this center; they become an ordered, meaningful cosmos by appearing as necessary links in the religious plan of salvation by taking a significant place in it. And from this one spiritual center the circle of interpretation gradually broadens.
> (Cassirer 1977b, p. 267)

Consistent with Cassirer's view of the mythic construction of "historical reality" taking "the redeemer as its fixed center"(1977b, p. 267), O'Keefe and Reno (2005) have explained how, historically (especially with regard to the Church Fathers), "Christ was the interpretive key" such that "the larger coherence of scripture was structured by the figure of Christ" and typological exegesis was used "to explore the larger coherence and describe the architecture of the text" so as to "develop a unified reading of the Old and New Testaments" that, in turn, "provided a means to bring Christian practice and experience into the structured economy of the scriptures, all drawing upon the central figure of Christ" (p. 69). Northrop Frye (1983) observes of this pattern of scriptural cross-referencing that "the two testaments form a double mirror, each reflecting the other" such that everything happening "in the Old Testament is a 'type' or adumbration of something that happens in the New Testament" (pp. 78–9). Banking on just such interpretive assumptions and replicating formally the shape and look of earlier expressions of devotional exercises, Day reclaims and reforms these old conventions of visuality in the service of giving Elizabeth's subjects new symbolic forms geared toward creating a uniform sense of purpose at once religious and nationalistic. The next section looks at how exactly he engineered and set in motion this triumph of English evangelical visuality.

Hemming in the text with memory images

As was demonstrated with reference to the emblems of *A Theatre for Worldings* in Chapter 4, Day did not erase or consign to oblivion the old imagery, but rather sought tacitly to overwrite and ascribe new sets of meanings to those same background mnemonics. In fact, this same creative and generative manipulation of imagery explicitly is recounted in Renaissance mnemotechnical treatises as being one of the key tactics for getting multiple uses out of a well-managed "artificial memory" scheme, which is to say, replacing a former set of images with new ones that then are slotted in sequence into the ready-made places or repositories (Engel et al. 2016, pp. 19–25). And in Day's case, the familiar old forms and myths were imbued with new associations all relating in some way to an evangelical view of God's all-encompassing salvific grace. A large number of people, some newly literate and some even learning to read using *Queen Elizabeth's Prayer Book*, thereby came to know these new associations as the basis for thinking about and practicing their faith in a reframed, reformed view of the truth of God's Word and of the divine scheme providentially prepared for humankind. Moreover, the next generation of English Protestants, those raised with these new associations and symbolic formations, no longer would need to make the substitutions of the old myths and images with the new.

In *Queen Elizabeth's Prayer Book*, Day takes as his focus—and subtly transforms—the quasi-narrative programs and boarder illustrations associated with the Catholic Book of Hours, Bible of the Poor, Mirror of Salvation, and Little Garden of the Soul, all of which had made the successful transition from manuscript to print culture.[9]

Regarding the latter (see Figure 5.2), this page taken from a cheaply produced Hortulus Animae (Little Garden of the Soul) includes border illustrations that follow an allegorical program independent of the text.[10] A grisly personification of cadaverous Death, with an hourglass balanced or held in place on its head symbolizing time's swift passage and the transitoriness of life, is cast here as a rather sinister looking reaper whose task is to harvest humanity. Below, in this vertical visual mini-narrative, a gentleman is heedless of the presence of Death just outside his field of vision. The well-dressed man, emblematized as being at the height of his powers, is oblivious to all that is taking place just above him from where he stands, self-satisfied, and, as he likely thinks, solidly grounded. We see what he cannot.[11] We see it all, the whole involved tableau and what it signifies—no text is required to convey the moral message. And so too from the margins of the book, readers are brought face to face as it were with the certain truth of mortal temporality, especially as regards how pride can blind us to what we should be heeding in the interest of incorporating into our own lives God's plan for redemption. This latter theme is reinforced by the folktale imagery of Chanticleer, a rooster enamored

Figure 5.2 Reaper *memento mori*. Little Garden of the Soul. *Hortul[us] Animae* (Mainz: J. Schöffer, 1514), fol. 147ʳ. Image used courtesy of the Newberry Library.

Compelling visuality of the Prayer Book   167

with his own crowing, and Reynard, the deceitful fox, depicted at the bottom of the page. This Aesopian analogue found its way deep into the pan-European literary imagination and was among the more popular works produced during the first age of print in England.[12] In effect then, in the margin as well as at the page-bottom, the overall Christian message of looking beyond the pride of life to higher spiritual matters comes through by diverse allegorical registers, both high and low, in easy-to-recognize emblematic tableaux.

The overall marginal program illustrated in this Hortulus Animae has other comparable iconographic reminders of the same *memento mori* motif by way of variations on the vanitas theme depicted on other pages.[13] One such typical vanitas vignette, for example, is featured at the top of a margin panel, as part of a sequence repeated throughout the volume (see Figure 5.3).

A woman gazes into a mirror, while below a decomposing body is egregiously represented, a jarring reminder of the inevitability of death. As such, it presents a kind of inverse mirror image of the same vain person but represented after the time of her projected future passing, thus symbolically and visually enacting what the motto *memento mori* imports, "remember you must die" (Engel 1995, pp. 77–80; Engel et al. 2022). Moreover, there is a larger allegory of visuality that is being played out here, one that was something of a metacritical commonplace of the age, namely, as our eyes stray from the prayers and guided meditations printed on the page containing serious devotional material, our attention wandering, we take in the picture of the vain woman looking at herself in the mirror and—metaphorically speaking—see ourselves reflected. This figurative *mise en abyme* involves our seeing the woman seeing a little face in the mirror looking back at her. In some ways, this experiential even performative way of reading the moral lesson in images, which incidentally sums the substance of many of the pious reflections recorded in this devotional manual, is even more effective in grabbing the viewer's attention. We do not need psychological studies to tell us that people's eyes reflexively tend to go to the pictures first before engaging with the words on the same page. The makers of manuscript and printed Books of Hours were attuned to this cognitive commonplace, and Day replicated it with the best equipment his printing house had to offer in making *Queen Elizabeth's Prayer Book*. Day's project thus fits well within the larger context of "a process of 're-forming' images" whereby "traditional religious iconography was exploited as a familiar channel through which to express the message of reform," essentially a "hijacking of traditional imagery, and associated manipulation of visual imagery," which was to become "an enduring form of Protestant propaganda" (Hamling 2020, p. 191).

Accordingly, I have singled out here the expressive images pertaining to the vanitas and *memento mori* themes found in earlier works to which Day's prayer book was visually and topically indebted because,

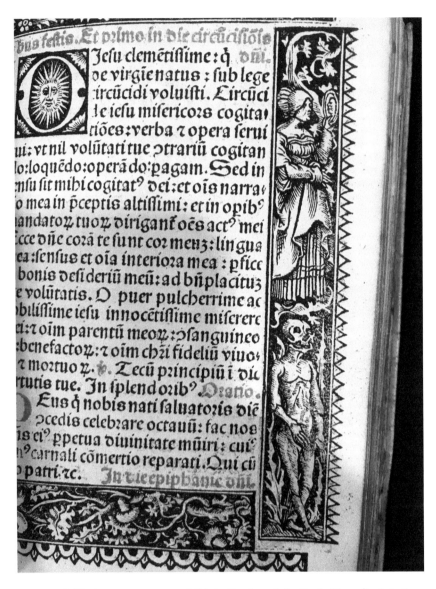

Figure 5.3 Vanitas *memento mori*. Little Garden of the Soul. *Hortul[us] Animae* (Mainz: J. Schöffer, 1514), fol.142ʳ. Image used courtesy of the Newberry Library.

as discussed in what follows, they will continue to play a persistent role in the underlying memorative and monitory messaging disclosed in his iconographic border-image program, culminating with the Apocalypse by way of a Protestant Dance of Death involving first men and then women. Davidson and Oosterwijk (2021) have provided ample precedents for seeing in their continental contexts how illuminations of the *Danse Macabre* functioned "as a decorative cycle" and "rapidly entered the visual repertoire" of "extant luxury books of hours" by the 1430s and, thereafter, "can be found as both a moralizing and decorative motif in the margins of other books of hours, particularly within the Office of the Dead, and it was especially used as such from the 1480s on by printers" (p. 58). The layout of such pages fully engages and makes much of the strategies associated with the typographical imaginary where memory is transformed from imagined, mental spaces to material physical spaces. Viewers thereby are induced to take in aspects of such compound emblems positioned along the page margins and, in effect, see themselves allegorically reflected. Vanitas and *memento mori* imagery act as spurs to motivate each person individually to reform by reminding them, once more, of the conditions of their ineluctable mortal temporality. The text alone should suffice, of course, to alert the reader of the precarity of one's mortal existence. And yet, since time immemorial, there has always been a nagging sense that images can convey in an instant, more immediately and directly, what we tend to lose sight of while reading words on a page. The prologue to the impressively illustrated *Ship of Fools*, one of the first truly trans-European popular books,[14] addresses this problematic straightaway with an account of why people need such insistent—and visually augmented—reminders:

> All lands in Holy Writ abound
> And works to save the soul are found,
> The Bible, Holy Fathers' lore
> And other such in goodly store,
> So many that I feel surprise
> To find men growing not more wise
> But holding writ and lore in spite.
> The whole world lives in darksome night,
> In blinded sinfulness persisting,
> While every street sees folks existing
> Who know but folly, to their shame,
> Yet will not own to folly's name.
> (Brandt 1944 [1497], p. 57)[15]

And so it was deemed important also to have this visual way of catching one's attention, unawares as it were, even and especially in a devotional work like the Hortulus Animae—or indeed in any of the comparable works that involve bimedially expressed messages intended for the betterment of one's spiritual condition. And these bimedial subgenres, to which Day's prayer book owes its amalgamated origins (the Book of Hours, Bible of the Poor, Mirror of Salvation, and Little Garden of the Soul), each in its own way, partakes of the principles associated with mnemonic bibles—along the lines discussed in Chapter 4 with special reference to the Book of Revelation expounded in a vision-driven emblem book. Each subgenre, following its own formal principles, is composed of carefully excerpted and thematically arranged images and descriptive textual extracts with the aim of serving devotional needs, whether private religious exercises (as with the Book of Hours and Little Garden of the Soul) or as handbooks initially for preaching and sermonic composition (the Bible of the Poor and Mirror of Salvation). Each provides users with "a readily applicable treasure trove of useful information, just as encyclopedias and commonplace collections did, with the significant difference of not having been written, but rather inculcated" (Kiss 2016, 23). Samuel Chew (1945) does not overstate the case when he contends that, as "a repository of traditional iconographical material," Day's prayer book "is unique among publications of the Elizabethan period" owing to its sheer copiousness (p. 293). In line with this 16th-century vogue for such collecting and compiling, exemplarily championed by Erasmus (as discussed in the Introduction), as Ann Moss (2002) has shown, "Renaissance authors speak the language of the commonplace-book" (p. 211). To this I would add that John Day, the printer as author, proves to be especially fluent in the language of commonplace mnemonic images of the period, transplanting into *Queen Elizabeth's Prayer Book* many flowers taken from many different gardens, consistent with Moss's view of Renaissance authors being "most visibly masters of their own creation when they assemble what they have gathered in patterns of their own devising" (p. 211).

By means of a veritable barrage of "tightly controlled illustrations" in *Queen Elizabeth's Prayer Book*, John Day was able to transform "the images of his borders from objects of reverence to reference" (Epstein 2021, p. 383 cf. Jørgensen 2018, p. 136). In this regard, the image "does not simply produce actions and reactions; it can also act" (Dekoninick 2017, p. 176). Toward this end, Day reshaped and edited the "visual content to suit the new religious and political reality" (Epstein 2021, p. 389), a process that both reflected and set the pace and tone for the incremental shifts in Tudor religious ideology and cultural identity. *Queen Elizabeth's Prayer Book* offers itself as an ideal case study for observing and commenting on how Day managed so effectively, copiously, and performatively to establish—and subtly to fix for future use—a new paradigmatic order of English Protestant iconography.[16] He compiled and made available a rich treasury of mnemonic images geared toward locating and presenting in a familiar way a host of doctrinally acceptable places to focus one's own religious practices, thereby reinforcing the foundation of English Protestant piety and belief.

In keeping with the through-thread of Day's evangelical agenda in all of his published works, *Queen Elizabeth's Prayer Book* enabled domestic devotional exercises to come further than ever before in defining a new kind of collective Protestant Memory Art in Tudor England.[17] Each person taking this book in hand gained access to a private window onto

Compelling visuality of the Prayer Book 171

the illustrated and glossed biblical stories, which omitted of course "the 'Romish' Miracles of Our Lady of the traditional French *Horae*" (Chew 1945, p. 294); panels depicting the performance of acts of "corporeal mercy," also changed somewhat from traditional Catholic expressions of the same (as discussed further below); allegorical personifications of virtues overcoming vices (Engel 2014, p. 25); and the revised Protestant sacraments, such as baptism (Epstein 2021, pp. 380–2), represented in the book's margins and page-footer vignettes (*A Book of Christian Prayers* 1578, sig. R1ᵛ). Individual consciousness thus coalesces with a shared communal consciousness, paving the way for—and reifying—a reformed religiously oriented collective memory that would take on nationalistic implications (see, for example, Figure 5.4, discussed below).

The compelling visuality of Day's newly adapted iconographic program supplied and repurposed imagery that was consistent with the most up-to-date developments in the doctrinal standards and curtailed ritual observances of the Elizabethan reformed Church.[18] The combined religious and aesthetic effect was to enrich private devotional practices in acceptable ways while at the same time contributing to, by helping mold and shape, a common experience among the faithful grounded in a series of shared memory images. Something similar can be seen to be at work in the books by Edmund Spenser (as treated in Chapter 4 with reference to *A Theatre for Worldings*), a comparable case being his *Shepheardes Calender* (1579), which "assembles medieval Catholic mnemonic systems together with classical hermetic mnemonics" such that "visual culture in Elizabethan Protestantism was not broken entirely but was reformed through the iconic centrality of the Elizabethan monarchy and its appeals to a British national consciousness" (Reid 2019, p. 92). Apropos of the assertion of "a British national consciousness" likewise at work in Day's prayer book, a few textual considerations will help bring out the conditions of possibility that inform the compelling visuality of *Queen Elizabeth's Prayer Book*.

First, the popular name for this work derives in part from the fact that an image of young Queen Elizabeth at prayer greets the reader upon opening the manual rather than, as had been the case with earlier Books of Hours of the Holy Virgin, an image of Mary, the mother of Jesus (Figure 5.4).[19] Second, a deluxe presentation copy intended for Elizabeth, with her portrait meticulously hand-colored in the style of earlier unique Books of Hours (see Figure 5.5),[20] uses the first person in the initial prayer, as well as in the "Prayer for wisdom to govern the realm" (sig. p2ᵛ–p4ᵛ).

Other unique press alterations in this copy include the Litany, "changing references to the Queen to the first person" (Harding 2010, p. 111). Likewise, the foreign language prayers (in French, Italian, Spanish, Greek, and Latin) are set in the first person, as if for the queen herself to recite aloud (Chew 1945, p. 293). Any given page in this section serves as a representative sample of the Latin part of the prayer book (Figure 5.6), like

172 *Compelling visuality of the* Prayer Book

Figure 5.4 Elizabeth at prayer. *A Book of Christian Prayers* (London, 1608), sig. ¶1ᵛ. Private collection. Photo credit © William E. Engel.

this one that happens to have border illustrations showing the end of the Dance of Death of men and the start of one of women, which includes a vignette of a queen as well as one lying in state at the page-bottom. Throughout, then, from first to last, the book is characterized especially as being linked to Queen Elizabeth.[21]

Compelling visuality of the Prayer Book 173

Figure 5.5 Elizabeth at prayer / prayer in first person. Hand colored presentation copy of *Christian Prayers and Meditations* (London: John Day, 1569). Image used courtesy of The Lambeth Palace Library.

It clearly had her approval for nationwide devotional use and was sanctioned for immediate circulation. In line with this, instead of including his own tell-tale *memento mori* printer's mark at the end *Christian Prayers and Meditations*, Day inserts a full-page image of Queen Elizabeth's royal coat of arms encircled by the Order of the Garter with the motto "*Honi soit qui mal y pense*" [Evil to those who evil think] associated with the quintessential medieval order of British knighthood dating back to the 1340s and of which the reigning monarch is the head (1569, sig. Qq2^r). Steadily, throughout her reign, Elizabeth went about adopting "the Garter device as her own" (Waddington 1993, p. 113). Further, her being linked to the most "distinguished and exclusive of the British chivalric orders" (p. 97) presented something of an "anomalous situation" with "a woman becoming the head of a male chivalric order," which, for Elizabeth, "stands as a microcosm of the problems and strategies of governing the nation itself" (p. 103). Thus, Day's prominent and public inclusion of the Garter belt and motto in the prayer book underscores his willing complicity in helping Elizabeth accede to the stature of being perceived as a puissant monarch in the style of her father, Henry VIII, thus implying (through the Garter association) a parallel between his

174 *Compelling visuality of the Prayer Book*

Figure 5.6 Dance of Death hemming in Latin prayers. Hand colored presentation copy of *Christian Prayers and Meditations* (London: John Day, 1569), sig. Oo2^v–Oo3^r. Image used courtesy of The Lambeth Palace Library.

sovereign mode of governance and church reform and hers. Apropos of which, she made several significant changes regarding how and to whom the Garter was bestowed, most notably instituting "Garter Feasts" held at Greenwich and later at Whitehall. "The change of venue made possible development of the Great Procession as another public spectacle, like the Accession Day Tilts, paying homage to the queen" further establishing her "dominance over the Order by changing the ceremony to her desire. As the ceremony was subject to alteration, so also could the history of the Order be rewritten" (Waddington 1993, pp. 107–8). The same held true for the Church of England, and Day used his press to bolster the reformed religious agenda under Elizabeth.

Most notably, the intimate frontispiece portrait (Figures 5.4 and 5.5) shows the sovereign in an unguarded moment of private piety, having set aside her crown to pray (Strong 2003, p. 56). This powerful visual statement, like the foreign language prayers (as in the presentation copy, Figure 5.6), and the overtly reformed content reinforce in a number of ways the connection of Elizabeth as the authoritative—if humbly portrayed—head of the Church of England (Epstein 2021, p. 370). Although more remains to be said, it is instructive at this stage in the

Compelling visuality of the Prayer Book   175

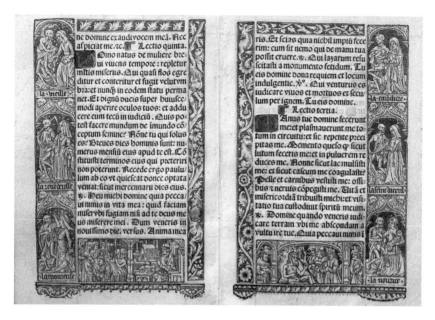

Figure 5.7 Dance of Death of Women. Book of Hours (Paris, c.1502). Loose page, printed on vellum. Private collection. Photo credit © William E. Engel.

analysis initially to compare this page from the Dance of Death of women to a comparable page from an earlier Northern French printed Book of Hours that circulated in England (see Figure 5.7) to notice and appreciate Day's acutely self-conscious imitation and strategic curation of this traditionally Catholic popular genre in his composition and production of *Queen Elizabeth's Prayer Book*.

The bimedial visual and narrative elements associated with the Dance of Death cycle can be seen to yield to Day's evangelical enterprise; for, in the end, the images, and especially that of the Queen in her piety, make the book as a whole "more Protestant, more transnational, and much more collective" (Shenk 2010 p. 35). Day thus successfully crafts and produces—indeed authors—what amounts to a "Protestant Book of Hours: a re-creation of a popular pre-Reformation format" (Harding 2010, p. 110). The commissioned pictures secured by John Day (and probably set in the press "forme"[22] by his son, Richard) have no direct correspondence to or bearing on the prayers printed on the pages on which they appear. The visual program thereby creates something of a separate book-within-the-book, serving as a devotional guide in its own right. And yet the illustrations, standing on their own, for all of their similarity in format to those in the Book of Hours (evident in Figure 5.7), do not serve the same essential function as they did in Roman Catholic devotional practices (Epstein 2021, p. 383). As already observed, Day literally manipulates the familiar mnemonic placeholders and cannily reassigns to them new visual referents, which are made all the more powerful because of their subtle link to and tacit supplanting of previous associations with Catholic daily use. Nora Epstein (2021) correctly points out that when we "contextualize the prayer books within Day's political network and print output, they appear particularly on-brand for this image-conscious book producer" (p. 362).

The overall composition of these two prayer books, *Christian Prayers and Meditations* (1569) and *A Book of Christian Prayers* (1578), "have too many textual and visual variations to be considered two editions of the same work"; and yet "their shared content and means of creation makes it imprudent to examine them in isolation" (Epstein 2021, p. 361). Owing to their overriding similarities, especially as regards the inclusion of mnemonic images in set sequences and the visual elements and distinctively Protestant iconographic depictions, which become more pronounced from 1569 to 1578, book historians and bibliographers traditionally refer to all five of the earliest editions of these two books collectively as *Queen Elizabeth's Prayer Book* (Chew 1945, p. 295).[23] And so while there are enough differences to warrant looking at these prayer books as two separate versions of a common ideational model, and given the decision to include Elizabeth's coat of arms with Garter belt in the first printing (1569) instead of his printer's mark, and notwithstanding the key role Day's son, Richard, played in improving the production of the 1578 version (Evenden and Freeman 2013, p. 258), the most compelling positive evidence that Day wanted to mark the 1578 prayer book as the product of his own ingenuity is the inclusion of his identifying *memento mori* colophon on the last leaf—with the advertisement about where the authorized book might now be purchased: "to be sold at his long shop at the west end of Paul's" (see again Figure 1.6). Within two years of its publication and circulation, Richard Day (whose inconsistent work had undermined his big break of supervising the 1576 third edition of *Acts and Monuments*) had left the printing trade in the wake of his stock and equipment being seized at his father's instigation and with the aid and approval of the wardens of the Stationers' Company.[24] Curiously, most bibliographers and rare book sellers still attribute the 1578 version to Richard.

At all events, these two versions of the prayer book (1569 and 1578), fundamentally similar in format, layout, and design (if differing occasionally in production decisions), are the only such examples of deluxe prayer books to appear in Elizabethan England (Chew 1945, p. 294). Insofar as the set of seven illustrated sequences hemming in the prayers (albeit varying somewhat in their ordering and in the number of times repeated from 1569 to 1578) do not serve as glosses or even accompaniments to the prayer-text, our focus will be on the visual elements of *Queen Elizabeth's Prayer Book*. Doing so will allow unfettered access to observe

John Day's comprehensive engagement with the typographical imaginary in his fabrication of a Protestant Memory Art. For, much like "the memory spaces of Spenser's *Calender*" (Reid 2019, p. 113), and like its late medieval predecessor, the almanac genre, frequently issued in the first age of English printing (Engel et al. 2022, entry I.2), Day's page layout in *Queen Elizabeth's Prayer Book* is an involved assemblage of visual images coupled with descriptive verbal tags that conform to the sanctioned Reformation wording. The prayer books (1569 and 1578, as well as subsequent reprintings, especially the 1608 version owing to the obvious care that was taken with the woodblock inking to get crisp and clean impressions), show every sign of being designed to guide—and, indeed, to train—readers to actively participate in the proper understanding of the imported meanings as iconographically and typologically presented for their consideration. Such a view is consonant with recent theoretical approaches to iconographic analysis, which take into account "the active life and performative agency" of imagery, whereby images are seen as not only representing but also doing things in the world, "as actors in social life, as mediators in social processes," intended "to change the world rather than merely to encode it" (Dekoninick 2017, p. 176).

Patterns of devotional reflection

Day's ingeniously arranged and crisply transferred border illustrations accompanying *Christian Prayers and Meditations* (1569), discussed in the previous section as a veritable book-within-the-book, constitute a series of well-thought-out visual narratives designed to reinforce distinctively Protestant themes notwithstanding their self-conscious imitation of pre-Reformation designs. Day's images on the margins sequentially trace stages in the trajectory of an individual's spiritual journey, implicating and involving viewers in a compelling visual narrative—along a discernable mnemotechnical track—wherein they see themselves and their inevitable end mirrored, thus making the whole a compelling and insistent reminder of what observant Protestants must do for the sake of their own salvation. In effect then, following the visual program (from memorable episodes in the life of Christ to the apocalyptic Four Last Things, immediately preceded by the socially relevant Dance of Death in which readers find themselves variously depicted by station, degree, and gender) is tantamount to undertaking a spiritual pilgrimage where the specific sites visited are not saint's tombs or relics but stages in one's own reformation. Although there are some variations in the order of the allegorical and iconographic designs from 1569 to 1608, all versions retain the same distinctive mode of border illustrations. The variable length of a visual sequence might well have been "determined not only by authorial and editorial dictate but also by the logistical demands of the printing process," owing to the casting off of pages (as was the case with the second edition of the *Book of Martyrs* discussed in Chapter 3) and "an unexpected need to add filler" such that the "aesthetics of the page" can help determine the resulting content, visual as well as textual (Evenden 2010, p. 90).

Seven distinct sequences constitute the overarching iconographic program of the border illustrations in *Queen Elizabeth's Prayer Book*—an orderly arrangement easily accommodated to one's own private Memory Theatre. Appropriately enough, given the Christological nature of this devotional text, the first sequence concerns the life of Christ, the primary "mythical figure" in Christianity, the "culture-hero, a bringer of light and salvation" (Cassirer 1977b, p. 204). Woodcut vignettes chronologically recount his miracles, teachings, passion, death, and resurrection. Then, second, we find a series of 22 Christian virtues personified as triumphing over their corresponding vices, with some variation to the number shown in later editions owing to exigencies of the printing process and paper supply (as mentioned above) and yet clearly also in some cases owing to doctrinal adjustments where, according to Epstein (2021), "we see Day's attempt to construct a new set of images to direct devotions and edify his readers" (p. 382). The third sequence in this seven-part iconographic program involves a series of images showing the acts of corporal mercy (derived from Matt. 25), but referred to here as "Charity," and supplemented with the occasional tag from an Old Testament prefiguration. Day unmistakably modifies the traditional Catholic list, cutting it from seven to six: "Charity feedeth the hungry," "Charity giveth drink to the thirsty," "Charity harboreth strangers," "Charity clotheth the naked," "Charity visiteth the sick," and "Charity visisteth prisoners" (1608, sig. T4^r–U3^r). The obvious omission from the Roman Catholic reckoning is the last, burying the dead. Even a hint of conjuring up this act might potentially awaken complicated responses from people still getting used to the Church of England's newly prescribed relationship of the living to the dead, which substantially redefined any duties owed to the departed.[25] As John S. Garrison (2018, p. 78) astutely has remarked in this regard: "Though the Reformation may have dismissed Purgatory, neither could its long history be elided nor its symbolic power assuage longing to connect with the dead." Correlatively, Peter Marshall (2002) observes of the demise of purgatory that it "must rank as one of the most audacious attempts at the restructuring of beliefs and values ever attempted in England, a kind of collective cultural de-programming" (p. 100). And Rory Loughnane (2022) points out that, following the Reformation, it became quite complicated how in fact the dead should be remembered and mourned. The fourth visual series features allegories of the five outward senses with edifying biblical mottoes. The final three sequences involve images pertaining to the Apocalypse, followed by the Dance of Death, first of men and then of women; and, lastly, a series depicting the four last things of Christian eschatology–death, judgment, heaven and hell.[26] Day confidently repurposes the same evocative image-clusters as those in its *ars praedicandi* predecessors, "depicting scenes that belonged more to the medieval than the Renaissance world, and perhaps the most striking and neatly executed borders to appear in an English book of this period" (Oastler 1975, p. 17).

Day's shrewd business sense in retaining old familiar textual forms, coupled with his unwavering promotion of evangelical principles in printing reformation-oriented books, led him to anticipate and hence to respond decisively to the need for a range of new Protestant texts with Elizabeth's accession (Evenden 2008, pp. 48–53). This was especially the case with works for domestic use, occasioned by the reintroduction of the Book of Common Prayer in 1559 (Cummings 2011, pp. xxxiv–xxxvi). Thomas Cranmer's 1552 prayer book was restored in connection with a revived Act of Uniformity (passed in 1559) which, among other allowances, sanctioned belief in the real presence of Christ in the Eucharist (Clegg 2016, pp. 94–8; cf. Marshall 2009, pp. 581–5). This iteration of the Act of Uniformity, which laid the groundwork for modifications in liturgical practices, in conjunction with the Elizabethan Act of Supremacy, set in train "the visual architectural transformation of churches across England from a Catholic to a more Protestant appearance" (Reid 2019, p. 92).[27] And Day's main models informing his realization in print of this transformation, in line with the typographical imaginary discussed above, were manuals designed as visual and mnemonic aids for individual spiritual exercises though still reminiscent of earlier texts used by those preaching God's Word who needed access to descriptive scriptural points of reference (Figure 5.8).

For example, in this typical page from a late-15th-century *Bible of the Poor*, the partitioned-off visual tableaux evoke memory images associated with the scriptural theme of providential and temporary confinement as part of God's plan: Joseph imprisoned in the well by his brothers to be sold to slavers (Gen. 37:12) and Jonah cast from the ship to the awaiting great fish (Jon. 1:15). Both episodes typologically anticipate Christ's entombment (Matt. 27:60), thus constituting one of the many such trios of linked memory images that Day transplants into the border narrative of the life of Christ (1608, sig. L1^v).[28]

Such an arrangement historically provided ready material for sermons and, in Day's prayer books, for devout contemplation of God's plan replete with a clear indication of the penitent's place within it. Consistent with the literary and rhetorical principles of biblical typology,[29] the illustrations show how past events divinely foreshadow future ones. Key moments in the linear narrative of Christian teleology explicitly are on display, while readers implicitly become attuned to a pervasive sense of providence guiding the movements in their own lives as well. Day's seven-fold program of pictorial elements clearly if selectively draws on and uses many aspects of the traditional Art of Memory, especially as the images are arranged in designated sequences and situated in clearly defined and uncluttered spaces (or *loci*) each with its own narrative integrity. Day's reform-oriented readers thus are furnished with a mnemonic itinerary,

180 *Compelling visuality of the* Prayer Book

Figure 5.8 Entombment typology. Biblia Pauperum. (*c.*1495). Loose page. Private collection. Photo credit © William E. Engel.

in many ways reminiscent of portable devotional objects such as ivory diptychs recounting the passion and resurrection of Christ in a series of partitioned set-scenes (Pentcheva 2020, pp. 267–73).

Perhaps more so than other mnemonic images, those that involve Christ's death, entombment, and resurrection provide especially poignant opportunities for reflection not only on God's plan for human redemption but also on individual stock-taking as regards one's own mortal temporality. As Elizabeth Morrison (2017) has pointed out in this regard, "narrative, both textual and visual, could serve as an especially efficacious method to impress on the reader that death was always both just around the corner and inevitable," and, furthermore, "books became in and of themselves active intercessors on the behalf of those who read them" (p. 94). Whereas earlier Books of Hours foreground prayers for the dead, the Office of the Dead section is noticeably absent from every version of *Queen Elizabeth's Prayer Book*. Moreover, Day's visual sequences that call death to mind absolutely eschew any lingering intimations of imagery relating to supernumerary clergy at the bedside of the dying, monks, paid mourners, priest performing the Mass of the Dead, and other remnants of Catholic ritual observances. Instead, consistent with the evangelical reliance on scripture alone (as discussed in Chapters 2 and 3), Day's commissioned illustrations are all grounded securely in biblical treatments of the death and resurrection of Christ situated with respect to—and in visual dialogue with—Old Testament typological prefiguration (Figure 5.9); and, where the Dance of Death is concerned, Day makes good use of the pan-European popular tradition after the fashion of acceptable Protestant imagery recalling works by Albrecht Dürer and especially by Hans Holbein, the Younger (see again Figure 5.6).[30]

The resurrection takes on special emphasis in "The Order for the Burial of the Dead" in Cranmer's revised Book of Common Prayer, a work foremost in Day's mind as he set about figuring out how best to illustrate *Queen Elizabeth's Prayer Book*. Cranmer's 1549 text includes petitions and supplications for the dead, but these are omitted in the 1552 printing never again to be seen in any of the later editions (Engel et al. 2022, entry II.2). What does remain, though, are the words of Christ, typologically bolstered by the Old Testament references to Job interwoven with those mainly from the Gospel of John and with chapter and verse indicated in the margin. What remains, consistent with Cassirer's contention about the reality of the redeemer as the fixed center, is the emphasis on the truth and trans-temporality of a living redeemer.

> I am the resurrection and the life (sayeth the Lord), he that believeth in me: yea, though he were dead, yet shall he live. And whosoever liveth, and believeth in me: shall not die forever. I know that my redeemer liveth, and that I shall rise out of the earth in the last day, and shall be covered again with my skin, and shall see God in my flesh: yea, and I, myself, shall behold him, not with other but with these same eyes. We brought nothing into this world, neither may we carry anything out of this world. The Lord giveth, and the Lord taketh away. Even as it pleaseth the Lord, so cometh things to pass: blessed be the name of the Lord.
>
> (1552, sig, X1ʳ)

182 *Compelling visuality of the* Prayer Book

Figure 5.9 Resurrection typology. *A Book of Christian Prayers* (London, 1608), sig. L2ᵛ. Private collection. Photo credit © William E. Engel.

The images that Day selected for his page illustrating the resurrection in the life of Christ sequence all serve to advance a reformed religious view of looking toward the afterlife in sure and certain faith rather than in terms of anything one must do for the dead (Figure 5.9). The center image shows Christ arisen from his tomb. The identifying scriptural tags positioned above and below the image come from Matthew 28:4-5:

Compelling visuality of the Prayer Book   183

"And for fear of him, the keepers were astonied, & became as dead men. But the Angel [answered, and] said to the women: fear ye not, for I know that ye seek &." (1608, sig. L2ᵛ). The ampersand ("&"), like the truncated biblical reference clarifying the situation depicted in the image, is intended to set up or cue the recall of the rest, namely, "Jesus which was crucified" (Geneva Bible 1560, DD4ᵛ).[31] This identifying trigger, as with all other such scriptural memory traces throughout the seven discrete iconographic sequences, derives ultimately from Tyndale's translation, which can be found, among other places, in the Matthew Bible that Day produced in 1551 (Chapter 3, n1; see again Figure 1.3), and which parallels all subsequent reformed translations especially the Geneva Bible (Daniell 2003, pp. 299–301). Day retains the wording of this evangelical account of the resurrected Christ, which can be noted especially in the choice of the word "keepers" (those keeping watch over the burial place) rather than "guards," and the use of the preterit form of the verb "astonied," meaning astonished and connoting to be stunned, from the Old French *estoner*. The latter perhaps carries along within it a bilingual pun on the sense of being dazed by an unexpected loud noise, like a clap of thunder. For, in the passage leading up to this one, after all: "there was a great earthquake: for the Angel of the Lord descended from heaven, and came and rolled back the stone from the door, and sat upon it. And his countenance was like lightning" (Matt. 28:2-3). At all events, this snippet of the verse is enough to signal—and mnemotechnically to trigger—the recollection of what precedes and what follows this scriptural explanation of the image presented.

As for the images themselves, much is achieved by Day's first-rate sculptor commissioned to create this woodblock as well as many others in *Queen Elizabeth's Prayer Book*, known to us only as "CI" (see again Figure 5.9, this monogram appears as if incised in the recessed arched space of the tomb to the left of the dazed keeper's leg).[32] The tomb keeper's armor is in the style of what Elizabethans generally imagined a Roman guard would wear. He is slumped over, as though dead—again, a clever if oblique allusion to Jesus's resurrection for he is arising from the dead to make it possible for the faithful to live eternally and hence not be utterly subjected to death. Moreover, the guard is situated at the most extreme lower right of the inset panel, such that the physical limits of the woodblock create a kind of *trompe l'oeil* wall supporting his buckled over body. Likewise, the bottom of that same panel provides a convenient floor to set the lower boundary of the tableau. What the philosopher of aesthetics, Jean-Luc Marion (2004), has said of Dürer's painting *The Virgin of Autun*, can be instructively applied to this tableau as well, namely, that it is "only partially governed by the organizing principle of perspective, which must acknowledge an irreducible margin—the forestage [*l'avant scène*]" such that "perspective clearly acts as a distinct limit of the visible, in accordance with a marked boundary that demands it, or better, excludes it; [...] perspective itself is invisible" (pp. 8–9). The overall effect of this representation of the keeper being pushed to the limit of what one can see in the panel and the triumphant Christ looming large so as to fill the visible space, is reminiscent in both composition and theme of the allegorical portraits of Protestant Christian virtues in the second sequence of the overall iconographic program. In this regard, especially, it calls to mind the figure of "Industry" standing—as if in triumph—over its corresponding opposite, the vice of "Sloth" (see Figure 5.10, left page).

The mottos assigned to each collaborate to convey a message regarding how to make the most of one's time in the world: "Industry gathereth reward. / Sloth bringeth sleep." (sig. S3^v). In the resurrection panel (Figure 5.9), Christ stands ready to undertake what amounts to superhuman feats in his tropological role as savior and redeemer who will conquer Death, while the guard, like the lazy ass, is as one dead. He is figured as being utterly oblivious to the unfolding of divine history going on right in front of him, reminiscent of another of the vices in Day's pictorial sequence, "Oblivion," which "is as a grave" (see again Figure 5.10, bottom right), set in opposition to—and being overcome by—Memory, which is "a treasure house."[33]

The Old Testament typological figures of the resurrection border images again represent Jonah (Figure 5.9; cf. Figure 5.8). But here, in this tableau concerning the theme of liberation, unlike in the previous

Figure 5.10 Industry over Sloth/Memory over Oblivion. *A Book of Christian Prayers* (London, 1608), sig. S4^v–S5^r. Private collection. Photo credit © William E. Engel.

page concerning imprisonment with an image of Jonah tossed to the great fish (a ghastly, and therefore quite memorable, sea creature with jaws wide open to receive him, strikingly reminiscent of traditional medieval depictions of the gaping maw of Hell-mouth), he is depicted glancing back at the peril he has just escaped owing to God's salvific aid. His hands are joined in an immemorial gesture of prayer, emblematic of gratitude for his deliverance.[34] Seen through a Protestant lens, the message is clear: it is though God's grace alone and not by his own merits that he has been redeemed. The parable of Jonah thus becomes in Day's prayer book a visual text affirming that there is nothing we can do to earn God's grace, for it is not by works but by faith alone that we are saved (Rom. 3:21-28). The scriptural gloss at the bottom of the page leaves no doubt that deliverance—which is to say, redemption—is the Lord's doing, just as God had prepared the fish to swallow Jonah in the first place: "And the Lord spake unto the fish, and it cast out Jonas, &." (Jon. 2:10). The overall architectural disposition of the page follows the format of the earlier Catholic Biblia Pauperum (Figure 5.8), with panels at the bottom divided into two compartments, which include scriptural verses referring to and identifying the images. Closely following the earlier block book designs, Day's border panels at the bottom of the page (Figure 5.9) disclose the commonplace scriptural links for the reader, serving as proof texts mutually validating the truth of the Christian message and also providing viewers with a mnemonic network of interlaced meanings aimed at stimulating further pious contemplation.

Specifically, the turbaned, stereotypical oriental-Hebraic figure (bottom left),[35] in a gesture of explication, relates the words from the book of the Old Testament prophet Jonah. The figure on the right, with a stern countenance and wearing a pointed hat associated with Jews in the later Middle Ages well into the 17th century, represents the Old Law.[36] He points the reader to the uppermost quotation, which corresponds to and identifies the top-most vignette encapsulating a key moment in the Samson saga when, once again, he avoids certain death by outsmarting his adversaries, this time getting the better of the people of Gaza who "decided to kill him at sunrise" (Judg. 16.2) by breaking out of the place where he had been confined: "Samson rose at midnight and took the doors, &." (sig. L2^v). This scriptural tag, combined with the image of a man displaying a feat of superhuman physical strength, is trigger enough for readers to understand the typological foreshadowing of Christ symbolic breaking the bonds of the tomb, rising up, and overcoming death. Each Old Testament vignette foreshadows the comparable event in the life of Christ (in this case, his resurrection), with the appropriate verse above and below that focal image to consolidate the intended Christian meaning.[37] As with all such pages in the life of Christ series, Jesus is given the central place in the margin-image triad, flanked above and below by typologically resonant images paralleling and visually reinforcing his place as *the central figure* in the story of humankind's redemption.[38] Such typological imaginary, for Christians, treats the Old and New Testament as mirrors facing each other, "each reflecting the other but neither the world outside" (Frye 1983, p. 79). In every way possible, Day's page layout gives centrality and priority to the New Testament scene, which the other two passages presage and anticipate. This closed-circuit modality of hermeneutic biblical elucidation provides visual cues for recalling the scriptural evidence of the fulfillment of God's plan played out through events in human history, culminating with the crucifixion, death, and resurrection of Christ. It supplies viewers with a series of memorable images and biblical passages, the recollection of any one of which cues the others, creating a network of glosses, exegetical interpretations, and doctrinal tenets seen now, in *Queen Elizabeth's Prayer Book*, through a distinctively Protestant lens.

Another parallel to Christ's resurrection is the temporary Triumph of Death, which, as discussed above, is a necessary part of God's plan for mankind's redemption. Instead of being just a typological foreshadowing, though, it is viewed as a dynamic and essential aspect of everyone's bid for redemption. Hence the extended and episodic *memento mori* sequence of the Dance of Death in the *Book of Christian Prayers* conforms, as we have seen, to the decorum of earlier such border decorations in devotional texts like the Books of Hours (see again Figure 5.7), but of course without the traditional Office for the Dead. Instead, these dynamically depicted cameos of people being yanked out of everyday life are made all the more compelling and hence easy to recall by virtue of the presence of these unsettling, surreal animated cadavers or *morts*, so-called in England drawing on the spry figure populating the French *danses macabres* found on church walls, cemetery murals, and eventually in block books (Gertsman 2010; Rublack 2017 Davidson and Oosterwijk 2021).

These woodcuts, possibly executed by Marcus Gheeraerts, derive their affective power from grisly visual parody, insofar as the viewer is confronted with personified images of death based on, as traditionally they are, the decay and decomposition of the human form.[39] Viewers see an arresting mirror image of themselves after death. The living thus are *mocked*, in every sense of the term, by the dead (see again Figure 5.6). The disturbing combination of allegorical—which is to say symbolic and mythic—imagery cutting into a domestic scene of quotidian tranquility produces a jarring effect. The perspective presented thus brings out the paradox that inheres in any visual presentation of what is visible, set in relief by the invisible—by what is outside the perceptible field of vision but present before our gaze nonetheless (Marion 2004, pp. 2–12). The last panel in the Dance of Death of men shows a *mort* taking a cradle-bound child by the wrist, ready to convey the infant from this world to the next: "Fear not me: / though I grisly be." Its shroud flaps dramatically in an unseen wind suggesting movement and haste. The iconographic attribute of a scythe, a tool for reaping, harkens to the sickle of Chronos, or Saturn, and is associated with the immemorial symbolic figure of

Father Time (Panofsky 1972, pp. 27–54). The words attributed to this animated skeleton sent to usher this infant away from life, in compliance with the divine plan, eerily are reminiscent of the words angels use when delivering a message from God: "Fear not me."[40] In the scriptural passage accompanying the resurrection panel (Figure 5.9), thus calling it back to the reader's mind, we read: "And for fear of him, the keepers were astonied, and became as dead men. But the Angel answered, and said to the women, *Fear ye not*: for I know that ye seek Jesus which was crucified" (Matt. 28:4-5) [emphasis added]. This is another indicator, marked by scriptural syntax—as a phonetic image (to recall the epigraph to this chapter)—that sets up an expectation that this mythic figure is an emissary or attribute God.[41] This *mort* in the Dance of Death then, like the angel at Christ's tomb, simply is carrying out God's work in the world. When the more encompassing scheme for redemption that God has set in motion for humankind is recalled by the faithful Christian, fear turns to comfort.

But still, the gesture of comfort and companionability remains somewhat troubling, existentially at least, in the Dance of Death sequence (see Figure 5.6). In the upper panel, for example, a *mort* familiarly—with the nonchalance of old friend—puts its arm around a well-dressed, ostensibly prosperous, young man, drawing him closer with the words: "Young and old, / Come to my fold" (1569, sig. Oo2^v). It is both a direct statement and an invitation that cannot be refused. And the panel at the bottom of the page recalls the transi tombs, where a sculpture on top of the sepulchre represents what the body enclosed within is in the process of becoming. As such, it presents a grim marmoreal mirror of mortality showing for all the world to see what the grave hides from view (Cohen 1973). But there is a hint in this representation that it is the *real thing*, the thing itself, and not a work of art being depicted; namely, a corpse recently placed on top of a tomb (cf. Figure 1.6). What starts out for the viewer as a typical *trompe l'oeil* image of a sculpted tomb figure of a corpse in short order reveals a visual touch of lingering life by virtue of the flowing hair—which the colorist painstakingly has highlighted (Figure 5.6). The burial shroud tousles open to reveal a figure showing only minimal signs of its imminent and ineluctable decomposition thereby making it seem in some ways *closer* to the viewer than would a skeleton or transi tomb: "Time to live, and time to die: God grant us life, eternally."

This same verse motto, though with a different image, makes the rounds in filling out the panels at the page-bottoms in the Dance of Death sequence (Figure 5.11).

The easy portability and apparent interchangeability of words applied to images in the more general expressions of *memento mori* accompanying the orderly Dances of Death sequence, while perhaps simply a result of printing house exigencies and last-minute production decisions, nonetheless provides for different yet still edifying ways for the viewer to attend to particularity amid the sameness of the recurring pattern. Moreover, this

188 *Compelling visuality of the* Prayer Book

Figure 5.11 Death visits Youth and Infant. *A Book of Christian Prayers* (London, 1608), sig. Gg4ᵛ. Private collection. Photo credit © William E. Engel.

woodcut of two men depicted as if pausing to remark on the tomb bears an unmistakable resemblance to John Day's *memento mori* colophon (Figure 1.6). As with Day's printer's mark, one viewer appears older than the other, an analogue to the relationship of the Master and Scholar as showcased in *The Cosmographical Glass* with Philonicus and Spaudaeus, and as marking the dialogic form of the Catechism with the Master and

Scholar (discussed in Chapters 1 and 2 respectively). The lesson being read and recited at the bottom of this page, however (Figure 5.11), concerns what is to be done quite literally in the face of death. The metaphorical text, as it were, consists visually of the mixed up remains of those now deceased thereby reinforcing the overriding and redundant theme of the erasure of individuality in death. Furthermore, the image of these two visitors at the tomb creates what amounts to a visual intertext with the other *memento mori* mottos in the prayer book such as, especially (as was seen in the panel titled "Of youth"), Death's implacable decree: "Young and old / Come to my fold" (see again Figure 5.6). The bearded, older man (coded as the more experienced and hence wiser of the two) points to the image, directing the youth's attention to something worthy of contemplation (Figure 5.11).[42] This indexical finger, like the pointing hands found in commonplace books marking a passage to be singled out for future remembrance (Hunter, 1951, pp. 171–5), also directs the reader's gaze to the motto that declares the meaning of the tomb—as well as of the entire visual assemblage on the page, and indeed of the entire Dance of Death sequence: "Time to live, and time to die: / God grant us live eternally" (1608, sig. Gg4^v).[43] These might well be words the older man says to instruct the younger, as the youth's hand is brought to his heart in a gesture signaling "What, me too?"; and, moreover, it also carries with it the gestural connotation of "this then I shall take to heart." The whole vignette in effect is a visual rendition of the classical expression of "*tu fui, ego eris,*" poetically rendered in English as the commonplace epitaph: "Pause stranger, when you pass me by, / *As you are now, so once was I.* / *As I am now, so you will be,* / So prepare for death and follow me" [emphasis added].[44] It also shows up as one of the verse mottos used in several of the page-bottom panels in the Dance of Death sequence, among other variations, the one depicting a lady and gentleman regarding a dead body (or perhaps a marmoreal effigy) atop a coffin bearing the epitaph "Behold the Squire as in a glass: / For as thou art so he was" (1608, sig. Kk3^r). The same formula is echoed in the words of a *mort* in the Dance of Death summoning a queen (see again Figure 5.6, recto page, bottom right): "Queen also thou dost see / As I am so shalt thou be").

What the old and young man behold atop the coffin, however (Figure 5.11), is not a tidy sepulchre. Rather, it is a jumbled grab-bag of *memento mori* symbols: a skeleton atop the tomb, a skull, some crossed bones, and a corpse tied up in a winding sheet—and the latter, as we have seen elsewhere in *Queen Elizabeth's Prayer Book*, is a familiar visual trope signifying "Oblivion" (Figure 5.10, sig. S5^r). The same motif of scattered human remains is picked up directly to the right of this panel in the purely decorative border design (Figure 5.11, bottom right). Heaped up fleshless bones, some of the skulls with empty eye sockets eerily looking out to the viewer, recall the charnel house where remains were stored when removed from the cemetery's hallowed ground to make room for new graves (Harding 2002, pp. 91–4). Further, the decorative

190 *Compelling visuality of the* Prayer Book

panels in the Dance of Death sequence in *A Book of Christian Prayers* (1578 and 1608) take on a decidedly more macabre ornamental accompaniment than the earlier 1569 *Christian Prayers and Meditations* (see, for example, Figure 5.6, verso page, right margin and top panel) with its fruited floral display, signifying growth and rebirth, along with classical visual tropes like a satyr's backside, Panesque statuary visage, stretched-out horned zoomorphic skull, and at the top of the page, a stylized ox skull. In later editions, exemplarily the 1608 printing (Figure 5.11, top right), the uppermost ornamental figure on the right margin presents viewers with an uncannily erect *mort* appearing as if vertically encoffined by virtue of the close-cropped panel design. With its rich head of hair and sturdy muscular legs, it looks more alive than dead, but still unmistakably a representation of one who is dead—"*tu fui, ego eris.*"[45]

Each of the central panels at the page-bottoms in the Dance of Death sequence may have variable and different rhyming admonishments, but all are concerned with conveying the same moral theme about human transience. In effect then, notwithstanding the repetitions and variations on the same theme play out in different configurations of word and image, the unfolding of the visual narrative of the Dance of Death sequence presents an allegory of life as a journey. But it is a composite one, as it were, enfolding all humankind, beginning with those at the very peak of the proverbial wheel of fortune, "The Emperor" and "The King," and then moving steadily down through the social stations. And so this progression is also figured as digression in its implicit simulation of movement, collectively, back in time—and memory. As with Ernst Haeckel's summary formula "ontogeny recapitulates phylogeny," viewers end up seeing their common origins paralleled in their common end, arriving finally at the panels "Of Youth" and "Of Infancy," which brings to a close the Dance of Death sequence of men (see Figure 5.6). Comparably, the Dance of Death of women, beginning with "The Empress" and "The Queen," ends with "The Infant" and "The fool" bereft of her sense and in effect oblivious to all around her including the *mort* (1608, sig. Ii3ᵛ). Along the way, viewers find themselves mirrored more particularly somewhere in that parade of humanity—a stirring reminder of what should be of paramount concern to all but which, in the bustle of daily life, tends most to be forgotten.

The repetition with a difference (the constant being the *mort* in each narrative panel) within this affectively presented iconographic sequence has an additional perhaps unexpected effect on the viewer. It is brought about owing to the shifting around of panels used for the page-bottoms and the trading out of the essentially decorative margin designs without verbal tags. The composite visual components thereby provide a slightly different look from what one already has seen in typical Dances of Death by affording a subtle glimpse of recognition—albeit with a difference—of the overarching focal message of the whole work, seen now in a new light and from a new, more encompassing perspective. Perhaps nowhere is this more evident—and metacognitively poignant—than in the panels stacked

Compelling visuality of the Prayer Book 191

one atop the other dedicated to "The Compositor" ("Leave setting thy page: spent is thine age") and "The Pressman" ("let printing stay: and come away") (Figure 5.12).

Compositors and pressmen make their livings keeping such words and images in circulation, and here are shown being pulled away from setting the very printed pages that make such representations of Death's message possible for readers to see and take to heart. Their going off to join Death's dance quite literally implies stopping the presses. But, of course, the message of the Dance of Death here *is* conveyed—the book manages to make it through the press process and now become part of the reader's experience in preparing for a good death. The same subtle and very personal engagement with the text is reinforced by other means in the central panel at the bottom of the page where readers find a recurring and familiar reminder of mortal temporality (discussed above) in the symbolic form of a woman's corpse atop a tomb. But here, in this particular printing, unlike the 1578 hand-colored version (Figure 5.6), it is all of one tone, white, the color of dried bone—and of paper. Moreover, the verse motto self-referentially looks to the end of all book production, in both senses of the word "end," meaning at once the aim or goal of printing and also its termination: "We printers wrote with wisdom's pen: / She lives for aye, we die as men" (1608, sig. Gg1^v).

The right-margin decorative border (which is to say the nonnarrative visual elements) on this page is a repetition of what was seen on one of the previously discussed pages, the jumble of skulls and bones below and the freestanding lively corpse with bushy hair (Figure 5.11). This feature, combined with the presence of the figure of death in the printshop on the left margin, calls attention to the transitoriness of things of this world— and, in this case, of the very means of production making possible the use of the prayer book.[46] As with Day himself being brought into the narrative flow of the *Book of Martyrs* (as discussed in Chapter 3 in connection with Foxe's encomium to the printing press and its place in God's providential plan involving the advent of Protestantism), here the viewer encounters a visual simulacrum, or virtual stand in, for Day's own base of operations and livelihood. The necessary machinery and tools associated with book publishing, including the compositor's stand and letter cases, press, and ink daubers (the latter held by the worker beside the pressman) come together to establish an indelible mnemonic place of invention that subtly causes the user of the prayer book to reflect on the material basis and physical conditions of how it has come about that they in fact are able to engage with this book of private devotional exercises. As with the Protestant emblems discussed in Chapter 4, the larger spiritual aim here is to look beyond the image—beyond that which is given to be seen—in order to apprehend the invisible, that which cannot be seen but which must be taken on faith.[47] After the fashion of the Protestant emblems that Day produced in *A Theatre*, here in *Queen Elizabeth's Prayer Book*—and exemplarily with the Dance of Death sequence involving people in the

192 *Compelling visuality of the* Prayer Book

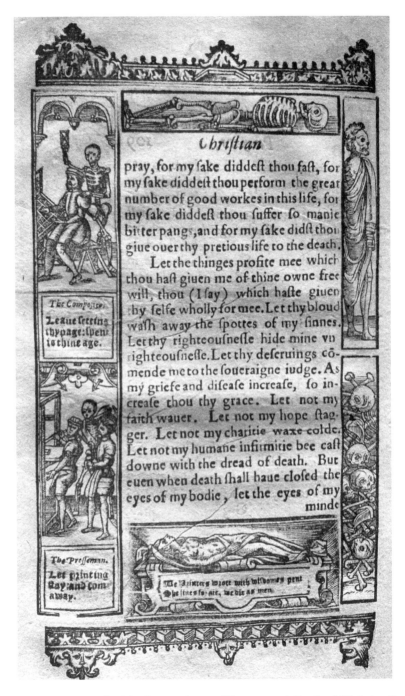

Figure 5.12 Death visits Compositor and Pressman. *A Book of Christian Prayers* (London, 1608), sig. Gg1ᵛ. Private collection. Photo credit © William E. Engel.

print shop having their work symbolically halted by death—he makes good on his life's work of reforming "the inherited images of medieval Catholicism," including the *Danse Macabre*, "internalizing and personalizing them, altering forever the person's relation to them" (Diehl 1986, p. 66). As a new take on *memento mori* symbolism evoking both the personal remembrance of death as well as the end of printing, Day's commissioned Dance of Death makes viewers mindful of their own end in a variety of self-referential and self-reflective ways, impelling them to make timely provision for a good death with the assistance of *Queen Elizabeth's Prayer Book*—no priest required. The book is one's intercessor. As such, this book serves as another stunning example of the way Day helped contribute to the creation, fixing, and setting in place of the framework for a Protestant Memory Art in Reformation England.

The circulation and transfer of memorable matter

By way of a coda, and thereby resuming the main mnemotechnical argument of both Chapter 5 and indeed this book as a whole, I would call attention to a series of hand-drawn images copied directly from the Dance of Death sequence and signs of Apocalypse in *Queen Elizabeth's Prayer Book* (Figures 5.13 and 5.14).

The pen-and-in blocks of linked panels headed "The triumph of death over all estates" and "Signs before the day of judgment" appear in a masterly maintained commonplace book kept by William Burch for his employer, Thomas Nettleton.[48] The entire work is descriptively titled: *A book of drawing of the shapes and forms of divers beasts, fowls, birds, fishes, monsters, serpents, trees, herbs, plants, and flowers with diverse accidents of antiquities, and armory.* Clearly, the Dance of Death and the cataclysmic End Times caught the attention of Nettleton, who had them copied out by Burch in the order they originally appeared in their respective iconographic sequences in Day's prayer book but arranged in a format appropriate to pages in a principally visual commonplace book. The same *memento mori* theme involving the resurrection is captured elsewhere in Burch's drawings (f. 142ʳ), including a serviceable rendering from the exceedingly popular and much-circulating "Imago Mortis" from the *Nuremburg Chronicles* (Figure 5.15).

The Dance of Death taken from *Queen Elizabeth's Prayer Book* had special appeal perhaps because of its easy portability to another medium. Arranged in this transposed layout that privileges the visual elements, the viewer is confronted more directly by the particularities of each recognizable type, one after another, without needing to turn so many pages to take in the visual program.

For example, on the lower tiers on Burch's page concerning authorities who must submit to Death's summons (Figure 5.16), the sergeant, attorney, mayor, sheriff, bailiff, constable, physician, and astronomer, all are treated equally by the *morts,* without regard to professional status

194 *Compelling visuality of the* Prayer Book

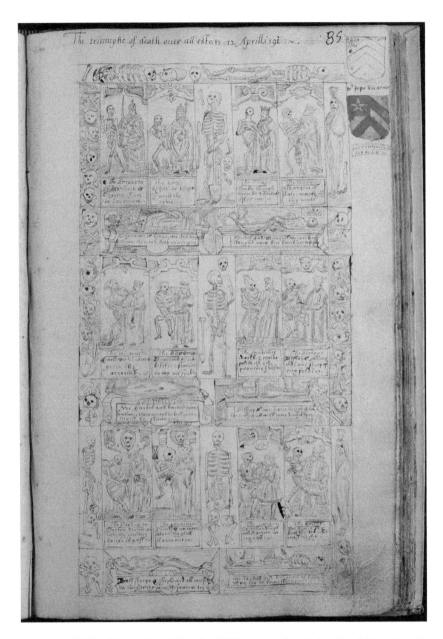

Figure 5.13 The Triumph of Death. William Burch, *A Book of Drawing* (*c.* 1590), fol. 85ʳ. Canterbury Cathedral Archives (Lit Ms/A/14). Image used courtesy of Canterbury Cathedral Archives.

Compelling visuality of the Prayer Book 195

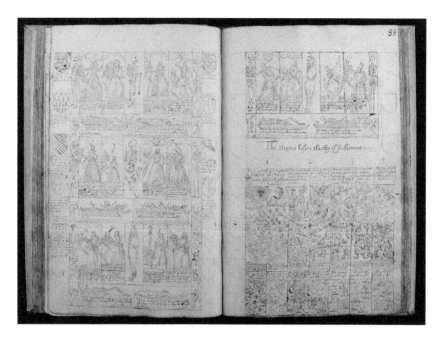

Figure 5.14 Day of Judgment. William Burch, *A Book of Drawing* (*c.* 1590), fol. 88ʳ. Canterbury, Cathedral Archives (Lit Ms/A/14). Image used courtesy of Canterbury Cathedral Archives.

except to taunt them with identifying attributes of their respective duties or trades—such as the physician's flask of urine held aloft as he is wryly told that death is the only cure for mortality. Owing to this feature of the Dance of Death, these images speak directly and simply to whoever looks at them. Burch shows an obvious interest in the Dance of Death and Signs before the Day of Judgment sequences, arguably Day's most arresting and compelling border images. For, other than the six acts of corporal charity (fol. 88v), none of the other sequences from *Queen Elizabeth's Prayer Book* are culled for this commonplace book. The images however that he does collect and arrange in a tight, orderly, and sequential visual display are all in accordance with the decorum for setting up and adorning panels in one's own Memory Theatre as outlined by mnemonists such as William Fulwood (1562) as discussed in both Chapters 2 and 3.

Burch clearly makes use of Day's book not for the prayers, but for the images—and for the more compelling and arresting ones at that. In effect, then, Burch moves what he would retain from one commonplace repository of images into another—from what he is treating as a printed visual anthology to the manuscript book he is charged with curating, compiling, and drawing for his patron. Whether Nettleton tasked

196 *Compelling visuality of the* Prayer Book

Figure 5.15 "Imago Mortis." William Burch, *A Book of Drawing* (c. 1590), fol. 141ᵛ. Canterbury Cathedral Archives (Lit Ms/A/14). Image used courtesy of Canterbury Cathedral Archives.

Burch with copying out these visual sequences specifically from Day's book, which he must have had on hand in his library, or whether he left the selection up to Burch, cannot be determined. What matters though is that the copying process in and of itself underscores the success of Day's program to fabricate and set in circulation a Protestant Memory

Compelling visuality of the Prayer Book 197

Figure 5.16 Death of Death Panels. William Burch, *A Book of Drawing* (c. 1590), fol. 85ᵛ. Canterbury Cathedral Archives (Lit Ms/A/14). Image used courtesy of Canterbury Cathedral Archives.

Art—and one wholly consistent with the commonplace book method of composition—which is especially evident in the borders of *Queen Elizabeth's Prayer Book*.

Burch's procedure for transferring and setting in a new context these images strikingly evokes the prescriptions for setting up and storing a range of stirring and lively images to adorn one's own Memory Theatre. Such artificial memory schemes depended on having access to a variety of well-circulated commonplaces. He follows Day in this, for (as has been discussed in Chapter 5), the images in *Queen Elizabeth's Prayer Book* have no direct link to the prayers on the page. As a result, a well-thought-out visual program constitutes something of a visual commonplace book within the prayer book in its own right, with the aim of offering readers a ready-made Protestant devotional mnemonic itinerary. Although there are many textual transcriptions from other works in Burch's *vade mecum*, it is Day's images, and not the text, that figure significantly in this made-to-order Book of Memory.

Focusing on the images alone permits the viewer to take in the sweep of the compelling stages in the Dance of Death and the End Times without the distraction of the prayer book's guided meditations. One can thereby more immediately contemplate the progress of death's triumph at a glance and see one's own place within it. In this transference of Day's images into a book having such very personal aims, we can catch a glimpse of something quite subtle about how and the extent to which printing gave rise to a special kind of artificial memory in the brave new paperworld of early modern England—with John Day leading the way.

Notes

1 On the stories of persecution in Foxe's *Book of Martyrs*, for example, being "imagined as supernaturally determined by an omnitemporal pattern" so that readers "in some sense should recognize history's truth as manifestly present among them," see Healy (2013, p. 128).
2 The "same form of objectivization as we found in language" referred to here is developed at great length in his first volume of *The Philosophy of Symbolic Forms* entitled *Language* (Cassirer 1977a).
3 On Christ as the "hero of the entire Bible narrative," see Frye (1983, p. 178).
4 Some readers may perhaps take umbrage at my reference to Jesus Christ as a "mythical figure," and no disrespect is intended in my critical pursuit of Cassirer's philosophical approach to understanding the organization of historically grounded symbolic forms in the Western cultural imagination in which Jesus Christ, indisputably, is the central figure, and whose story requires and is itself bolstered by a range of other closely related "mythical figures" including, for example, the Antichrist, Virgin Mary, God the Father, Lucifer (or Satan) the Adversary, and Adam and Eve. Cf. Frye (1983, p. 225):

> Literally, the Bible is a gigantic myth, a narrative extending over the whole of time from creation to apocalypse, unified in a body of recurring imagery that "freezes" into a single metaphor cluster, the metaphors all being identified with the body of the Messiah.

5 In tandem with Day's attention to visuality in the *Book of Martyrs*, see Healy (2013) on Foxe's use of *historia* (the narrative of history) as "the life of memory" in establishing "remembrance" among early readers of *Acts and Monuments*: "Foxe's method is to investigate the details of an event's circumstances and narrate these so that they reinforce how the incident typifies an established model" (p. 130).
6 On the appearance of the foliated head of the "Green Man" tucked away in church architecture beginning in the later Middle Ages, stemming from earlier folk lore and seasonal rites of the so-called "Old Religion" that predated the advent of Christianity in Britain, see Basford (1998).
7 See Wandel (2015) on early Reformation recourse to typology and visual allegory to accommodate to human understanding what "is neither narrative nor, in its immediacy, eternally present" (p. 191); and the view that, for Calvin and his followers, "Christ's death occurred one time only—Christ was not 'in

time' as human beings experienced it. [...] There could be no assumed affinity between human bodies and Christ's; there was no ontological foundation for representation of Christ" (pp. 196–7).

8 Cf. Frye (1983, p. 81): "The backward movement reminds us of, and is not impossibly connected with, Plato's view of knowledge as *anamnesis*, or recollection, the *re*-cognizing of the new as something identifiable with the old" [original emphasis].

9 On Day's purposefully harnessing "old forms to smuggle in the new religion," see Duffy (2006, pp. 170–2); and on Day's appropriation of lay devotional formats, such as French Catholic Horae especially those printed in Paris, see Epstein (2021, p. 362). See Wieck (1997, p. 51) on the typical structure of a Book of Hours, at the very heart of which was a series of prayers called the Hours of the Virgin (pp. 138–40), an aspect of the devotional format that Day studiously avoided including in the visual register of his prayer books; on the Biblia Pauperum being "reproduced rapidly and inexpensively because of the entrepreneurial instinct of printers and booksellers who found a market for their products," see Labriola and Smeltz (1990, p. 5); on the Speculum Humanae Salvationis becoming "widely available because of rapid and inexpensive production as a blockbook" that enabled "its readers to infer, multiple interpretations of its visual and verbal contents" with the aim "of educating the common folk in a manner commensurate with their level of understanding," see Labriola and Smeltz (2002, pp. 5–6); and on the Hortulus Animae as an example of early printed Protestant devotional works coopting the Catholic Horae tradition, with special reference to its early appearance in England, see Butterworth (2017, pp. 18–27).

10 The Hortulus Animae was a subgenre of continental devotional manuals, frequently produced in the vernacular; but, as the text printed in Latin here indicates (see again Figure 5.2), this particular book was intended for more widespread distribution than just regional German speakers from the Rhineland where it was produced, in Mainz—a major center of printing and, beginning in 1477, home to a large university attracting students and clergy from across Europe.

11 This commonplace allegory partakes of the same sort of visual register as the panoramic, privileged perspective discussed in terms of the bird's eye view of reconstructed scenes of historical martyrdom treated in Chapter 3 (see again Figure 3.1).

12 For a modern adaptation (at once charming and also indicative of sound scholarly endeavor) of the main stories and legends that grew up around this motif based on Caxton's 1481 English translation of the Middle Dutch, see Avery (2020, pp. 27–38). On Caxton's *Aesop's Fables* and its appeal to English readers "stirred by the currents of the Italian Renaissance," see Ford (2020, p. 18).

13 It must be mentioned however that, perhaps to satisfy the desire for variety, some of the margin panels sport comically grotesque designs of strangely morphed body parts and unusual creatures, thus making this printed book further reminiscent of the imaginative border ornaments adorning manuscript Books of Hours; see Camille (1992, p. 40). And, incidentally, on Camille's subjects as being less concerned with "the ethical and the aesthetic 'edges' of medieval culture," as with, for example, "the scatological borders of a book of hours in Trinity College, Cambridge," see Reeve (2017, pp. 164–6).

14 For more precise data concerning the reach, range, and extraordinary influence of this book, "one of the first truly international best-sellers at the beginning of the age of print," see Evans (1996, p. 48).

15 On the widespread impact of this book in continental Europe, and on the earliest English versions that began circulating by 1509, see Engel et al. (2022), entry IV.1.

16 Cf. Dryness (2004, p. 101) with reference to how, using "the images in catechisms, the bible and Foxe's 'Book of Martyrs' one might describe the beginning of a Protestant iconography" (p. 101), and the analysis in Chapter 1 of Day's use of images in his Matthew's Bible, in Chapter 2 on the catechism, and in Chapter 3 on the much expanded second edition of *Acts and Monuments* (1570), a richly illustrated work being prepared for press at the same time as *Queen Elizabeth's Prayer Book*.

17 On *Queen Elizabeth's Prayer Book* assimilating a wide range of traditional material from "primers, the Catholic liturgy, and continental texts into a new Protestant context of private devotions, a context evoked by the domestic setting of the image of the queen at prayers," see Luborsky and Ingram (1998, p. 315).

18 Much of the text that is printed in the first part of Day's prayer book (1569) is modeled quite closely on *Christian Prayers and Holy Meditations* (1568) by Henry Bull, who was a steadfast reformer closely associated with John Foxe and who likewise was compelled to leave a post at Oxford owing to his nonconforming religious convictions.

19 On the substitution of the image of the Virgin Mary with that of the Virgin Queen, Elizabeth I, see Collinson (1986, p. 23), King (1989, p. 114), Engel et al. (2016, p. 247), and Epstein (2021, pp. 368–70); on other related deific representations involving the queen in Tudor iconography, see Strong (2019, pp. 48–9); and for a close reading of this depiction of Elizabeth as a pious, learned queen, as "a Queen Solomon," see Shenk (2010, p. 23).

20 This particular copy most likely was hand colored by artists in Matthew Parker's workshop based at Lambeth Palace; on Day's longtime connection with Archbishop Parker, see Chapter 1, and on this particular book as well as other deluxe religious works given to Elizabeth by Archbishop Parker, see Evenden (2008, p. 107). Evidence of Parker's flourishing workshop around this same time comes from a letter written in 1573 to Lord Burghley, William Cecil: "I have within my house in wages, drawers and cutters, painters, limners, writers, and book binders" (Harding 2010, p. 111). On the role of the Earl of Leicester, Robert Dudley (mentioned in the previous chapters as being an early and consistent patron of Day's projects) in the dissemination of and possible subsidization of *Queen Elizabeth's Prayer Book*, see Epstein (2021, pp. 367–8).

21 Another reason why the book has been considered *Queen Elizabeth's Prayer Book* is because there is some basis for conjecturing that she may have written some of the prayers (Marcus et al. 2000, pp. 143–4). However, cf. Shenk (2010, p. 21):

> We have no autograph copy of these prayers to prove Elizabeth's authorship, and indeed, I am not convinced that Elizabeth composed them herself. What these prayers and the apparatus of other prayers in the text do provide, however, is an important political *image* of Elizabeth, one that the queen clearly accepted [original emphasis].

22 On the stages involved in arranging type-font alongside the selected woodblocks for inking, such that the galleys were positioned face-up in a frame, or "forme," see Lyons (2011, p. 59); also, it remains a historical curiosity in the nomenclature of wooden handpress production that the forme was situated on a flat stone positioned within a "coffin," namely, the wooden frame enclosing and holding in place the press stone (Gaskell 2015, pp. 118–19).

23 On the identity of possible candidates perhaps responsible for compiling the evangelical texts comprising *Christian Prayers and Meditations* (1569), see Clement (2008) and Stróbl (2012).

24 After having been more or less forced out of printing, Richard sought ordination in the Church of England, briefly holding the post as a vicar in Essex, which he resigned in 1584 and thereafter apparently living off income from patents bequeathed to him in John Day's will—although not without some litigation. On Richard Day's efforts to exercise more freedom as a printer and the various obstacles he encountered toward this end, see Oastler (1957, pp. 65–86) and Evenden (2008, pp. 151–80).

25 On the rejection of Purgatory in the reformed faith and how it changed daily life in early modern England, with special reference to death and burial customs, see Gittings (1984), Duffy (1992), and Cressy (1997).

26 For an account of the various ways this theme typically was handled in post-Reformation England, see Engel et al. (2022), Introduction.

27 Cf. Duffy (2004, pp. 429–32) on "Anglican self-identity" as never simply or unequivocally Protestant, where lay and clerical conservatives resisted the removal of the remains of the old religion, such that "vestiges of the Catholic past were embedded like flies in amber in the Prayer Book liturgy," in church buildings, and in their attitudes and memories. On the long-lasting political consequences of the parliamentary settlement of religion of 1559, which in the Acts of Supremacy and Uniformity recognized the monarch as the supreme governor of the English Church and required worship according to "the only slightly modified, indisputably Protestant second Prayer Book" (the first being instituted under Edward VI), see Cross (2017, pp. 1–6).

28 For a more detailed if preliminary discussion of this typological mnemonic triad of images and scriptural tags, see Engel (1995, pp. 161–5), the recollection of any one of which being sufficient to trigger recall of the others, thus creating "an internal network of intertextual glosses" (p. 165).

29 On biblical typology, in theory and practice and with reference to its origins and later uses, see Frye (1983, pp. 78–138), Smalley (1984, pp. 196–263), and O'Keefe and Reno (2005, pp. 69–88).

30 On the numerous reprintings of Holbein's *Dance of Death* before 1562 as the model for the Dance of Death sequence in Day's prayer book, which instead of a round dance produces "a series of separate images in which Death, in the form of a skeleton, approaches individuals or small groups, unexpected, and unseen," see Sillars (2015, p. 125). Furthermore, Holbein's artistic influence was strongly felt in early Tudor England, both because of his commissioned portraits of Henry VIII and members of the royal family as well as of aspiring courtiers and people of consequence, and also owing to his role in producing the title page of the Coverdale Bible printed in 1535; cf. Dryness (2004, p. 98).

31 The 1560 Geneva Bible is referenced in this chapter because it would have been among the most recently printed and readily accessible versions available to Day and his print setters and compositors; also the wording inserted in the spaces left open in the woodblock panels for this purpose in both *Christian Prayers and Meditations* (1569) and *A Book of Christian Prayers* (1578) appears to be following this text.

32 Two other sets of initials are visible on select woodcuts. The bottom panels in the Dance of Death sequence have the initial "G" in the lower left corner—perhaps Marcus Gheeraerts the Younger, who (as discussed in Chapter 4), likely was in Day's employ during the late 1560s, around the same time as when *Queen Elizabeth's Prayer Book* was being prepared for production. The initials "CT" appear in the lower left of the final set of images, namely, the panel depicting the first of the four last things, the scripturally necessary theme of the Triumph of Death preceding Christ's subsequent victory over Death in the End Times (1608, sig. Oo1^v).

33 On the iconography of this border image and its wider implications, see Engel (1995, pp. 248–9); and for a treatment of the same image in the context of interpreting Shakespeare's *As You Like It* (2.7.166–7), see Holland (2021, p. 104).

34 An immemorial visual trope in its own right, the focal image of "praying hands" was given an especially powerful Protestant valence and attained widespread popularity in the sixteenth century with Dürer's now famous picture *Betende Hände* (c. 1508), originally "a direct study for the hands of an apostle in … the *Heller Altarpiece*" (Robinson and Schröder 2013, p. 176).

35 For further insights on "imagining the Jews," as the "production of culturally shaped and conditioned ideas about the Jews in England," see Holmberg (2011, p. 5).

36 Regarding the "shift in the construction of Christianity's relationship to Judaism" beginning with "humanist approaches to biblical study and the integration of these new methodologies into Reformation reading practices," as well as the never quite entirely abating "impulse to cast Jews as antique relics," see Shoulson (2013, p. 70).

37 On the appropriation of the Jews—and especially the Old Testament—as an index of the truth of Christianity, see Guibbory (2010, p. 27):

> Christians interpreted the survival and restoration of the biblical Jews to glory and the true worship of God, foretold by the prophets, as referring not to the Jews who returned from Babylon or to some future condition of the Jews brought back from their Diaspora, but to the Christian Church.

38 On the central place accorded to the savior and redeemer in the cultural formation of mythical thought, see Cassirer (1977b, p. 204); and on the various ways this motif more specifically is figured in Christian exegetical thought and writings, see O'Keefe and Reno (2005, p. 69).

39 For a more detailed treatment of this aspect of the continental figural tradition involving death, with special reference to the English context, see Engel et al. (2022, Introduction, "The Visual Proliferation of the Death Art").

40 The same rhetorical formula ("fear not") is used regularly in the Bible to set at ease those visited by angels; for example, in the prophesying of John the Baptist's birth to his father Zacharias (Luke 1:13) and of Jesus's birth to Mary (Luke 1:30).

41 On "decoding the appearance of angels mentioned in Scripture, including the Hebrew testament," especially as pertains to later typological figuration of the Annunciation, see Gill (2014, pp. 6–7).
42 For a comparable if more succinct analysis of this image in the context of the memory arts in Renaissance England, see Engel et al. (2016, p. 253).
43 The same applies to the other mottoes used with this same woodblock inserted into the open space left for this purpose using miniscule Gothic type: "Death wins the field, / All arms must yield" (1608, sig. Aa4^v, Ff3^r, and Ll2^r; used three times in the repetition of the sequence).
44 On the place of this "doubly chiastic statement of temporal displacement" in "early English epitaphic inscriptions," see Newstok (2009, p. 110); and for a subtle exploration of "the many paradoxes of the *tu fui*" in early modern England, see Sperry (2022, ch. 5).
45 This macabre decorative figure, it must be noted, bears a striking resemblance to the classically garbed man with lush hair likewise postured in the originary 1569 edition (Figure 5.6, recto page); perhaps both were cut by the same artist or perhaps by someone else using the older inset woodblock as a model—as one might with a design taken from a program book—for creating the decorative margin filler for later editions.
46 Day was not the first, of course, to include the printing press in a Dance of Death—indeed it was featured in what often is considered the earliest printed *Danse Macabre* (1499); see Engel (1995, pp. 77–9). He was however the first to situate it within a distinctively Protestant context.
47 See Marion (2004, pp. 1–13, 25–30) on "the crossing of the visible," especially as regards what is "given" to be seen: pictures essentially are paradoxical in their reminding viewers, by virtue of illusionistic perspective play, of what they cannot see. And see Diehl (1986, p. 66) on the emblematic image pointing away from itself such that when readers see the emblematic image and use it properly, they are seeing "through or beyond the material image" and, in effect, remembering "another world," substituting "spiritual for physical sight."
48 Attribution is based on internal textual and visual evidence; for example, at the bottom of fol. 106^v, we find "John Nettleton the owner of this book, his coat of arms" followed by a smaller version of the arms painted on the verso of the title page. Basically, the main work on this book was carried out between 1590 and 1591 by William Burch (or Burke) under the patronage of Nettleton who had compiled a library of printed books and medieval manuscripts mainly on natural history, coins and medals, and especially heraldry. Burch seems to have been hired on the basis of his having already distinguished himself as an arms painter.

References

Primary Sources

A Book of Christian Prayers. 1578. London: John Day. STC 6429.
A Book of Christian Prayers. 1608. London: [H. Lownes]. STC 6432.
Book of Common Prayer. 1552. London: R. Grafton. STC 16285.5.
Brandt, S. 1944 [1497]. *The Ship of Fools*. Edwin H. Zeydel, trans. New York: Dover.

Bull, H. 1568. *Christian Prayers and Holy Meditations*. London: T. East. STC 4028.
Burch, W. 1590. *A book of drawing of the shapes and forms of diverse beasts, fowls, birds, fishes, monsters, serpents, trees, herbs, plants, and flowers, with diverse accidents of antiquities, and armory*. Canterbury Cathedral Archives (Lit Ms/A/14).
Christian Prayers and Meditations in English French, Italian, Spanish, Greek, and Latin. 1569. London: John Day. STC 6428.
Foxe, J. 1570. [...] *Acts and monuments*. London: John Day. STC 11223.
Fulwood. W. 1562. *The Castle of Memory*. London: R. Hall. STC 12191.
Hortul[us] Animae. 1514. Mainz: J. Schöffer.
Spenser, E. 1579. *The Shepheardes Calender*. London: H. Singleton. STC 23089.
The Bible and Holy Scriptures. 1560. Geneva: R. Hall. STC 2093.

Secondary Sources

Acciarino, D. 2021. Between Renaissance and Reformation: Grotesques and the Debate on Images. In: D. Acciarino, ed. *Paradigms of Renaissance Grotesques*. Toronto: Centre for Renaissance and Reformation Studies.
Avery, A.L. 2020. *Reynard the Fox*. Oxford: The Bodleian Library, University of Oxford Press.
Basford, K. 1998. *The Green Man*. Rochester, NY: D.S. Brewer.
Butterworth, C.C. 2017. *The English Primers (1529–1545): Their Publication and Connection with the English Bible and the Reformation in England*. Philadelphia: University of Pennsylvania Press.
Camille, M. 1992. *Image on the Edge: The Margins of Medieval Art*. Cambridge, MA: Harvard University Press.
Cassirer, E. 1977a [1923]. *The Philosophy of Symbolic Forms*. Vol. 1: *Language*. R. Manheim, trans. New Haven: Yale University Press.
Cassirer, E. 1977b [1923]. *The Philosophy of Symbolic Forms*. Vol. 2: *Mythical Thought*. R. Manheim, trans. New Haven: Yale University Press.
Chew, S.C. 1945. The Iconography of *A Book of Christian Prayers* (1578). *The Huntington Library Quarterly*. **8.3**, 293–305.
Clegg, C.S. 2016. The 1559 Books of Common Prayer and the Elizabethan Reformation. *The Journal of Ecclesiastical History*. **67.1**, 94–121.
Clement, J. 2008. The Queen's Voice: Elizabeth I's *Christian Prayers and Meditations*. *Early Modern Literary Studies*. 13.3, 1–26.
Cohen, K. 1973. *Metamorphosis of a Death Symbol: The Transi Tomb in the Late Middle Ages and the Renaissance*. Berkeley: University of California Press.
Collinson, P. 1986. *From Iconoclasm to Iconophobia: The Cultural Impact of the Second English Reformation*. Reading: University of Reading.
Cressy, D. 1997. *Birth, Marriage, and Death: Ritual, Religion, and the Life-Cycle in Tudor and Stuart England*. Oxford: Oxford University Press.
Cross. C. 2017. The Political Enforcement of Liturgical Continuity in the Church of England 1558–1662. In: R. Bethmont and A. De Mézerac-Zanetti, eds. *The Book of Common Prayer, Studies in Religious Transfer. Revue Française de Civilisation Britannique*. **22.1**, 1–13.
Cummings, B., ed. 2011. Introduction. *The Book of Common Prayer: The Texts of 1549, 1559, and 1662*. Oxford: Oxford University Press.

Daniell, D. 2003. *The Bible in English: Its history and influence*. New Haven and London: Yale University Press.
Davidson, C. and Oosterwijk, S. 2021. Introduction. In: C. Davidson and S. Oosterwijk, eds. *John Lydgate, "The Dance of Death," and its model, the French "Danse Macabre."* Leiden: Brill.
Dekoninick, R. 2017. The Anthropology of Images. In: C. Hourihane, ed. *The Routledge Companion to Medieval Iconography*. London and New York: Routledge. pp. 175–83.
Diehl, H. 1986. Graven Images: Protestant Emblem Books in England. *Renaissance Quarterly*. **39.1**, 49–66.
Dryness, W.A. 2004. *Reformed Theology and Visual Culture*. Cambridge University Press.
Duffy, E. 1992. *The Stripping of the Altars: Traditional Religion in England 1400–1580*. New Haven: Yale University Press.
———. 2004. The Shock of Change: Continuity and Discontinuity in the Elizabethan Church of England. *Ecclesiastical Law Journal*. **7.35**, 429–46.
———. 2006. *Marking of the Hours: English People and Their Prayers, 1240–1570*. New Haven: Yale University Press.
Engel, W.E. 1995. *Mapping Mortality: The Persistence of Memory and Melancholy in Early Modern England*. Amherst: University of Massachusetts Press.
———. 2014. The Decay of Memory. In: C. Ivic and G. Williams, eds. *Forgetting in Early Modern English Literature and Culture: Lethe's Legacies*. London and New York: Routledge. pp. 21–40.
Engel, W.E, Loughnane, R., and Williams, G. 2016. *The Memory Arts in Renaissance England: A Critical Anthology*. Cambridge: Cambridge University Press.
———. 2022. *The Death Arts in Renaissance England: A Critical Anthology*. Cambridge: Cambridge University Press.
Epstein, N. 2021. Illustrating Authority: The Creation and Reception of an English Protestant Iconography. In: N. Lamal, J. Cumby, and H.J. Helmers, eds. *Print and Power in Early Modern Europe (1500–1800)*. Leiden: Brill. pp. 361–89.
Evans, R.C. 1996. Forgotten Fools: Alexander Barclay's *Ship of Fools*. In: C. Davidson, ed. *Fools and Folly*. Kalamazoo: Medieval Institute Publications. pp. 47–72.
Evenden, E. 2008. *Patents, Pictures, and Patronage: John Day and the Tudor Book Trade*. Aldershot, UK; Burlington, VT: Ashgate.
———. 2010. Closing the books: the problematic printing of John Foxe's histories of Henry VII and Henry VIII in his *Book of Martyrs*. In: J.N. King, ed. *Tudor Books and Readers: Materiality and the Construction of Meaning*. Cambridge: Cambridge University Press. pp. 68–91.
Evenden, E. and Freeman T.S. 2011. *Religion and the Book in Early Modern England*. Cambridge: Cambridge University Press.
———. 2013. *Religion and the Book in Early Modern England: The Making of John Foxe's "Book of Martyrs."* Cambridge: Cambridge University Press.
Ford, J.A. 2020. *English Readers of Catholic Saints: The Printing History of William Caxton's "Golden Legend."* London and New York: Routledge.
Frye, N. 1983. *The Great Code: The Bible and Literature*. New York: Harcourt.
Garrison, J.S. 2018. *Shakespeare and the Afterlife*. Oxford: Oxford University Press.

Gaskell, P. 2015. *A New Introduction to Bibliography*. New Castle, DE: Oak Knoll Press.

Gertsman, E. 2010. *The Dance of Death in the Middle Ages*. Turnhout, BE: Brepols.

Gill, M.A. 2014. *Angels and the Order of Heaven in Medieval and Renaissance Italy*. Cambridge: Cambridge University Press.

Gittings, C. 1984. *Death, Burial and the Individual in Early Modern England*. London: Croom Helm.

Guibbory, A. 2010. *Christian Identity, Jews, and Israel in Seventeenth-Century England*. Oxford: Oxford University Press.

Hamling, T. 2020. Memorable Motifs: The Role of "Synoptic" Imagery in Remembering the English Reformation. In: A. Walsham, B. Wallace, C. Law, and B. Cummings, eds. *Memory and the English Reformation*. Cambridge: Cambridge University Press. pp. 185–206.

Harding, R. 2010. The Prayer Book of Elizabeth I. In: R. Palmer and M.P. Brown, eds. *Lambeth Palace Library: Treasures of the Collection of the Archbishop of Canterbury*. London: Scala. pp. 110–11.

Harding, V. 2002. *The Dead and the Living in Paris and London, 1500–1670*. Cambridge: Cambridge University Press.

Healy, T. 2013. "Making it True": John Foxe's Art of Remembrance. In: A Gordon and T. Rist, eds. Farnham, UK; Burlington, VT: Ashgate. pp. 125–40.

Holland, P. 2021. *Shakespeare and Forgetting*. London: Bloomsbury.

Homberg, E.J. 2011. *Jews in the Early Modern English Imagination*. Farnham, UK; Burlington, VT: Ashgate.

Hunter, G.K. 1951. The Marking of *Sententiae* in Elizabethan Printed Plays, Poems, and Romances. *The Library*. 5th series, 6.3–4, 171–88.

Jørgensen, H.H.L. 2018. The Image as Contact Medium: Mediation, Multimodality, and Haptics in Medieval Imagery. In: L. Liepe, ed. *The Locus of Meaning in Medieval Art: Iconography, Iconology, and Interpreting the Visual Imaginary of the Middle Ages*. Kalamazoo: Medieval Institute Publications. pp. 128–58.

King, J.N. 1989. *Tudor Royal Iconography: Literature and Art in an Age of Religious Crisis*. Princeton: Princeton University Press.

Kiss, F.G. 2016. Introduction. In: F.G. Kiss, ed. *The Art of Memory in Late Medieval Central Europe*. Budapest-Paris: L'Harmattan.

Labriola, A.C. and Smeltz, J.W. eds. 1990. *The Bible of the Poor*. Pittsburgh: Duquesne University Press.

———. 2002. *The Mirror of Salvation*. Pittsburgh: Duquesne University Press.

Loughnane, R. 2022. Afterword. In: W.E. Engel and G. Williams, eds. *The Shakespearean Death Arts: Hamlet Among the Tombs*. New York: Palgrave Macmillan.

Luborsky, R.S. and Ingram, E.M. 1998. *A Guide to English Illustrated Books, 1536–1603*. Tempe: ACMRS.

Lyons, M. 2011. *Books: A Living History*. Los Angeles: Getty Publications.

Marcus, L.S., Mueller, J., and Rose, M.B., eds. 2000. *Elizabeth I: Collected Works*. Chicago: University of Chicago Press.

Marion, J.-L. 2004. *The Crossing of the Visible*. J.K.A. Smith, trans. Stanford: Stanford University Press.

Marshall, P. 2002. *Beliefs and the Dead in Reformation England*. Oxford: Oxford University Press.

———. 2009. (Re)defining the English Reformation. *Journal of British Studies.* **48.3**, 564–86.
Morrison, E. 2017. The Light at the End of the Tunnel: Manuscript Illumination and the Concept of Death. In: S. Perkinson, ed. *The Ivory Mirror: The Art of Mortality in Renaissance Europe.* Brunswick, ME: Bowdoin College Museum of Art; distr. by Yale University Press. pp. 83–105.
Moss, A. 2002. *Printed Commonplace-Books and the Structuring of Renaissance Thought.* Oxford: Oxford University Press.
Newstok, S.L. 2009. *Quoting Death in Early Modern England: The Poetics of Epitaphs Beyond the Tomb.* New York: Palgrave Macmillan.
Oastler, C.L. 1975. *John Day, the Elizabethan Printer.* Oxford: Oxford Bibliographical Society.
O'Keefe, J.J. and Reno, R.R. 2005. *Sanctified Vision: An Introduction to Early Christian Interpretation of the Bible.* Baltimore: Johns Hopkins University Press.
Panofsky, E. 1972. *Studies in Iconology: Humanistic Themes in the Art of the Renaissance.* London: Routledge.
Pentcheva, B. 2020. Visions of the Passion imagined through the agency of voice and icon. In: A.O. Lam and R. Schroeder, eds. *The Eloquence of Art: Essays in Honour of Henry Maguire.* London and New York: Routledge. pp. 267–82.
Reeve, M.H. 2017. Michael Camille's Queer Middle Ages. In: C. Hourihane, ed. *The Routledge Companion to Medieval Iconography.* London and New York: Routledge. pp. 154–71.
Reid, P. 2019. *Reading by Design: The Visual Interfaces of the English Renaissance Book.* Toronto: University of Toronto Press.
Robinson, A. and Schröder, K.A. 2013. *Albrecht Dürer: Master Drawings, Watercolors, and Prints from the Albertina.* Munich: Prestel Verlag.
Rublack, U. ed. 2017. *Hans Holbein: The Dance of Death.* London: Penguin.
Shenk, L. 2010. *Learned Queen: The Image of Elizabeth I in Politics and Poetry.* New York: Palgrave Macmillan.
Shoulson, J.S. 2013. *Fictions of Conversion: Jews, Christians, and Cultures of Change in Early Modern England.* Philadelphia: University Pennsylvania Press.
Sillars, S. 2015. *Shakespeare and the Visual Imagination.* Cambridge: Cambridge University Press.
Smalley, B. 1984. *The Study of the Bible in the Middle Ages.* Oxford: Oxford University Press.
Sperry, A. 2022. "As thou art, I once was": Death and the Bodies in *2 Henry IV*. In: W.E. Engel and G. Williams, eds. *The Shakespearean Death Arts: Hamlet Among the Tombs.* New York: Palgrave Macmillan.
Stenner, R. 2019. *The Typographic Imaginary in Early Modern English Literature.* London: Routledge.
Stróbl, E. 2012. *The Queen and Death: An Elizabethan Book of Devotion.* In: K. Földváry and E. Stróbl, eds. *Early Modern Communi(cati)ons: Studies in Early Modern English Literature and Culture.* Newcastle upon Tyne: Cambridge Scholars Publishing. pp. 10–31.
Strong, R. 2003. *Gloriana: The Portraits of Queen Elizabeth I.* London: Pimlico.
———. 2019. *The Elizabethan Image: An Introduction to English Portraiture, 1558–1603.* New Haven: Yale University Press.
Waddington, R. 1993. Elizabeth I and the Order of the Garter. *Sixteenth Century Journal.* **24.1**, 97–113.

Wandel, L.P. 2015. Incarnation, Image, and Sign: John Calvin's *Institutes of Christian Religion* and Late Medieval Visual Culture. In: W. Melion and L.P. Wandel, eds. *Image and Incarnation: The Early Modern Doctrine of the Pictorial Image.* Leiden: Brill. pp. 187–202.

Wieck, R.S. 1997. *Painted Prayers: The Book of Hours in Medieval and Renaissance Art.* New York: George Braziller.

Conclusion
Making history

> If we seek a general heading under which we are to subsume historical knowledge we may describe it not as a branch of physics but as a branch of semantics. The rules of semantics, not the laws of nature, are the general principles of historical thought. History is included in the field of hermeneutics, not in that of natural science. [...] It is obvious that history cannot describe all the facts of the past. It deals only with the "memorable" facts, with the facts "worth" remembering. But where lies the difference between these memorable facts and all the rest which fall into oblivion? [...] In our historical knowledge—which is a semantic knowledge—we do not apply the same standards as in our practical or physical knowledge. A thing that physically or practically is of no importance at all may still have very great semantic meaning.
>
> (Cassirer 1992, pp. 195–7)

A conscious sense of symmetry accounts for the final epigraph of this study bookending the long quotation from Ernst Cassirer in the Introduction. From first to last, I am indebted to his trenchant analysis of the historical interplay of memory, myth, and language in the philosophy of symbolic forms. This book has dealt selectively and critically with the "memorable" facts, with the facts "worth" remembering, in early modern English book history, especially as regards John Day, master printer, as having given rise to—as having authorized and, in effect, authored—a host of works that had profound nationalist and historical consequences.

John Day made history in every sense of the phrase. First, his building up of the stature of the printing press in England, principally in the service of promoting Protestant beliefs and practices, was truly pioneering in terms of the completion of unprecedentedly large book projects (difficult to manage materially and risky to produce financially) and had an enormous historical, political, and religious impact, the ripple-effect of which we are still experiencing today. Second, he stands out as being associated with some of Britain's book history "firsts," including the first book printed in England to be illustrated with etchings, and also the first Renaissance emblem book published in England, *A Theatre for Voluptuous Worldings*. In addition to giving Euclid to the English-speaking people, he also supplied them with the first viable, deluxe handbook of nautical navigation with *The Cosmographical Glass*, as well as what amounts to—in visual terms—the first Protestant Book of Hours with *Queen Elizabeth's Prayer Book*. In tandem with such adventurous publishing events, he assembled and innovatively used a wide variety of type fonts, including musical notation for *The Whole Book of Psalms*. His attention to both the aesthetics of image selection and overall page design was uniquely trendsetting, with the effect of bringing English printing on par with, and in some cases exceeding, what was being done on the continent. He also made history through his *Short Catechism* with his acquisition and securing of licenses, patents, and monopolies, paving the way for what today we would recognize as the protection of intellectual property. Moreover, and more literally, with Foxe's *Book of Martyrs*, he made history by reimagining it from an evangelically reformed perspective. With Foxe, Day successfully consolidated and spread a view of history, as "the life of memory," and "history's truth as manifestly present" and "supernaturally determined by an omnitemporal pattern" among his early modern readers (Healy 2013, p. 128), including those new to literacy or in the process of acquiring it using the compelling images and descriptive tags from this work. More fundamentally still, with the *Short Catechism* and *Book of Psalms*, Day taught Tudor England not only how to read but also how to interpret authoritatively what was being read, in alignment with the Protestant faith and true to the Word of God as disclosed solely in scripture.

This sweeping and quick *montage* of the key texts—historical events in their own right—covered in *The Printer as Author* is not intended as adulation for Day but simply to restate some standout "facts" in English book history. And had it not been Day, it would have been somebody else. Oswald Spengler (1996), unimpressed by the recorded historical feats of so-called "great men," reminds us how little in fact the "logic of Destiny needs particular instances, better men or situations" for, in the end, the same theme, "to use the language of music, could have been 'worked out' in other ways" (pp. 144–5). We do well to recall that competition in the London printing trade and book business was extremely keen during Elizabeth's reign, with all involved parties striving to gain, maintain, and expand their portion of an albeit ever-increasing market, which often meant encroaching on one another's territory.[1] Be that as it may, as it happened, in many key instances, it was Day who got there first.

Part of what made Day's expertly illustrated works stand out from those of his competitors, however, was a result of his scrupulous attentiveness to the material conditions of print technology and labor relations with artisans from the continent, both of which afforded him a wider range of options for creating, implementing, and activating long-lasting visual memory cues—coupled of course with a shrewd head for business. My goal throughout has been to show how he drew on the prevailing mnemotechnic commonplaces of the day in the process of plying his trade and promoting the Protestant cause. As mentioned in Chapter 3, if ever there was a case to be made about the rise of capitalism and Protestantism going hand in hand, then it is John Day.[2] The cumulative result of Day's craft—of the printer as author—can be seen in his fabrication of a Protestant Memory Art, the material traces of which are discernible in the products of his technical ingenuity.

Imagining Derricke's *Image of Ireland* (1581)

It is therefore fitting to conclude with a parting glance at one of the last major works to come from his shop while he was still overseeing day-to-day operations (Day died July 23, 1584).[3] We need to bear in mind that a never-ending flow of his monopolized publications continued to issue from his presses, including books of sermons, the catechism and metrical psalms, as well as a fourth, much expanded, edition of the *Acts and Monuments* (1583). His bringing *The Image of Ireland* (1581) to the English nation can be seen as the culmination of a lifetime of his striving to produce the highest quality printed images using the most up-to-date techniques while seeding his works with well-managed nationalist propaganda for a queen who, in many ways, was behind his successful career from the very beginning of her own. There was a symbiosis between this printer and Queen Elizabeth that is difficult to quantify but, as I have demonstrated, quite verifiable.

John Derricke's *The Image of Ireland*, "mainly a poem in varied parts" concerning the colonial project, "is known, above all, for its woodcuts" (Herron et al. 2021, p. 1). Whatever else might be said about the complex cross-cultural misunderstandings propagated as a kind of "afterimage" in this bimedial book, the 12 woodcuts form a coherent series that, for 16th-century book production, is exceptionally innovative in its treatment of historical writing and artistic representation (Knapp 2003, p. 207).[4] What James Knapp has discussed as cultural "afterimages" that linger in the mind's eye as a result of certain printed images being circulated in early modern England, I have been referring to in *The Printer as Author* as memory traces—the stuff of mnemotopes as discussed in the Introduction.

Further, as Andie Silva (2021) astutely obverses, the illustrations of *The Image of Ireland* are significant and "interesting not only for their visual design but also for their material history" (p. 136), showcasing "a number of remarkable approaches for multimodal reading practices" typically found in other productions by John Day (p. 135). As I have shown throughout, Day's choices, even as regards border illustrations, demonstrate a commitment to involving his readers in a Protestant Memory Art that draws on an evangelically informed belief system, affective stylistics,[5] and the promotion of a new, engaging, and recursive modality of visual literacy. Indeed, for Day, "Protestant devotion could not be separated from the act of diligent reading," and which, Silva continues, "could only

212 Conclusion: making history

be accomplished through recursive and selective analysis, using a number of navigational tools to produce distinct reading experiences" (p. 137). Day's backlog of experience in publishing—his innovative approach to illustrating, indexing, and setting up tables, headings, and textual glosses using special-made fonts and well-positioned features of his house printing style, all contributing to his putting in place a series of interlinked mnemonic nodes—provided "Derricke with a unique perspective on how to manufacture the multipart, multivalent *Image of Ireland*" (pp. 146–7).

In keeping with Day's tactical emphasis on setting up easy-to-follow mnemotechnical metaphors and symbolically charged emblematic designs, Derricke characterizes his project overall as a vast memory image: "Diverse were the causes (good Reader) that moved me first to take in hand, the carving forth of this Image…" (sig. b1^v). Day too, historically, knew a thing or two about the carving of images; the mnemic energies generated and memory traces set in motion by virtue of the images he commissioned for his publications, no less than the overall layout and page design, also left lasting marks on the print trade in Elizabethan London and the cultural imaginary of early modern Britain. He was responsible for the look, style, and authorized content of a significant body of English Reformation printing—including the culturally complicated *Image of Ireland*,[6] which, as another "first" in English book history, features "some of the only contemporary images of the early modern Irish and the city of Dublin we have today" (Herron et al. 2021, p. 1). *The Printer as Author*, unlike previous treatments of Day's place in early modern book history, has focused on his finely honed mnemotechnical sensibilities that informed his hybrid role as printer, publisher, stationer, and yes—ultimately—author.

Notes

1 For example, as discussed in Chapter 1, even as Day printed the catechism in Latin without proper licensing, and likewise printed musical notes in his psalter even though others held the monopoly on "all books of music" (Loewenstein 2002, p. 29), so too, as treated in Chapter 2, he called out specific publishers and printers for surreptitiously selling 10,000 copies of his patented *Catechism* and further charged three others, including "two senior members of the trade with printing yet another 15,000 pirated copies" (Green 2003, p. 175).
2 See again Weber (2002), regarding Luther's notion of "calling" and the Calvinist belief in predestination as preparing the groundwork for the emergence of "the capitalist spirit."
3 On Day's final years, death, and memorial, see Evenden (2008, pp. 166–76).
4 On Day's primacy in the production of *The Image of Ireland*, see Knapp (2000, p. 417; and 2003, pp. 208–12). For the program of the 12 woodcuts, see Herron (2021, p. 203).
5 As discussed in the Introduction, see Stanley Fish (1970) on "meaning as event" in his development of "affective stylistics," apropos of Day's calling upon, co-opting, and mobilizing in his books a wide range of affectively displayed

mnemotechnical commonplaces—whether visual or verbal, whether religious or folkish in origin.
6 See Soderberg (2021): "rather than being simply a justification of conquest, the poem and accompanying woodcut illustrations are fully entangled in the contradictions and anxieties of Elizabethan Ireland and colonial encounters more generally" (p. 49).

References

Primary Source

Derricke, J. 1581. *The Image of Ireland*. London: John Day. STC 6734.

Secondary Sources

Cassirer, E. 1992 [1944]. *An Essay on Man: An Introduction to a Philosophy of Human Culture*. New Haven, CT, and London: Yale University Press.
Evenden, E. 2008. *Patents, Pictures, and Patronage: John Day and the Tudor Book Trade*. Aldershot; Burlington, VT: Ashgate.
Fish, S. 1970. Literature in the Reader: Affective Stylistics. *New Literary History*. **2.1**, 123–62.
Green, I. 2003. *Print and Protestantism in Early Modern England*. Oxford: Oxford University Press.
Healy, T. 2013. "Making it True": John Foxe's Art of Remembrance. In A. Gordon and T. Rist, eds. *The Arts of Remembrance in Early Modern England: Memorial Cultures of the Post Reformation*. Farnham; Burlington, VT: Ashgate. pp. 125–40.
Herron, T. 2021. Irish Apocalypse: Derricke, Dürer, and Foxe. In: T. Herron, D. Iammarino, and M. Maroney, eds. *John Derricke's "Image of Irelande, with a Discoverie of Woodkarne": Essays on Text and Contexts*. Manchester: Manchester University Press. pp. 201–28.
Herron, T., Iammarino, D., and Maroney, M. 2021. Introduction. In: T. Herron, D. Iammarino, and M. Maroney, eds. *John Derricke's "Image of Irelande, with a Discoverie of Woodkarne": Essays on Text and Contexts*. Manchester: Manchester University Press. pp. 1–20.
Knapp, J.A. 2000. "That moste barbarous Nacion": John Derricke's *Image of Ireland* and the "Delight of the Well Disposed Reader." *Criticism*. **42.4**, 415–50.
———. 2003. *Illustrating the Past in Early Modern England: The Representation of History in Printed Books*. Aldershot; Burlington, VT: Ashgate.
Loewenstein, J. 2002. *The Author's Due: Printing and the Prehistory of Copyright*. Chicago, IL: University of Chicago Press.
Silva, A. 2021. "Framed and clothed with variety": Print Culture, Multimodality, and Visual Design in Derricke's Image of Ireland. In: T. Herron, D. Iammarino, and M. Maroney, eds. *John Derricke's "Image of Irelande, with a Discoverie of Woodkarne": Essays on Text and Contexts*. Manchester: Manchester University Press. pp. 135–49.
Soderberg, J. 2021. Animals Make the Man: Violence, Masculinity, and the Colonial Project in Derricke's *Image of Irelande*. In: T. Herron, D. Iammarino,

and M. Maroney, eds. *John Derricke's "Image of Irelande, with a Discoverie of Woodkarne": Essays on Text and Contexts*. Manchester: Manchester University Press. pp. 49–64.

Spengler, O. 1996 [1926]. *The Decline of the West*. C.F. Atkinson, trans. New York, NY: Knopf.

Weber, M. 2002. *The Protestant Ethic and the Spirit of Capitalism*. P. Baehr, ed. and trans. London: Penguin.

Index

ABC 67, 70, 75–7, 83, 99–100; *see also* catechism
Agricola, R. 4–5, 23, 27
Alciato, A. 141, 145, 155
allegory 2, 22, 48, 51–2, 54, 56, 66, 78, 111, 147, 149–51, 154, 164–5, 167, 171, 174, 177, 184–6, 190, 198–9; *see also* emblems; hermeneutics; myth
Antwerp 26, 32, 49, 133, 158
Apocalypse 35, 85, 103, 108–9, 131, 144, 146–7, 151, 153–7, 168, 177–8, 193, 198, 213; *see also* eschatology; teleology
Aristotle 3, 17, 21, 48
Art of Memory *see* memory
Articles of Religion 74–5, 83, 108; *see also* Protestantism
Ascham, R. 56, 59

Bacon, F. 62, 120, 138, 152, 156
Bakhtin, M. 10, 24
Baldwin, W. 104, 136
Bale, J. 146, 156
ballad 70, 86, 88–94; *see also* meter
baptism 67, 171; *see also* Protestantism
Barthes, R. 40, 57, 59–60
Bateman, S. 156
Becon, T. 33, 97–8, 105, 135
Beza, T. 141, 144
Bible 3–4, 32, 34, 41, 59, 67, 72–3, 76, 82, 90–94, 101, 106, 108, 112, 125, 132, 136, 169, 198, 202, 205, 207; Authorized Version (King James) 38; 41, 67–8; Coverdale 133, 201; Geneva 111, 150–1, 183, 202, 204; Hebrew 71, 84, 89, 94, 98, 203; Luther 83, 95, 155, 167; Matthew 35–8, 68, 103, 105, 114, 133, 189, 200; Vulgate 114; *see also* biblical mnemonics; psalms; typology
Bible of the Poor (Biblia Pauperum) 165, 169–70, 179–80, 185, 199; *see also* Book of Hours; Little Garden of the Soul; Mirror of Salvation
biblical figures: Adam 198; angels 149, 183, 187, 202–3, 206; Antichrist 130, 132, 146–7, 149, 155, 198; David 59, 88–9, 95, 98; Elijah 164; Elisha 164; Eve 198; Jesus Christ 14, 34, 76–7, 109, 124, 128, 134, 144, 154, 161, 163–4, 177–87, 198–9; Job 181; John the Revelator 103, 109, 131, 147, 151, 155; Jonah 179; Joseph (son of Jacob) 92, 179; Mary 14, 76, 171, 184–5; Moses 76; Pharaoh 76; Solomon 200; Samson 76, 185; Satan 150, 198; Stephen 114; Whore of Babylon 147–9, 151, 202; *see also* hermeneutics; typology
biblical mnemonics 68, 71–2, 93, 98, 108, 164, 171, 178–9, 183, 186; *see also* Bible; Bible of the Poor; memory arts
Billingsley, H. 43, 59
Book of Common Prayer 64, 67, 69–70, 97–8, 100, 108, 179, 181, 203–4; *see also* Cranmer
Book of Hours 162, 165, 167, 169–71, 175, 181, 186, 199, 205, 208, 210; see also Bible of the Poor; Little Garden of the Soul; Mirror of Salvation
Book of Martyrs see Foxe
booksellers 3, 31, 43, 46, 57, 76, 102, 136, 199; Day's "Sign of

216 *Index*

the Resurrection" 36; *see also* printshops
Brinsley, J. 82, 98
Bruegel, P., the Elder 14, 28
Bull, H. 200, 204
Bullinger, H. 146, 153, 156
Burch, W. 48, 193, 203–4
Burghley, Lord *see* Cecil, W.
Burton, R. 78, 98
Bynneman, H. 24, 143–4, 148, 154, 156
Byrd, W. 42, 57

calendars 34, 118, 124, 126, 141; *see also* martyrs; memory arts
Calvin, J. 88, 153–4, 198; works by 66–8, 98–9, 156; *see also* Protestantism
Calvinism in England 14, 69, 110, 117, 135, 145–6, 212
Camden, W. 34, 57, 59
Camillo, G. 15–16, 23; *see also* memory arts; memory theatres
Cassirer, E. 1–2, 9, 11, 22–3, 25, 28, 65–6, 99, 120–1, 136, 160–1, 164, 178, 198, 202, 204, 209, 213
catechism, 7, 10, 18, 33, 56, 64–84, 95–9, 106, 143, 162, 164, 188, 200–12; *see also* ABC; *Short Catechism*
Catholicism 6, 32, 66, 74, 117–18, 142, 151, 155, 178–9, 201; devotional practices 12, 31, 34, 104, 116, 121, 145, 153, 162, 165, 171, 175–6, 181, 185, 199–200
Caxton, W. 6, 99, 117, 134–5
Cecil, W. 69, 84–5, 125, 128, 154, 200
Charles V, Holy Roman Emperor 32
Chaucer, G. 39, 59
Christ *see* biblical figures
Cicero 17, 21; *see also* rhetoric
commonplace books 5–6, 17, 23, 149, 170, 189, 193–7
copia *see* rhetoric
Cranmer, T. 32, 64–7, 69, 73, 75, 97–8, 114, 134, 179, 181
culture 2, 5, 10–11, 126: definitions of 118–19; Protestant Christian 66, 116–20, 161, 164, 178; material aspects of 21, 110; of memory 2–6, 12–13, 19, 97–8; as shaped by printing 2–3, 57, 107, 135, 165; and symbolic forms 1, 120–21, 148, 161, 164, 198, 209; visual 123, 171, 199; *see also* myth; paperworld
Cunningham, W. 24, 42, 46, 49–50, 59, 112, 134

Dance of Death 53, 168, 172, 174–5, 177–8, 183, 186–7, 189–91, 103, 195, 198, 201–3; *see also memento mori*; vanitas
Danse Macabre see Dance of Death
Day, J.: base of operations 32, 36, 85, 95, 104–5, 146, 167; business acumen 7, 33, 41, 50, 69–70, 83–5, 96, 104, 106, 128, 130, 133, 143, 210; collaboration with Foxe 97, 104, 109, 111, 115–16, 120–1, 123, 125, 135, 141–2; colophon and printer's mark 14, 34, 36, 41, 47, 52–6, 83–4, 173, 188; imprisonment 6, 128; lifespan 6–8, 10, 70, 211; partnership with Seres 32, 41, 57, 93, 146; patrons 32, 46, 68, 128, 155; and Stationers' Company 3, 30, 32, 129, 177; *see also* monopolies
Day of Judgment 193, 195; *see also* eschatology; history; teleology
Day, R. 70–1, 85, 129, 144, 154
Day's Service Book 105
Derricke, J. 14, 22, 24, 211–12
dogs: symbolic meaning of 78, 80–1
Dudley, J. 69, 97
Dudley, R. 46, 68, 123, 134, 155, 200
Dürer, A. 80–1, 85, 181
Dutch Revolt *see* Eighty Years' War

Edward VI, King of England 32, 41, 66, 69, 73, 85–6, 93, 134, 201
Eighty Years' War 116, 143, 154
Elizabeth I, Queen of England 22, 47, 50, 68, 70, 73, 84, 86, 115, 124–5, 127, 134, 142, 150, 171–2, 200, 211; and the Order of the Garter 173–4, 176; as supreme head of the English Church 67, 93, 125, 179, 201
emblems 10, 14, 19–20, 52, 55, 67, 78, 105, 112, 133, 141–2, 144–6, 148, 151, 153–5, 169
emblem books 15, 52, 70, 129, 132, 142–3, 145–6, 152–5, 162, 170, 209
End Times *see* Apocalypse
engrams 11–12, 30, 96, 98; *see also* mnemic energy; mnemotopes; psychograms

epic 94, 121; *see also* romance
Erasmus, D. 17–19, 51, 70, 108, 155; *see also* pedagogy; proverbs
eschatology 109, 118, 147, 155, 178; *see also* Apocalypse; teleology
etchings 3, 144, 155, 209; *see also* woodcuts
eucharist 31, 67, 89, 97, 179; *see also* Protestantism
Euclid: *Elements of Geometry* 43, 45, 47, 54, 209
Eusebius 109–10, 116, 124
Evangelism *see* Protestantism

Fish, Stanley 15, 212
Foucault, M. 9, 13, 40, 57
Foxe, J.: *Acts and Monuments* 12, 97, 105–7, 116–21, 124–33; collaboration with Day 84, 97, 104, 109, 111, 115–16, 120–1, 123, 125, 135, 141–2; on the continent 115, 124–5; early works 103, 107–9, 111, 115; last works 131; left Oxford 200
Frye, N. 164, 186, 198–9, 201
Fuller, T. 88–9
Fulwood, W. 98, 123, 134, 195

Geneva 88–9, 110; *see also* Bible
Gheeraerts, M., the Elder 142–3, 186, 202
Golden Legend 112, 117–18; *see also* Caxton
"Green Man" 162, 198

Hanmer, M. 109, 112, 124, 136, 155
heaven 108, 124, 149, 178, 183; *see also* hell; purgatory
Hegel, G.F.W. 20–1
hell 178, 185; *see also* heaven; purgatory
Henry VIII, King of England 32, 75–6, 85, 173, 201
hermeneutics 1, 12, 21, 48, 54, 77, 164, 186, 209; *see also* allegory; Bible; typology
historiography 12, 142
history 11, 21, 116–18, 121, 164, 198, 210; of the book 9, 119, 212; Christian 88–9, 97, 104, 106–9, 115, 120–1, 124, 131–2, 161, 184; and remembrance 10, 123, 210; as Theatre of God's Judgment 105–6, 141, 160, 186; of thought 9, 13; *see also* calendars; providence

Holbein, H., the Younger 58, 181, 201
Hooper, J. 65, 127
Hopkins, J. 42, 70, 84–6, 88–90, 94; *see also* metrical psalms; Sternhold
Horace 19, 39, 57, 145
humanism 2–3, 5, 7, 17, 19, 46, 51, 58, 72, 92, 95, 104, 142, 147, 202; *see also* pedagogy

iconoclasm *see* Protestantism (attitudes toward images)
iconography 9, 11, 17, 47, 58, 65, 98, 117, 142, 156, 162, 164, 167–8, 170, 176–8, 184, 187, 190, 193, 200
icons 121, 123, 151, 154, 171
ink 86, 103, 130, 177, 192, 201; *see also* paper; printing

Jacobus de Voragine *see Golden Legend*
James VI and I, King of Scotland and of England 8, 38; *see also* Bible
Jesus *see* biblical figures
Jews 77, 185, 202
Jonas, J. 65–7; *see also* catechism

Kempe, W. 82, 99; *see also* memory arts; pedagogy

Lambeth Palace 200; *see also* Parker, M.
Latimer, H. 41–2, 59, 67, 105, 111–12, 114–15, 126–7, 134
Leicester, Earl of *see* Dudley, R.
literacy 77, 82, 87–8, 94, 119; spread of 58, 68–9, 120, 165, 210; visual 58, 133, 152
Little Garden of the Soul (Hortulus Animae) 165–70, 199; *see also* Bible of the Poor; Book of Hours; Mirror of Salvation
London 30, 37, 64, 83, 86, 95, 125, 127–8, 133, 152; foreigners in 32, 56, 59, 65, 133, 142–4; guilds and companies 31, 46, 86, 127, 210
Luther, M. 4, 6, 32, 67, 75, 83, 87, 96, 98, 135, 153, 155, 212; *see also* Protestantism

Mainz 199
Manutius, A. 58
Marion, J-L. 55, 183, 186, 203

Index

martyrdom 64, 110, 114, 116–17, 120, 134, 199
martyrs 76, 103–12, 114–15, 118, 121, 125, 129, 137–8, 141–2, 146, 149, 151; *see also* Foxe; Hanmer; Oxford Martyrs; Protestantism
Mary I, Queen of England 6, 41, 64, 73, 107, 110, 133, 153
Melanchthon, P. 4, 67
memento mori 34, 52–4, 56–7, 84–5, 95, 105, 166–9, 186–9, 193; *see also* Dance of Death; vanitas
memory 1, 4, 209; the art of 13, 15, 20, 89, 110, 141–2, 152, 179; artificial 5, 90, 93, 97, 107, 146, 155, 165, 197–8; collective 3, 5, 8, 66, 96, 115, 170–1, 176; communal 2, 86–7, 96, 120, 171, 183, 198; cultural 5, 96, 123, 179; national 2, 8, 106, 116, 171, 177; personification of 184; visual 112, 130, 146, 153, 164, 169, 210; *see also* history; memory arts; mnemotechnics; oblivion
memory arts 89, 94–5, 107, 109, 112, 115, 117, 123, 134, 141–2, 152, 154–5, 161–2, 179, 203;
see also memory; memory theatres; mnemonics; mnemotechnics, rhetoric
memory theatres 112, 123–4, 142, 147, 149, 151–2, 154, 178, 193, 156–7; *see also* memory arts; mnemotechnics
Meres, F. 15, 17–18, 23
meter 42, 84, 86, 88–90, 93–4, 98; *see also* ballad
metrical psalms *see* psalms
Mirror of Salvation (Speculum Humanae Salvationis) 165, 169–70, 199; *see also* Bible of the Poor; Book of Hours; Little Garden of the Soul
mnemic energy 10, 12, 96, 98, 117, 212; *see also* engrams; mnemotopes; psychograms
mnemonics 3, 7–8, 11, 13, 21, 23, 72, 82, 112, 170–1, 180; devotional 68, 90–1, 114, 123, 151–2, 160, 169, 171, 179–80, 197, 201; place systems 15, 17, 92, 94–5, 98, 115, 117–18, 176; tableaux 56, 114, 147, 150–1, 165, 167, 179, 183–4; itineraries 15, 17, 56, 147, 149, 179–80, 197; *see also* biblical mnemonics; calendar; memory arts; memory theatres
mnemotechnics 11, 14, 17–21, 55, 93, 97, 108, 110, 112, 141, 149, 183; combinatory 14, 17, 112, 161, 165, 186; cultural work of 142, 170, 200, 209; *see also* memory; mnemonics
mnemotopes 9–10, 12, 14, 22, 42, 96, 98, 118, 120, 211; *see also* engrams; mnemic energy; psychograms
monopolies 22, 32, 42, 48, 50, 63–70, 83–5, 96–7, 105, 210–11; *see also* printing
Montaigne, M. 5, 23
Mulcaster, R. 78, 81, 97
myth 1, 8, 11–12, 14–15, 20, 120–1, 160, 165–6, 198, 209; *see also* culture
mythography 48, 121

nonconformity 114–15, 123, 200; *see also* martyrs
Norton, T. 69, 94, 154
Northumberland, Duke of *see* Dudley, J.
Norwich 46, 112

oblivion 165, 209; personification of 184, 189; *see also* memory
Oxford Martyrs 41, 105, 114, 134; *see also* martyrs; Protestantism

Panofsky, E. 11, 85, 97, 187
paintings 14, 55, 59, 134, 183; *see also* Protestantism (attitudes toward images)
paper 125, 191; cost of 84, 127, 130; quality of 125; supply of 103, 126–7, 178; *see also* ink; printing
paperworld 5, 18, 21–2, 31, 38, 40, 43, 69, 198; *see also* booksellers; culture; printing
Parker, M. 125, 154; workshop 33, 56, 200
Parr, Katherine, Consort of Henry VIII 76, 86, 97, 114, 135
patents *see* printing
pedagogy 5, 51, 66; early modern practices 5, 15, 66–7, 69, 78, 81–3; schoolrooms 49, 77–80, 92; *see also* catechism; humanism
Philip II, Consort of Mary I and King of Spain 115

Plantin, C. 49
Plat, H, 82, 97, 115
Plutarch 51
Ponet, J. 33
pride 149–50, 165, 167; see also vanity
primers 6, 42, 67, 69, 72, 75, 130, 200
printing: advent of 3, 39, 107, 130–1, 155; early modern practices 2–7, 22, 85–6, 175, 201; licenses and patents 7, 12, 22, 30, 33, 41–2, 46–7, 49–50, 70, 83–5, 121, 144, 210; piracy 30, 70–1, 77, 95, 212; see also ink; monopolies; paperworld
printshops 20–1, 32, 43, 51, 72, 95, 104, 115, 187, 191–3; see also booksellers; ink; paper
printing press 2, 86, 106, 131, 191, 203, 209; see also typeface
Protestantism 4, 13, 22, 67, 72, 76, 108, 112–14, 128, 130, 155, 191, 211; Anglicanism clarified 8, 201; attitudes toward images 110, 145, 155; Church of England 96–7, 103, 108, 106, 125, 174, 201; as expressed in England 32, 34, 42, 46, 49–50, 69–70, 82, 93, 95, 104, 106–7, 171; and national consciousness 3, 8, 96, 106, 119, 141, 171; sacraments 67, 89, 171; scripture alone (*sola scriptura*) 72, 76, 110, 112, 128, 130, 181; see also culture; Calvin; Luther; martyrs
proverbs 13–15, 17–19, 65, 96; see also Erasmus
providence 114–15, 128, 130–2, 160, 163, 165, 179, 191; see also history; Protestantism
psalms 84–9; metrical 68, 84, 88–90, 93; singing of 57, 86–9, 95–6; see also Bible; Hopkins; Sternhold; *Whole Book of Psalms*
psalter 6, 84–6, 87–8, 93, 110, 143, 212
psychograms 9, 12, 14, 96, 98, 117–18; see also engrams; mnemic energy; mnemotopes
purgatory 6, 74–5, 108, 134, 178, 201; see also heaven; hell

quadrivium 47–8, 58; see also humanism; pedagogy

Ramus, P. 3, 82
Recorde, R. 49, 59
resurrection 14, 34, 36, 55–6, 76, 161–4, 178, 180–7, 193; see also allegory; myth; teleology
rhetoric 89, 147, 180; canons of 15, 20; classical 7, 15, 19, 97; copia 19, 71, 170; formulas of 202, 111; and humanism 7, 20; simulated dialogues 51, 72; see also commonplace books; memory arts
Ridley, N. 111–14, 124, 134
romance 38, 120–1; see also epic; myth

sacraments see Protestantism
Samuel, W. 90–3; see also biblical mnemonics
Semon, R. 10; see also mnemic energy
Seres, W. 99, 156; partnership with Day 32, 41, 57, 93, 146
sermons in print 41, 57, 67, 89, 105, 146, 156, 179, 211; see also Protestantism
Seznec, J. 11, 13
Shakespeare, W. 40–1; *As You Like It* 202; *Cymbeline* 74; *Macbeth* 156; *Two Gentlemen of Verona* 77; see also memory theatres
Short Catechism 67, 71, 75, 79–80, 83, 96; see also catechism; monopolies
Spengler, O. 20, 210
Spenser, E. 14, 22, 77, 171; *Complaints* 155–6; *Faerie Queene* 93–4, 150; *Shepheardes' Calendar* 39, 171; *Theatre for Worldings* 144–5, 147, 149; as a translator 144–5
Stationers' Company see London
Sternhold, T. 42, 70, 84–6; see also Hopkins; metrical psalms
Stradanus, J. 3, 23
Stringers' Company see London

Tallis, T. 42, 57
teleology: Christological 118, 132, 147, 161, 164, 17; see also Apocalypse; eschatology; history
Ten Commandments 67, 76, 82, 86; see also Bible; biblical mnemonics; catechism
theatre 74, 82, 109, 151, 156; as metaphor 142, 154: see also history; memory arts

Index

Tyndale, W. 35, 103, 105–6, 127, 133–4, 183; *see also* Bible; martyrdom
typeface: compositors use of 104, 126, 191, 154; 202; creation of 49, 59, 104; inking of 86, 130, 177, 201; setting in place of 173, 201; *see also* printing press; typeface fonts
typeface fonts: Anglo-Saxon 32, 38, 49, 56, 60; black letter (or Gothic) 49, 58, 71–5, 96, 94, 203; double pica 49, 61; Greek 49, 69, 71, 81, 144, 157, 171, 204; Hebrew 71, 84, 89, 98, 144; italic 49, 58, 71–3; music 42, 57, 86–7, 98, 101, 212; pica 46, 61; roman 10, 49, 54, 70–3; *see also* printing press; typeface
typography 6–7, 43, 49, 70, 72, 75, 94, 96, 112, 134–5, 155, 169; *see also* printing press; typeface
typographic imaginary 27, 136, 139, 161–2, 164, 177–9, 207; *see also* mnemonics
typology 70, 72, 75–6, 163–4, 179–82, 184–6, 198, 201, 203; *see also* Bible; biblical mnemonics; hermeneutics; myth

Van der Noot, J. 24, 129, 132, 142–7, 150–1, 153–6, 159; *Theatre for Worldings* 22, 142–4, 147, 153–9, 165, 171, 191, 209; *see also* Apocalypse; emblem books; etchings; woodcuts
vanitas 167–9; *see also memento mori*; vanity
vanity 145, 151; *see also* pride; vanitas

Warburg, A. 2, 11, 17, 24, 28; *see also* culture; myth; psychograms
Weber, M. 135, 140, 212, 214
Whitchurch, E. 85–6, 99, 139
Whole Book of Psalms 68, 84–9, 93–6, 99, 102, 106, 210; *see also* Hopkins; metrical psalms; Sternhold
Willis, J. 141, 150, 153–4, 157; *see also* emblems; memory theatres
Wolfe, R. 33, 59, 69
woodcuts 50, 106–7, 110, 116–17, 121, 123, 127, 129, 133–4, 144–5, 152, 155, 186, 202, 211–12; *see also* etchings; printing press

Yates, F. 7, 16, 20, 23, 29, 82, 102, 107, 140

zoomorphism 190